Routledge Revivals

The Touch-Stone

The Touch-Stone:
or,
Historical, Critical, Political, Philosophical, and Theological Essays on the reigning Diversions of the Town With a Preface, giving an Account of the Author and the Work.

The Second Edition

James Ralph

First published in 2010 by ECCO Print Editions

This edition first published in 2018 by Routledge
2 Park Square, Milton Park, Abingdon, Oxon, OX14 4RN
and by Routledge
52 Vanderbilt Avenue, New York, NY 10017, USA

Routledge is an imprint of the Taylor & Francis Group, an informa business

© 2010 by Taylor and Francis

All rights reserved. No part of this book may be reprinted or reproduced or utilised in any form or by any electronic, mechanical, or other means, now known or hereafter invented, including photocopying and recording, or in any information storage or retrieval system, without permission in writing from the publishers.

Publisher's Note
The publisher has gone to great lengths to ensure the quality of this reprint but points out that some imperfections in the original copies may be apparent.

Disclaimer
The publisher has made every effort to trace copyright holders and welcomes correspondence from those they have been unable to contact.

A Library of Congress record exists under ISBN:

ISBN 13: 978-0-367-24878-9 (hbk)
ISBN 13: 978-0-367-24881-9 (pbk)
ISBN 13: 978-0-429-28487-8 (ebk)

The touch-stone: or, historical, critical, political, philosophical, and theological essays on the reigning diversions of the town. ... With a preface, giving an account of the author and the work. The second edition.

James Ralph

The touch-stone: or, historical, critical, political, philosophical, and theological essays on the reigning diversions of the town. ... With a preface, giving an account of the author and the work. The second edition.
Ralph, James
ESTCID: N045850
Reproduction from Huntington Library
Anonymous. By James Ralph. With a half-title.
London : printed for J. Crokatt, 1729.
[2],xxviii,237,[1]p. ; 12°

Eighteenth Century
Collections Online
Print Editions

Gale ECCO Print Editions

Relive history with *Eighteenth Century Collections Online*, now available in print for the independent historian and collector. This series includes the most significant English-language and foreign-language works printed in Great Britain during the eighteenth century, and is organized in seven different subject areas including literature and language; medicine, science, and technology; and religion and philosophy. The collection also includes thousands of important works from the Americas.

The eighteenth century has been called "The Age of Enlightenment." It was a period of rapid advance in print culture and publishing, in world exploration, and in the rapid growth of science and technology – all of which had a profound impact on the political and cultural landscape. At the end of the century the American Revolution, French Revolution and Industrial Revolution, perhaps three of the most significant events in modern history, set in motion developments that eventually dominated world political, economic, and social life.

In a groundbreaking effort, Gale initiated a revolution of its own: digitization of epic proportions to preserve these invaluable works in the largest online archive of its kind. Contributions from major world libraries constitute over 175,000 original printed works. Scanned images of the actual pages, rather than transcriptions, recreate the works ***as they first appeared.***

Now for the first time, these high-quality digital scans of original works are available via print-on-demand, making them readily accessible to libraries, students, independent scholars, and readers of all ages.

For our initial release we have created seven robust collections to form one the world's most comprehensive catalogs of 18th century works.

Initial Gale ECCO Print Editions collections include:

> ***History and Geography***
> Rich in titles on English life and social history, this collection spans the world as it was known to eighteenth-century historians and explorers. Titles include a wealth of travel accounts and diaries, histories of nations from throughout the world, and maps and charts of a world that was still being discovered. Students of the War of American Independence will find fascinating accounts from the British side of conflict.

Social Science
Delve into what it was like to live during the eighteenth century by reading the first-hand accounts of everyday people, including city dwellers and farmers, businessmen and bankers, artisans and merchants, artists and their patrons, politicians and their constituents. Original texts make the American, French, and Industrial revolutions vividly contemporary.

Medicine, Science and Technology
Medical theory and practice of the 1700s developed rapidly, as is evidenced by the extensive collection, which includes descriptions of diseases, their conditions, and treatments. Books on science and technology, agriculture, military technology, natural philosophy, even cookbooks, are all contained here.

Literature and Language
Western literary study flows out of eighteenth-century works by Alexander Pope, Daniel Defoe, Henry Fielding, Frances Burney, Denis Diderot, Johann Gottfried Herder, Johann Wolfgang von Goethe, and others. Experience the birth of the modern novel, or compare the development of language using dictionaries and grammar discourses.

Religion and Philosophy
The Age of Enlightenment profoundly enriched religious and philosophical understanding and continues to influence present-day thinking. Works collected here include masterpieces by David Hume, Immanuel Kant, and Jean-Jacques Rousseau, as well as religious sermons and moral debates on the issues of the day, such as the slave trade. The Age of Reason saw conflict between Protestantism and Catholicism transformed into one between faith and logic -- a debate that continues in the twenty-first century.

Law and Reference
This collection reveals the history of English common law and Empire law in a vastly changing world of British expansion. Dominating the legal field is the *Commentaries of the Law of England* by Sir William Blackstone, which first appeared in 1765. Reference works such as almanacs and catalogues continue to educate us by revealing the day-to-day workings of society.

Fine Arts
The eighteenth-century fascination with Greek and Roman antiquity followed the systematic excavation of the ruins at Pompeii and Herculaneum in southern Italy; and after 1750 a neoclassical style dominated all artistic fields. The titles here trace developments in mostly English-language works on painting, sculpture, architecture, music, theater, and other disciplines. Instructional works on musical instruments, catalogs of art objects, comic operas, and more are also included.

The BiblioLife Network

This project was made possible in part by the BiblioLife Network (BLN), a project aimed at addressing some of the huge challenges facing book preservationists around the world. The BLN includes libraries, library networks, archives, subject matter experts, online communities and library service providers. We believe every book ever published should be available as a high-quality print reproduction; printed on-demand anywhere in the world. This insures the ongoing accessibility of the content and helps generate sustainable revenue for the libraries and organizations that work to preserve these important materials.

The following book is in the "public domain" and represents an authentic reproduction of the text as printed by the original publisher. While we have attempted to accurately maintain the integrity of the original work, there are sometimes problems with the original work or the micro-film from which the books were digitized. This can result in minor errors in reproduction. Possible imperfections include missing and blurred pages, poor pictures, markings and other reproduction issues beyond our control. Because this work is culturally important, we have made it available as part of our commitment to protecting, preserving, and promoting the world's literature.

GUIDE TO FOLD-OUTS MAPS and OVERSIZED IMAGES

The book you are reading was digitized from microfilm captured over the past thirty to forty years. Years after the creation of the original microfilm, the book was converted to digital files and made available in an online database.

In an online database, page images do not need to conform to the size restrictions found in a printed book. When converting these images back into a printed bound book, the page sizes are standardized in ways that maintain the detail of the original. For large images, such as fold-out maps, the original page image is split into two or more pages

Guidelines used to determine how to split the page image follows:

• Some images are split vertically; large images require vertical and horizontal splits.
• For horizontal splits, the content is split left to right.
• For vertical splits, the content is split from top to bottom.
• For both vertical and horizontal splits, the image is processed from top left to bottom right.

THE
TOUCH-STONE:

OR,

Historical, Critical, Political, Moral, Philosophical and Theological

ESSAYS

Upon the reigning Diversions of the Town.

THE TOUCH-STONE:
OR,
Historical, Critical, Political, Philosophical, and Theological
ESSAYS
On the reigning Diversions of the Town.

Designed for the Improvement of all AUTHORS, SPECTATORS, and ACTORS of OPERAS, PLAYS, and MASQUERADES.

In which every Thing antique, or modern, relating to

Musick,	Criticks,	Prize-Fighters,
Poetry,	Balls,	Italian Strollers,
Dancing,	Ridottos,	Mountebank Stages,
Pantomimes,	Assemblies,	Cock-Pits,
Chorusses,	New Oratory,	Puppet-Shews,
Cat-Calls,	Circus,	Fairs, and
Audiences,	Bear-Garden,	Publick Auctions,
Judges,	Gladiators,	

Is occasionally handled.

With a PREFACE, giving an Account of the AUTHOR and the WORK.

―――― *Ridiculum Acri*
Fortiùs & meliùs magnas p'erumque secat res.
HORAT. Sat. Lib. 1. Sat. x.

*Non hic Centauros, non Gorgonas, Harpyiasque
Invenies: Hominem pagina nostra sapit.*
MARTIAL Ep. iv. Lib. x.

The SECOND EDITION.

LONDON: Printed for J. CROKATT, at the *Golden Key* opposite to *Chancery-Lane*, in *Fleet-Street* M DCC XXIX.

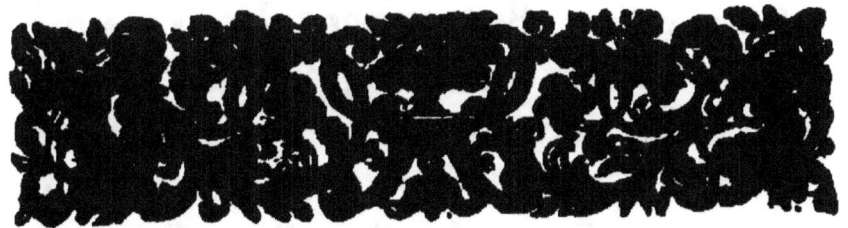

EPISTLE DEDICATORY.

To the Right Notable

----- *PAYNE*, Esq;

Supervisor General of the Mall, Political Censor of Great-Britain, and Heir Expectant of a very great POST.

Wonderful SIR!

SHOULD Essays of this publick, private, general, particular, grave, merry *Nature*, appear under the Protection of any Name but the illustrious 'Squire *Payne*, the World would so far resent my Choice of a *Patron*, as not even to read my

Epistle Dedicatory.

PREFACE: But when the Town is assur'd that your Approbation was Midwife, as your Person stands *Godfather* to this Infant; without Hesitation, or Perusal, they'll of course allow it all the *Quantums* and *Quales* of your Body and Mind.

YOUR Solemnity of Countenance prognosticates its Wisdom, and your Air of Insinuating Address its Penetration; your laughing at great People, and little People's laughing at you, are manifest Tokens of its Humour and facetious Disposition. From your good Breeding they depend upon its Politeness; from your easy Conversation, its being the Standard of sheer Wit; and from your picquant Reflections, they expect in it the sharpest but justest *Satyr*.

To you then, Sir, the *Criterion* (to the Vulgar, the *Touch-Stone*) flies for Refuge. Point out to the ignorant World its Beauties, and excuse to the Learned its Errors. Shield it from the piercing Tongue, and blasting

blasting Breath of the Malicious and Envious. Let it retreat under the Shelter of your Eye-Brows, and cover it with the Wings of your Authority; so shall it remain as snug and safe as a Murderer in a Catholick Church.

Pardon, dear Sir, my being thus busy about my Book, that I have forgot you: In this widely differing from most modern Dedicators, who designedly neglect themselves, in order to have an Opportunity of talking more largely in Praise of their Patrons. But not to be quite dead to the Fashion—— I must have a Touch at your Honour; though I fear, that even in this Case, I shall prove the Reverse of our present Set of Authors; for they generally attribute to their Patrons a Rag-man-roll List of Virtues, positively in the Affirmative, tho' uncertain in every Point; whilst I shall, in the Negative, absolutely suppose you adorn'd with all Perfections that I ought to know, or can desire you capable of.

As to your noble Family, it may be of older Date than History it self can go back to; nor can any Man say, but that every illustrious Branch of it may have been loaded with prime Ministers, Generals, Admirals, Bishops, and Judges; tho' some spiteful Persons have falsely advanc'd, that you never had any *Ancestors*, because you are universally acknowledg'd to be an *Original.* As to your Parts and Prudence, we cannot deny, but you might have shone out a *Wolsey*, or *Richlieu*, had any Prince put the same Confidence in you, and brought your Capacity to the Test. If our publick Papers are silent, as to any remarkable Proofs of your Courage, yet who's the Man that ever worsted you in the Field, or dares affirm, that he saw you fly from Danger? This we may modestly assert, That let your Family be ever so eminent, you are undoubtedly the most extraordinary Person of it; which few modern *Panegyrists* can

Epistle Dedicatory.

can plead in Favour of their Patrons, without stretching the Truth on too large a Last.

LET not my Forgetfulness obliterate the Wonders of your Hand, as made apparent in those valuable Sentences, wise Apopthegms, and immortal Maxims, so long and learnedly carry'd on in Behalf of our Constitution, to the Honour of our Country, and to the utter Ruin of its and your Foes. These fine Precepts are the most curious Medley of Zeal, publick Spirit, Learning, Wit, Humour, Politicks, Religion and necessary Nonsense, prudently adapted to the *British* Taste. What Pity it is, that like the Prophecies of the *Sybils*, they are only deliver'd to us on the Leaves of Trees, or the Sides of the *Mall!*

THE mentioning of which warns me, not to incroach upon those Moments, the least of which is of the utmost Consequence to the Nation, and gives me an Opportunity of wishing, viii *Epistle Dedicatory.*

wishing, that you may long live to enjoy (at least in Imagination) those Posts you are certainly capable of adorning.

SIR,

I am, with the profoundest

Respect, your most

Devoted humble Servant,

A. Primcock.

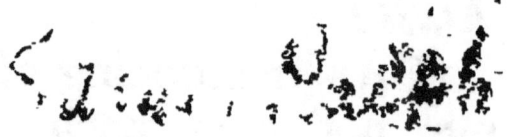

THE PREFACE:
OR,
INTRODUCTION.
Giving a particular Account of the AUTHOR and the WORK.

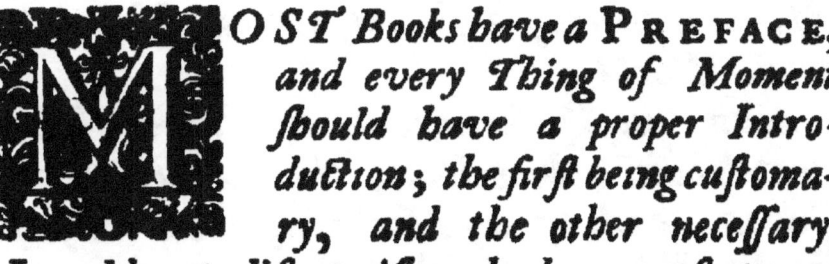OST *Books have a* PREFACE, *and every Thing of Moment should have a proper Introduction; the first being customary, and the other necessary, I could not distinguish which is most to my Purpose; therefore give the World both in one. This the Criticks may fall upon, either as an Absurdity, or Innovation: But my Writings*

tings are as far out of the Power of their *Criticisms*, as my *Fortune* is of their *Ill-Nature*. It is sufficient for me to let them know, that I write for the universal Benefit of my Country; that is, to improve one Part, and get the other Bread. But if these learned Snarlers bite their Nails at this Beginning, they may chance to eat their Fingers before they come to the last Page.

As the Generality of Readers would willingly pry into the most material Secrets relating to an Author (being very inquisitive about his Birth, Life, Circumstances and Conversation) so on the other hand, he is very often as much upon the Guard, to screen himself in all those Particulars, from their curious Search. But in order to gratify both my self and them at the same Time, I shall vary from the common Method of proceeding; and by telling positively who I am, keep my self, as hitherto, absolutely conceal'd from the whole World.

I am lineally sprang, by my Father's Side, from *Adam's* chief Root, the Family of the *Cocks*; and, by my Mother's, from the first *Welsh Kings*: So that the Antiquity and Gentility that run in my Veins, admit of no Dispute, or Rival, in Heraldry. I am the only Son of a younger Brother, of the Branch

of

of the Primcocks; which is noted for producing very fine Gentlemen, and generally great Favourites with the Ladies. The Laycocks are very numerous, and most commonly Females: They bear the Character of being Romps of the first Magnitude, and were the Inventors of the Game of Hot-cockles. The Allcocks are of an amorous Disposition; and though but low of Stature very often, yet by standing on Tip-toe, and other Devices, they exceed those who seem larger, by several Inches. The Stopcocks are altogether given to the Study of Physick and Surgery; their Knowledge in these Sciences, is of manifest Advantage in most Diseases particularly incident to the Family of the Cocks. The Handcocks are their nearest Relations, and are employ'd in those Affairs, under them, which require manual Operation. Several of these last, who are settled abroad, give mightily into a monastick Life. The Halfcocks enjoy the greatest Fortunes, and are allow'd to be the best dress'd Branch of the Family. We have but few Nococks in England, and they are generally esteem'd for their fine Voices, and acknowledg'd by us all to be the best Singers. The Smartcocks have naturally a fierce Air, and a strong Inclination to a military Life; tho' they often affect a lac'd Hat and red

red Coat, when they do not belong to the Army. The Lobcocks are thoroughly vers'd in Multiplication, and breed so fast, that they exceed all the other Tribes in Numbers: They are as fond of an Ecclesiastical State, as their Cousin-Germans the Woodcocks are of a Country Life; few of whom rise higher in Power, or Title, than a Justice of Peace, or an Esquire. Most of these two last Branches are got upon Hay-cocks. As for the Cock-a-Hoops and Cockneys, they are at best but Bastards of our Family; nor could their Wealth, or pretended Courage, ever prevail upon us to call Tradesmen and Bullies the legitimate Issue of the Cocks. In short, our Family has spread so wonderfully, that in some Respect we are allied to every Man in Europe; from L——s of B——n to Tom Tram.

Being descended from Parents more illustrious than rich, my Education was becoming a Gentleman's Son, but conducted in a Method rather learned than polite. Losing, when at School, both Father and Mother, I was left to the Care of an Uncle, who soon after died, and bequeath'd me a small Estate in Wales. Having by this Time attain'd my Eighteenth Year, a strong Inclination to seeing the World seiz'd me: Upon which I sold my little Fortune in the Country, and came up to Town

Town with a borrow'd Name, under which I purchas'd a moderate Annuity, and after a short Stay in London, *went abroad. In about the Space of five Years, I made the Tour of those Parts of* Europe *which are most worthy a Traveller's Curiosity. This I performed in a manner as reasonable as agreeable. My Genius (encourag'd by what I saw in other Countries) prompted me to an Improvement in my Travels, which may seem too trifling in one who was brought up to severer Studies. I div'd not into the political Principles of any State, but knew to a Tittle, what City had the most elegant Buildings, the best judg'd Amusements, or the finest Women. I troubled not my Head about the endless Controversies in Religion, nor enquir'd where I came, which flourish'd, which was tolerated, or which oppress'd. But I narrowly inspected the Architecture and Ornaments of their Churches; observ'd how the Rules of the Antients and Moderns agreed, and compar'd the Beauties and Proportions of the several Orders. I never sought the Conversation of their Divines, Philosophers, or Astrologers; but became intimate with every Poet, Critick, Painter and Statuary, each different Country call'd eminent. In short, I principally study'd the Fundamentals of the publick Amusements*

b *most*

most follow'd, wherever I came; I judiciously weigh'd the minutest Particulars in all Entertainments exhibited in OPERA *or* PLAY-HOUSES; *both on this, and t'other Side the* Alps. *I read attentively all the* French *and* Italian *Criticks: I could repeat the greatest Part of three hundred and thirteen* German *Commentators; and went to the Bottom of all the* Low-Dutch *Authors who commented upon them. Then considering that Speculation is but barely a Foundation in every thing, which Practice can only compleat, I sung the chief Part of an* OPERA, *at* Paris, *a whole Winter, and with equal Applause appear'd as the Hero of a Tragedy, at* Amsterdam. *Thus loaded with critical Learning, and cloath'd with necessary Experience, I return'd to my native Country, and have, since that Time, liv'd in publick, yet unknown, making my Studies my Amusements, always pleasing and improving my Mind by the noted Entertainments of the Town. I am now near my grand Climacterick, and have for above thirty Years, thus play'd Hide and Seek with the World: I am rarely known to two Persons by the same Name, and to no body, by my true one. I frequently change my Lodgings,*

and

and in them all, go generally by the Title of the strange Gentleman.

Tho' I seldom quit the Bills of Mortality, yet I rarely go into a Tavern: My Evenings are devoted to the publick Amusements; nor do I ever miss Operas *or* Plays, *that are good, or new. My Daylight is divided betwixt the Booksellers Shops (where I am welcome to pick out the Learning I cannot purchase, in Return of the little I buy) and those Coffee-Houses, where all critical Affairs are bandy'd* pro *and* con; *there I am oftener a Hearer than Speaker. I make frequent Visits to* Fleet-Ditch, Moor-Fields *Rails, and* Holborn-Bars, *where I spend many agreeable Hours, in meeting with Wit, Truth and Reason, conceal'd from that Part of Mankind, who scorn to look for them there; and unknown to that Part, who condescend to look, but cannot find them out. Having for so long a Space, nicely canvass'd, and maturely consider'd all things premis'd in my Title-Page, I cannot but look upon my self as a Person every way adequate to the Undertaking, and may, without Vanity affirm, that by Genius, Study and Experience, I am sufficiently qualify'd to inspect, criticise, and determine upon the reigning Di-*

versions

versions of the TOWN. *I blush not to own, that I was the famous* Trunk-Maker, *of whom the* TATLER *so often made just and honourable Mention: As I then gave Laws to the Realms of both* THEATRES, *I am now the only Body that can awe the Footmens* GALLERY *into any tolerable Degree of Order; nor am I less noted for being universally call'd upon, as an infallible Umpire, in all Disputes that happen betwixt Men or Brutes, at the* BEAR-GARDEN.

I thought it would be proper to inform the World of every Circumstance in my past Life, that was preparatory to my being an Author. I shall next, in the Out-lines of the following Work, give them a general Idea of the various Parts that compose the whole, so conclude this necessary Introduction.

My Manner of Criticizing, as observ'd in these ESSAYS, *differs widely from any thing that has yet appear'd under that Name: Both Censure and Panegyrick are introduc'd after a Method entirely new. I could never give into the slovenly, canting Reflections of* Pryn, *the arbitrary malicious Learning of* Collier, *the enthusiastick, insipid Arguments of* L----w, *or the severe, tho'*

tho' justifiable Rules of *Rymer and Dennis.* I hope my *Animadversions* upon all polite *Entertainments,* will be allow'd more agreeably just, if not so deeply Learned. Were we to be regulated by these Reformers and Criticks, we must with one Party demolish all *Stage-Entertainments,* upon account of some few bold *Licences,* which no Man will pretend to countenance; and, with the others, cramp every enterprizing Genius within the narrow Bounds of *Art,* blind to the *Charms* of the most beautiful *Irregularities.* The first would remedy some *Disorders* in our *Stage-Plays,* as if a Surgeon should cure a *Mortification* in a poor Fellows great *Toe,* by cutting off his Head; and the last are resolv'd to allow no *Coin* to be current but what comes from their own Mint. But I shall place these *Affairs* in another Light, and by some Hints tolerably uncommon, point out to the *World,* what I judge perfect, and what wants Amendment in these *Amusements,* at the same time proposing the most probable Remedies.

I am so far perswaded of the *Innocence* and *Use* of all our publick *Diversions,* taking them either in a moral, or religious Sense, that I shall endeavour to remove all *Prejudices* rais'd against them by unthink-

ing Zealots. This I hope to accomplish, either by giving pertinent and satisfactory Answers to the most material Objections of Consciences truly scrupulous, or by well-judg'd Alterations and Abolitions, bring about that Reformation in our Pleasures, as must of Course silence the specious Cavils of the most Inveterate.

As we cannot reasonably expect to be ever all of a Mind, as to the Principles of Religion or Politicks, I should be glad, we might in some Respect, be look'd upon as an united People, that we may at least agree in Singing and Dancing, since we cannot in Preaching and Praying.

My Lucubrations being principally confin'd to the most taking Diversions of the Town, no POETRY comes under my Consideration, but Dramatick; nor any MUSICK, but the Royal Academick. I flatter myself, that the Method observ'd in the following ESSAYS, will be thought pretty exact in the Point of Decorum; tho' I have ventur'd to introduce Sounds before Wit. 'Tis true, as a Scholar, I must maintain, that POETRY is the Head of all the fine Arts that ever were, or can be; the utmost Perfection that human Nature can excel in: But then as a Man of the Town, and one that has seen the World,
and

and all that, I must give MUSICK *the right Hand, because fine Gentlemen, and fine Ladies, always allow it the first Place; they both liking and understanding it best. Thus in my first* ESSAY *I shew my good Breeding, and in the second, my good Sense.*

The OPERAS *therefore being look'd upon as the Centre of the* Beau Monde, *I begin with them; in an historical Manner trace them to their first Rise: I make manifest their Beauties; how shocking the* Italian *Performance and Language are to some* English *Ears; shew what is wanting, what superfluous, and what Alterations or Additions are requisite to suit them to all Capacities, and adapt them to the Taste of this Nation in general.*

In the second ESSAY, *I consider the Instruction and Delight given by* Dramatick Poetry, *its great Merit, and the Esteem paid it by the Antients, why degenerated and despis'd in the present Age. That the Stage has so many Enemies, imputed to Poets, Actors and Auditors; the most reasonable Remedies propos'd for all Disorders in the Constitution of this fine Art, as occasion'd by the Writers, Managers, or Spectators of Plays.*

I then naturally slide into a third, but not contemptible, Theatrical Entertainment

ment, viz. Grotesque, *or* Dramatical Dancing; *in which I introduce an historical Account of the old* Mimes *and* Pantomimes; *with a just Comparison betwixt them, and their modern Imitators, the Race of* Arlequins, Scaramouches *and* Punchinellos. *I endeavour to shew how far this Art may be render'd of general Use, from what has been done in it; then conclude with some necessary Reflections and Documents of a publick and private Nature, tending to form a compleat Dancer.*

I next proceed to take Notice of our total Neglect of the most beautiful Appendix to the foregoing Entertainments, viz. A Grand Chorus, *always judg'd of the greatest Importance to the Stage, by Antiquity; their Magnificence and Use in* OPERAS, PLAYS, *and* DANCES, *explain'd; as approv'd of by the most learned of the Moderns: To which is added, a short Chronology, with the Nature, Use and Design of the* British Chorus of Cat-calls.

In the Fifth ESSAY *I enter into that Part of the Second, which relates to the Decay of Dramatick Poetry, being occasion'd by its Spectators and Readers: I there animadvert upon our* AUDIENCES, *as to the Articles of Behaviour and Judgment, both within Doors and without.*

out. *After having properly distinguish'd the several Orders and Degrees that form a regular Audience, I throw in some Hints and Rules for their Conduct, necessary to their future Amendment; then conclude with an Examination of Criticism in General, and a full Account of the several Kinds of Judges and Criticks.*

I next vary my Subject, without quitting the Stage, by enquiring into the Original, Use, and Danger of MASQUERADES *in General, I there demonstrate their great Antiquity, their pernicious Consequences, as now practis'd, and how far capable of being render'd as beneficial as agreeable: Several Arguments advanc'd and supported, to prove their Importance to the publick Welfare, if turn'd into a right Channel. To this Amusement, I tack some small Remarks upon that of going to* C———h, *ending with a modest Proposal in Behalf of the* O——ry *in* N————t M——t.

In my last ESSAY, *I run over concisely, the Rise, Progress, Studies and Exercises of the Old Grecian* GAMES; *their* GYMNASIA, STADIA, *&c. set apart for training their Youth up to these Martial Amusements. In the next Place, I shew, that from them sprung the*
CIRCUS,

CIRCUS, NAUMACHIÆ, AMPHITHEATRES, *and* CAMPUS MARTIUS *of the Romans, being of a-piece, in Design, Sports, and Improvement.*

Upon a Parallel with the antient CIRCUS, *I fix the* BEAR-GARDEN, *being a finish'd Copy of that great Original; or rather being descended from the same Illustrious Family: Its present Conduct defended with a Demonstration of a farther Improvement, if properly encourag'd. To this is annex'd a just Comparison betwixt the* PRIZE-FIGHTERS *and* GLADIATORS; *the* Italian Strolers *and* Mountebank-Stages: *The Whole concluding with some particular Observations upon* COCK-PITS, FAIRS, PUPPET-SHEWS, *and* Publick Auctions.

It is probable, that my Method of Writing will not be sufficiently surprizing, or out of the Way, to take with the English *Nation. I would rectify their Errors, and make even their Pleasures advantageous, by rational Courses; I speak to them as Men, and hope for a Man-like Reformation. I suppose no flying Islands, enchanted Castles, or fancy'd Regions, to amuse them. I bring home no Pygmies of six Inches, or Giants of sixty Foot, to moralize and talk Politicks to them; nor speaking Brutes to preach to them. Every Fool can furnish us with Countries and Chimæras hatch'd in his own Brain, and form a Speech out of mysterious Nothingness, and a Jargon not even to be pronounc'd; luckily judging, that by the Majority of Readers (who only skim the Surface of a Work, and are fond of strange Monsters) he must be held wise, who is unintelligible. My Remarks upon the Errors in our Conduct, my Reasons for Amendment, and my Method for attaining it, are drawn from Nature and Experience. Happy if I can but point out one wrong Step to be avoided; or that my rude Scheme may serve as a Hint to a brighter Genius, equally willing with me to promote the publick Good.*

Some Politicians, Informers, Reformers, and small Wits, may be very inquisitive about my half Blanks, whole Blanks, or mutilated Sentences: But I can assure my Readers, they need not dread any Scandal, Treason, or Impiety being couch'd in them. I am sensible most People love to meet with such Gaps, in order to fill them up If every Thing was set down plain, and at full Length in any Work; no Words to be guess'd at, or no Obscurity in the Sense, it would be thought

thought only proper for the perusal of a School-boy, and argue an Author's Assurance, in his giving no fair Play to a Reader's Penetration. Many dull Things, in suitable Expressions, have been admir'd, for the sake of those which were left out, and of course suppos'd to be very witty: The first and last Letters of Words, no Words at all, a Dash, or an Asterism, may contain more Merit than any Thing the whole Alphabet can produce in a regular Way. To this End were design'd the Mysteries, Hieroglyphicks, and Ænigmas of the Antients, to sharpen the Imagination, imploy idle People, and enhance the Value of any Thing discover'd. Moreover, as no Author can pretend, in Writing, to please the various Humours and Desires of Mankind; let him but leave some Parts of his Work imperfect, and every Man, in finding out the Meaning, will undoubtedly strive to please himself. In short, to ride Post thro' any Treatise, without Stop, Guess-work, scratching the Noddle, or grope in the Dark, is as insipid as a Fox-chace without Fatigue, a Victory without Danger, or a Wedding-night without a M--n---d.

THE

THE CONTENTS.

ESSAY I.

F *Musick; particularly Dramatick. The Original of Operas look'd into. An historical Account of their Progress in this Nation The Objection to the Italian Operas answer'd; and some Rules proposed for adapting them to the English Taste in general.* p. 1.

ESSAY II.

O*F Poetry; particularly Dramatick. The Decay of those Entertainments enquir'd into: Imputed*

puted to Poets, Actors, and Spectators: Their Mistakes set in a true Light, and some of the most probable Amendments to those Grievances proposed. p. 41.

ESSAY III.

OF Dancing, religious and dramatical. An historical Account of the Mimes and Pantomimes of the Antients; with a short Parallel betwixt them and our modern Arlequins and Scaramouches; and a learned Criticism on our present Grotesque Dances. To which are added, some Reflections upon Dancing, of a publick and private Nature; with a Side-step towards Tumblers, Posture-Masters and Rope-Dancers. p. 86.

ESSAY IV.

OF Chorusses, Antique and Modern; in great Esteem with the Antients; neglected by the present

sent Age. Of their Use and Beauty in all Stage Entertainments. To which are added, some Reflections upon the English *Chorus of Cat-Calls.* p. 115.

ESSAY V.

*O*F *Audiences; the several Orders of Spectators that form an* English *Audience. Their Behaviour in the Theatres consider'd. Their Manner of judging, in Publick and Private, set in a true Light. With a particular Account of the whole Race of Criticks.* p. 136

ESSAY VI.

*O*F *Masquerades; their great Antiquity; their Use and Abuse; capable of being contriv'd so, as to prove of vast Advantage to the Publick: With an Examen of the bare-fac'd Masquerades, call'd Ridottos, and Private Assemblies. To which is added, a Proposal for the Encouragement of the Oratory.*
p. 168.

ESSAY VII.

OF the Gymnasia, *Theatres, Amphitheatres*, Naumachiæ *and* Stadia *of the Antients*; *but particularly of the antique* Circus, *and modern* Bear-Garden: *A Comparison between the Gladiators and our Prize-Fighters*; *the* Italian *Strolers, and our Mountebank Stages: With a small Sketch of our Cock-Pits, Puppet-Shews, Fairs, and Publick Auctions.* p. 179.

ESSAY I.
OF MUSICK;

Particularly DRAMATICK.

The Original of OPERAS *look'd into. An Historical Account of their Progress in this Nation.* The *Objection to the* ITALIAN OPERAS *answer'd; and some Rules proposed for adapting them to the* ENGLISH TASTE *in general.*

OF all the fine ARTS, (excepting POETRY) none has exceeded MUSICK, or shewn a great *Genius* in a more distinguished way.

POETRY has the Advantage of delivering to its Readers or Hearers the finest Precepts of Morality, nay, Religion it self, in the most insinuating Manner, so, by pleasing, it instructs, as, some Diseases

cafes are cured by being tickled. It is indeed the utmoft Perfection human Nature can arrive at, to give or receive what is truly profitable with Delight. This is the happy Talent of POETRY, either *Epick* or *Dramatick*: And certainly of all other Arts a compleat OPERA comes nearest that perfect State of POETRY, becaufe you may there enjoy a finifhed regular *Fable*, accompanied with the moft exquifite *Harmony*.

As to the Antiquity of thefe Half-Sifters, I fhall not here prefume to make any Parallel. By all Accounts, facred and profane, both are very ancient; though moft People feem inclined to give *Mufick* the Preference, and amongft others, for the following weighty Reafon. The Foundation of our publick Entertainments of all kinds, is undeniably owing to fome Part of the Religious Worfhip of the firft Ages, this is notorious beyond any Ground for a Difpute, in MUSICK, POETRY, DANCING, and even all the Diverfions of the *Bear-Garden*, which we have certainly borrowed from the Ancients.

Now the earlieft Accounts we have of any Adoration paid to a fupreme Being, either in facred or profane Hiftory, inftructs us, That the Performance was mufical, either in Hymns or Songs, or by the Sounds of Inftruments, and as the Notions of a Divinity were naturally unplanted in the Minds of Men, fo their Expreffions of that Knowledge firft employed their leifure Hours, and it is probable, by MUSICK. And I am apt to think, that the Meafures of that Art firft gave the Hint and Model for the Numbers of POETRY.

This we are certain of, that in all Ages of the World, nothing has fhewn a greater Power over the Paffions in general, than MUSICK: It commands the Soul, and moulds the Heart at Will; it forces Mankind to be gay or grave, a-
morous

morous or religious, effeminate or brave, according to its Beauty, Justness or Variety: The Master's Skill inspiring us with Sentiments artfully thrown into our Minds, and all over our Bodies, by thrilling Notes, and captivating Sounds.

Now since a compleat OPERA is a regular musical DRAMMA, and approaching very near to the Excellency of POETRY, (because Virtue may be there inculcated by a proper Fable) I shall in this *Essay* confine my self to OPERAS alone, all other kinds of MUSICK, which are not perfect theatrical Entertainments, being entirely foreign to my Design.

But before I proceed any farther in canvassing our present harmonious Amusements, I believe it will be necessary to look back a little into the Original of OPERAS, which will be at best but Guess-Work, or a Grope in the Dark, without the Assistance of the smallest Star to guide us, then I will present my Readers with a more regular Sketch of the Rise and Progress of OPERAS in this Island, from their first rude Establishment, to that State of Perfection we now enjoy them in.

It will prove a difficult Task to form any true Judgment of the Original of OPERAS, especially how far the *Italians* (where certainly they first arrived to any tolerable Degree of Perfection) are indebted to the Ancients, or other modern Nations for this Musical *Dramma*. From *Italy* and *France* we have borrowed whatever has appeared on our Stages in that Way: We must then travel thither in search of the Hints which first gave Life to this Entertainment.

DRYDEN (who was one of our greatest Criticks, as well as Poets, and who has given us three *English* OPERAS in a different Taste) owns, he could not, by the nicest Scrutiny, get any just Light, either as to the Time, or the first Inventers

ters of OPERAS. He imagines *that the* Italians, *observing the Gallantries of the* Spanish Moors, *at their* Zambras, *or Royal Feasts,* (*where* MUSICK, SONGS *and* DANCING *were in Perfection, together with their Machines at their running at the Ring, and other Solemnities*) *might have refined upon those* Moresque *Amusements, and produced this pleasing kind of Dramma, by leaving out the warlike Part, and forming a poetical Design for to introduce more naturally the* MACHINES, MUSICK *and* DANCES. Then he proceeds, *that however the* OPERAS *began,* MUSICK *has for some Centuries flourished principally in* Italy, *and he believed, their* OPERAS *were first intended for the Celebration of the Marriages of their Princes, or the magnificent Triumphs of some general Time of Joy; and accordingly the Expences upon these Occasions were out of the Purse of the Sovereign or Republick, as has been often practised at* Turin, Florence, Venice, *&c.*

IN this last Point, it is very probable, he is justly exact, but as to the first, he allows it himself to be but conjectural; and, indeed, I think so too; therefore, begging Pardon for dissenting from so great an Authority, and for whose Judgment I have the utmost Deference, I must say, that in my Opinion, the Conjecture is mightily strained, and the Supposition very far fetch'd, and that the *Italians* had not the least Regard to, or Notion of a *Moorish* Solemnity, in bringing OPERAS on the Stage.

LET us thoroughly consider this Entertainment in all its Parts, and we shall readily perceive, they could only have an Eye to Antiquity, in its Invention and Establishment, particularly to the MAGNIFICENCE, MACHINES, MUSICK and DANCING of the old *Grecian* CHORUS, they (allowing for the different Design and Manner of their being

being introduced) answering exactly in the most essential Parts that compose one and the other.

DRYDEN himself, in a Postscript to the Preface of *Albion* and *Albanius*, recants and owns, *That possibly the* Italians *went not so far as* Spain *for the Invention of their* OPERAS, *they might have taken the Hint at Home, and formed this Dramma, by gathering up the Shipwrecks of the* Grecian *and* Roman *Theatres, which were adorned with* MUSICK, SCENES, DANCES, *and* MACHINES, *especially the* Grecian, *adding, that though they are a modern Invention, yet they are built on the Foundation of* Ethnick *Worship.*

Now indeed he speaks to the Purpose, and gives us the justest Idea of their Original, then pray, from what Part of the Shipwreck of the *Grecian* or *Roman* Theatres could the Design of an OPERA be plan'd out, but that of the Chorus? only what was but an Interlude, or a necessary Part of a Stage-Play with the Ancients, they enlarged, and swelled into a compleat Entertainment.

But there remain still two Points not yet taken Notice of by any Critick, which bear some Relation to the Birth of OPERAS, and weigh very much with me.

THE first is, the frequent Mention made in all Authors, (who treat of the Antiquities of *Greece*) of their *Odeum*, or Musick-Theatre, every one speaks of it, and describes its Magnificence, especially that of *Athens*, which was looked upon as the most sumptuous Building of that noble City, they mention it separately from the other Theatres, and call it, in a significant way, the *Musick Theatre*, which certainly must imply a Theatre where Musical Entertainments alone were performed. This has a Face of Probability, though none of the Authors who describe the Place, let us into the Secret, what the Nature of the Entertainments was, that appeared upon that Stage, but I humbly submit my private Opinion to be canvassed, and censured, or approved by the learned World.

'T is true, Mr. *Kennet*, in his *Roman Antiquities*, takes Notice of the *Odeum* at *Rome*, built in the ordinary Form of other Theatres, but (as he says) *only made use of for their Actors and Musicians to exercise themselves privately in, before they appeared upon the Stage*, a Custom parallel to our Rehearsals. If this was the sole Intent of the *Odeum* at *Rome*, I shall not pretend to determine, but if we may judge from the imperfect Accounts we have of the *Grecian* Odeum, it is impossible we should believe it designed for that Purpose, and, to corroborate my Assertion, I call upon his Quotation from *Plutarch*, who says, "That as to the "Contrivance of the *Odeum*, the Inside was full of "Seats, and Ranges of Pillars, and, on the Outside, "the Roof or Covering was made from one Point "at top with a great many Bendings, all shelving "downwards, in Imitation of the King of *Persia*'s "Pavilion." Now if they encouraged this extravagant Expence, only that the Actors and Musicians might privately rehearse the Pieces they were obliged to present on the Stage, what glorious Edifices must the Theatres themselves be: Or if the Grandeur of these sort of Buildings was confined to those Theatres alone where they rehearsed, and they publickly performed in wooden Booths, we can only liken them to a Man, who would put on his Shoes and wash his Hands in a Brocade Night-gown, then dress himself in Rags, in order to go abroad.

THE other Head (that I would instance here, and which has been hitherto unobserved) is, that I have some Grounds to believe, that the *Italians*, in their first modelling their OPERAS, had partly ly in their View the Conduct of the famous Priests of *Cybele*, at least, if we may judge from the Majority of their present Performers, and the Conduct of their Entertainments both in *Italy* and *Britain*. These Priests of *Cybele* bore various Names, but generally were known by the Denomination of the *Galli*.

THEIR Ceremonies were all performed in Publick, and consisted entirely of MUSICK, vocal and instrumental, intermixed with portable Machinery and all kinds of Dances, their Performers were all Eunuchs, and positively Foreigners to the *Roman* State, being all *Phrygians*. Whether this Description corresponds with OPERAS, as shewn abroad, is not my Business to assert, but in most Respects it tallies with what we have at Home.

BUT of all our Variety of Conjectures on this Subject, there is but one we can fix upon with any tolerable Look of Certainty, which is this: The *Italians*, in attempting to restore the Grandeur of the ancient *Grecian* and *Roman* Theatres, instead of the Magnificence of the old Tragedy, with a suitable Chorus, they revived that Part which they imagined would prove most generally entertaining, and being then infected with *Gothick* Whims, Licences, and trifling Ornaments in every thing polite, in place of a musical Chorus, which was the great Embellishment of the old Stage, they trump'd up an Entertainment to consist wholly of MUSICK, DANCING, and MACHINERY.

WHILE I am tracing the Original of OPERAS, it will be expected that I should, at least in a cursory manner, take some Notice of the MUSICK of the *Ancients*, both Vocal and Instrumental: But, I confess my self altogether at a Loss to produce any thing upon that Head, either in the way of Study or Conversation, that will prove satisfactory to my Readers. I have canvassed many Authors,

Authors, in order to make some regular Remarks upon their Composition, Harmony, and Difference of Instruments, as used singly, or in Consort, but found the Affair so puzling, and my Guides so blind, that, despairing of Success, I quitted the Search. The prodigious Force of Sounds we often meet with in all their Poets, exaggerated to the most miraculous Degree, and stretched beyond the Bounds of Probability: But we are sensible, that with them every thing was envelop'd in mysterious Allegories. Thus moral Instructions were convey'd to the People in the Fables of *Amphion*'s Lute's building the Walls of *Thebes*, *Orpheus*'s Lyre's taming the most savage Beasts, and *Arion*'s Harp's charming the Monsters of the Deep into a Tenderness unknown to Mankind. Yet, setting all Fiction aside, though instructive, this we may take for granted, that the trembling Strings, touched by *David*'s artful Hand, calm'd into Gentleness the raging Tyranny of froward *Saul*, and the Conqueror of the World was subdued by *Timotheus*'s Notes, the skilful Master raising and lowering his Spirits, or whirling him from Passion to Passion, just as he pleased to exert his Power.

VOICES were in great Request with the Ancients, and were frequently used at most publick Festivals, or private Feasts, Marriages, Funerals, &c. nay, even in War. We find the Names of many Instrumenss on Record, as Organs, Drums, Trumpets, Tymbrels, Cymbals, Psalters, Lutes, Harps, Lyres, Sack-buts, Dulcimers, and all sorts of Pipes, but particularly the Flute, which was the Instrument principally made use of at all solemn Games, or indeed at all Seasons, where either Grief or Joy required the Relief or Assistance of MUSICK. Of Flutes there were many different Kinds, which were varied as the Occasion demanded,

demanded, the *Phrygian*, the *Lydian*, the *Carian*, or the *Mysian*, some were right-handed, some left, some to be play'd singly, others doubly. But as this Instrument in particular has raised endless Disputes in the learned World, which we can enter into with small Prospect of Improvement (Authors being strangely divided in their Opinions about it, and all leaving us in a blind State of Uncertainty,) I think it will be more essential to the Affair in hand, to pass on to the past and present State of modern MUSICK, an Article, in which, I believe, we far excel the Ancients: For even the strongest Prejudice must allow, that in several Respects, they were a Parcel of *dull Dogs*, compared to this more brilliant Age.

As to the Rise and Progress of OPERAS at Home, I hope my Readers will not be displeased with the following concise Chronology of them, it being the most exact Account my Reading or Observation have made me Master of.

THE first regular OPERA (as I take it) that *England* could ever boast of, was performed in the Time of the great Rebellion, when Hypocrisy was called Religion, Anarchy, Government, and Enthusiasm Wit. Sir *William D'avenant*'s poetical Genius being debarr'd from entertaining the Town with the usual Theatrical Representations; he, under the Notion of an innocent musical Performance, introduced the Siege of *Rhodes*, in two Parts, the Model of which was rather taken from the *French*, than *Italian* OPERAS: But whether there were any more of this kind presented during that Scene of Villany, Confusion, and Nonsense, I could never discover, nor is it very material to our Purpose.

BEFORE I proceed any farther, I beg Leave to observe, that in the three Reigns preceeding the Æra just now mentioned, there were often performed

formed privately in the Royal Palace, and by the Gentlemen of the Inns of Court, MASQUES, contrived by the greatest *Poets, Musicians* and *Archetects* of that Age, which were in effect a kind of Drammatick Opera, or an Imitation of the old *Chorus*, being composed chiefly of MUSICK, MACHINERY and DANCING, but these will not in Propriety be looked upon as OPERAS.

AFTER the Restoration, we had at different Times several Entertainments, which were then stiled *Drammatick Operas*, which were indeed regular Stage-Plays larded with Pieces of occasional MUSICK, vocal and instrumental, proper to the Fable, and introduced either in the Beginning, Middle, or End of an Act, by single Voices, two or three Part Songs, and Chorus. These were likewise embellished with Scenes, Machines, *French* Dancing-Masters, long Trains, and Plumes of Feathers: Of this sort were the *Fairy Queen and Tempest*, alter'd from *Shakespear*; *Dioclesian* and *Island Princess*, from *Beaumont* and *Fletcher*, *Dryden*'s *Fall of Man*; never acted, and King *Arthur*, *D'avenant*'s *Circe*, *Granville*'s *Brittish Enchanters*; *Dennis*'s *Rinaldo* and *Armida*, and *Durfey*'s *Kingdom of the Birds*. These I believe were the principal, if not the whole that appeared upon our Stages of this Kind of Dramma: and, as I remember, during their Possession of the Stage, nothing was admitted in any other musical Way, excepting *Dryden*'s *Albion* and *Albanius*; which consisted altogether of MUSICK in Recitative and Airs, tho' I believe more after the *French* than *Italian Gou*, being set to Musick by a *Frenchman*. This I look upon as the second Age of OPERAS, as we then stiled them, but I absolutely deny them that Title, that Term implying a regular, compleat musical Entertainment, which they never could arrive at, till they entirely came into a finished

nished *Italian* Plan, nor do we bestow the Name of OPERA on any Dramma, but those where every Word is sung.

INDEED the only Merit they could boast of, was their claiming a kind of Resemblance or Relation to the old *Grecian* Tragedy and Chorus, and could they have supply'd the necessary Expences essential to the Grandeur of such a Design, I must own their Performances would have proved no bad Imitation even of the *Grecian* Stage in its greatest Lustre.

HOWEVER, in this State remained our Theatrical MUSICK, or the Shadow of an Opera-Stage for several Years, one House striving to out-do the other, or ruin Wit by Sound and Shew, till Mr *Clayton* happily arriving from *Italy*, introducing at once OPERAS after their manner, that is, *English* Words, with *Italian* Airs, true home-spun *British* Manufacture, cut out in the *Trans-alpine* Fashion. *Arsinoe, The Temple of Love,* and some others of that Stamp, pleased as long as they were a Novelty, but they only instructed us to have a Relish for better MUSICK, so some Operas of the best *Italian* Masters were translated into *English*, and the MUSICK preserved, as *Camilla, Thomyris,* &c. These succeeded tolerably well, till grown too familiar, and that we began to understand them, then an *Italian* Singer or two crept in by degrees, to charm us with something new and unintelligible, and this pretty motly Performance pleased for some Time, but some good Sense still remaining amongst us, the Absurdity of that Conversation *a la Babel* was so notorious, that it was look'd upon as more inexcusable, than having the whole Performance in one proper, though foreign, Language: This of Consequence threw us into entire *Italian* OPERAS, both as to Language, Musick and Performers, which gradually has work'd them

them up to that high Pitch they now shine triumphant in, and, we may boldly say, we excel any thing *Italy* ever knew, (as to one particular Stage) both in Composition and Performance: For several Years they have kept their Ground, against all vain Attempts to dislodge them, only allowing for some small Recesses for breathing Time: And as an *Italian* Opera can never touch the Comprehension of above one Part in four of a *British* Audience, it is very probable their Theatre will be crowded as long as we are a Nation.

BUT since the bare Name of an *Italian* Opera, as established at present amongst us, is to the last Degree shocking to the Ears of many honest Inhabitants of this METROPOLIS. In order to remove all groundless Prejudices, let us briefly and impartially, is possible, state the Case betwixt the contending Parties, by considering the most material Objections to this Entertainment, and framing a just Method of answering them: Thus wipe off, or at least compound for, those things they look upon as Absurdities or Impositions.

I think the Objections of greatest Weight may be reduced to four Heads. The first exclaims against an Opera's being performed in a Language so little understood Its Enemies cry out against this as a thing highly unnatural —— *What! be attentive to what is Gibberish to us!* —— *Chatt'ring Monkies!* —— *Ridiculous Apes! We spend our Money and lose our Time, and perhaps only to be cursed or laughed at!* —— The second is started by those who are charmed with the MUSICK, particularly the Airs, but nauseate the odious *Recitative:* —— Or that the Whole of an Opera should be sung —— *They die with Laughing to hear a Tyrant rage and storm in a vast Regularity of Sounds, a General sing at the Head of an Army, or a Lover, Swan-like, expire at his Mistress's Feet,* and that

there

there is not an imperial Mandate, a Word of Command, or Billet-doux delivered but in expressive Flats and Sharps. The third bears hard with a most general Out-cry upon the exorbitant Prices we pay the Performers, especially the Foreigners: —*Intolerable!*—*so many Hundreds!*—*for a Thing of nothing!*——*a Voice!*—*a meer ha, ha!*—*nasty Pusses, odious filthy Things!*—*Let them stay at home and starve, or sing at reasonable Rates*—— The fourth is altogether critical, and raised by those Gentlemen who are Masters of so much good Sense, and just Criticism, that they are obliged to be displeased with every thing that will not stand the Test of ARISTOTLE and RAPIN. *An Opera throws them into Convulsions, one Part is ridiculous, another improbable, a third unnatural; a fourth improper; a fifth irregular,—— and so they run themselves out of Breath*—— *Zounds, no Unity in Time, Place or Action observed!*

LET me now, as briefly as I stated these Objections, animadvert upon them, according to the Sentiments of those who are professed Admirers of our present OPERAS: Then I shall naturally throw in my private Opinion, and, like a true Critick, point out both Beauties and Blemishes, stand up in Defence of what is right, and propose Remedies for what is wrong.

As to the first Objection, The musical Part of this and all other modern Nations have agreed, that the *Italian* is undoubtedly the most proper Language to be joined to Sounds, for Reasons so obvious, that it would be Impertinence to mention them. But, not to tire my Reader with Quotations, let us hear what one of our greatest Refiners and Improvers of the *English* Tongue says, and every Man will allow DRYDEN to be a Judge. *All,* says he, *who are conversant in that noble Language, the* Italian, *cannot but observe, that it is the softest, sweetest, and most harmonious, not only of any modern Tongue, but even beyond any of the Learned. It seems to have been invented not only for* POETRY, *but* MUSICK, *the Vowels so abounding in all Words, especially in the Terminations, that, excepting a few Monosyllables, the whole Language ends in them. Then their Pronunciation is so sonorous, that their very Speaking has more* MUSICK *in it, than* Dutch POETRY *and* SONG: *And if we must call it barbarous, it is the most beautiful and most learned of any* Barbarism *in the modern Tongues.*

In the next place we cannot have native Performers for our Mother Tongue, but what will fall far short of the excellent Voices and Taste of those we are supplied with from Abroad: Some Women we boast of, and Boys; but the first generally lose their Voices before they begin to learn, and are then ill taught, as the latter are obliged by Nature to part with theirs, by the time they know any thing of the Matter: A tolerable Bass Voice we may meet with by Chance in an Age: But as we are denied the Liberty of artificially tuning the Pipes of those Performers who are neither Men nor Women, and who are the Foundation of the *Italian* OPERAS, I do aver, that I think it impossible to form a perfect and compleat Musical Entertainment of our own People, or in our own Language.

NOT to go any farther back than last Winter, the Attempt of introducing *English* Operas at L——n's-Inn-F——ds Theatre, will sufficiently justifie my Assertion. Their Endeavours, though headed by a great Master, and supported by some People of the best Fashion and Interest, in a few Weeks did but expose to the Ridicule of every body, that had any Notion of MUSICK, their wretched ed Performance, and even then, those that made the best Figure on their Stage were Foreigners: 'Tis true, that Representation had a Run, (as they term it) and brought several full Houses, but I speak of its Merit, and not its Success, the first was obvious to every Ear; the last was forced by a Party, during the Vacation of the *Italian* OPERAS.

NOTHING but the Wantonness of Plenty from the lowest Necessity, could have thrown People into such an Absurdity, thus profusely to squander away on bad Voices, what was got by clever Heels, and to choose that Season, when the whole of *English* MUSICK was at the lowest Ebb, and the OPERAS at the H—y-M—t at that Height, (both as to Composition and Performance) which no ancient Theatre could ever have an Idea of; nay, it is almost unknown to *Italy* it self.

I was so unfortunate, as to be oblig'd once to sit Ca———la out, to the great Disquiet of my Ears, nor have I perfectly got rid of the Head-ach it gave me, yet; and I vow, had it not been for Mrs. B———ter, and my old Friend L———dge, I could have swore the Stage had returned the Favour the Audience sometimes does them, and play'd a full Choir of Cat-calls upon us.

THIS Season they reviv'd *Thomyris* at L———n's *Inn*-F———ds, but that being rather a better OPERA, and more justly performed than the other, the Town would not go near it

So finding their Finances run very low, by striving to do well, they thought it absolutely necessary to do something very bad, in order to retrieve their undone Affairs.

THIS indeed they have happily effected in Conjunction with a great Poet, and by giving us something more execrable in relation to MUSICK, than the World ever dreamt of seeing on any Stage, they are Made, and we run mad with Joy in being so agreeably disappointed.

THE *Beggar's Opera*, by robbing the Performers at *Pye-corner*, *Fleet-ditch*, *Moor-fields* (and other Stations of this Metropolis, famed for travelling Sounds) of their undoubted Properties, has reinstated them in Wealth and Grandeur, and what shock'd most Ears, and set most Teeth on edge, at turning the Corner of a Street, for half a Moment, when thrown into a regular Entertainment, charms for Hours.

I must own they never appear'd to that Advantage in any musical Light as this OPERA of *Beggars*: Their Rags of POETRY and Scraps of MUSICK joining so naturally, that in whatever View we consider it as to Character or Circumstance, its Title is the most *apropos* Thought upon Earth.

THE second Objection, at first Sight, may appear very plausible, but, upon Examination, very ill grounded; for it is impossible to have a perfect musical *Dramma*, without Recitative: No Ear can support the Whole being all Air, therefore if you take away the Recitative, it is no OPERA: And the best Judges value a Master as much upon the Merit of one as the other: The Recitative is but a tuneable Method of speaking; and in the Article of MUSICK, but refines upon Speech, as far as polite Comedy excels common Conversation, or Tragedy in Heroicks, the ordinary Stile of the Great. As for the critical Part of the Objection against Recitative, I desire that our Poets, Criticks, and Fine Gentlemen, banish first greater Absurdities and Inconsistencies from their Stage-Plays, for I cannot

cannot imagine, that to sing all the Parts of an OPERA is by half so unnatural, as the sparkling Nonsense, gilded Fustian, and pompous Bombast in most, if not all our Tragedies; nor so improper as the quaint *Double Entendres*, and forc'd Similies, squeez'd out in the midst of Misfortunes, or at the Point of Death: The Heroes there quietly and stupidly sleep over four Acts in a dull regular Way of Life, till by Danger they are rouz'd from their Lethargy into a State of Wit, like the Prince born dumb, whose Tongue was never loosen'd, till the Sword was at his Father's Throat. In short, nothing is ridiculous that executes a regular Design: That of an OPERA, is to represent to us, in the Drammatick Way, some instructive *Fable*, where the Words are all to be deliver'd in MUSICK, therefore a King must rule, a General fight, a Lover sigh, in Harmony: Nor is there wanting in this Art a Variety to touch the different Passions, as justly as any Kind of POETRY. Nor can I observe any thing in singing a Conversation-Piece, more absurd or ridiculous than a familiar Dialogue in Heroick *Rhime*.

THE third Objection indeed carries great Weight with it. Our Prices are immoderately extravagant, and all we can say to justify them is, that we are arrived now to so picquant a *Gou* in MUSICK, that nothing but what is superexcellent will pass. What pleases at *Venice* or *Rome* may chance to be hiss'd at the H---y-M--t. If we must have those of the greatest Merit, they will be paid accordingly. If they don't meet with more Encouragement here than at Home, who will run the Hazard of coming near us? Should we pay them double, still the Odds is against them; an English Morning or Evening may

may ruin them for ever, and a North-East Blast in *July* rob them of their Bread at once: 'Tis but just, that if our Ears demand the best Performers, that our Purses should pay the highest Prices; else 'tis culling the choicest Fruit at *Leaden-Hall* and *Covent-Garden* Markets, and expect it as cheap as the withered Refuse of a blind Alley-Stall.

THE exorbitant Expences occasion'd by introducing an *Italian* OPERA amongst us, may be reduc'd to two Heads: *First*, the vast Salaries given to the Singers by the Academy. *Secondly*, what the Audience pays to the Academy, which is the natural Consequence of the other. As to the first, I think it fully answer'd before, nor is the Academy in the least to blame, our Taste is so refin'd, and our Judgment so solid in relation to all Parts of MUSICK, that such an Entertainment cannot be supported but by the Tip-top Performers of the World, and they will have Prices equal to their Merit. As to the second, it would be highly unreasonable to expect that the Directors of the H———y-M———t Th———e should amuse us at their own private Expence, they run a great Risque to please us, in engaging for vast Sums, whilst it is left to our Choice whether we'll come or no, to ease them of Part of the Burden: Nor can they with the highest Prices be certain of coming off clear one Season, unless they have crowded Houses every Night

THE fourth Objection is altogether critical, and carry'd on in the stiff pedantick Rules that Tribe have settled, by which they form a Judgment on every thing polite, and of consequence damn all Amusements where Spirit and Life prevail over their unanimated Works of Clay. These merry Gentlemen would reduce OPERAS to the Standard

OF MUSICK.

Standard of *Aristotle* and *Rapin*. Should these Entertainments in any Point prove Malefactors, they are for bringing them before improper Judges, it is carrying the Cause into as wrong a Court of Judicature, as trying a Pyrate for Murder in *Chancery*, or a Highwayman in *Doctors-Commons* An OPERA borrows no Helps from their *Poeticks*, is not built upon the Foundation of their Stages, nor must their Rules interfere with any Part of the Superstructure: Were it otherways, why should not this Amusement as well as others, upon Occasion, plead the Benefit of their Clergy, and when it is guilty of what is irregular or unnatural, excuse it, by calling it a bright Thought and bold Beauty It has ever been granted by those who allow an OPERA any Existence at all, that things wholly super-natural and marvellous are warrantable in this Kind of *Dramma*, though they would be damn'd in a regular Tragedy or Comedy: AN OPERA may be call'd the Tyrant of the Stage, it is subject to no poetical Laws, despises the Power or Limitations of a Parliament of Criticks, and subsists altogether by absolute Sway, and its own uncontroulable Prerogative: It has Liberty to range Heaven, Earth, and Hell, call Gods, Spirits, and Devils to its Assistance, and all this unbounded Freedom is taken for the Probable, or rather what is necessary in this Entertainment

But let me corroborate my Opinion on this Head by the Words of one even of our most eminent Play-Wrights and Criticks, who says, *That an* OPERA *is a poetical Tale or Fiction, represented by Vocal and Instrumental* MUSICK, *that the suppos'd Persons of this Musical Dramma are generally supernatural, as Gods, Goddesses and Heroes The Subject therefore being extended beyond the Li-*

mits

mits of human Nature, admits of that fort of marvellous and furprizing Conduct, which is rejected in other Plays. Humane Impoſſibilities are to be receiv'd as they are in Faith, becauſe where Gods are introduc'd, a ſupreme Power is to be underſtood, and ſecond Cauſes are out of Doors. But ſtill Propriety muſt be obſerv'd even here, the Gods muſt manage their peculiar Provinces; and what was attributed by the Heathens to one Power, ought not to be perform'd by any other ——— This laſt Part (which implies a proper Decency) is the only Reſtriction that OPERAS are laid under.

BUT after this Defence of OPERAS in general, our muſical Stage is rarely guilty of ſuch Faults as may incur a critical Cenſure: Thoſe Licences and Allowances, in my Mind, are too ſparingly made uſe of in that Theatre, and their Modeſty too great, in rejecting ſuch juſt and beautiful Alliances, which I cannot avoid conſidering, as Appendixes abſolutely eſſential to ſuch Entertainments.

I had ſome Thoughts of adding to theſe Objections, a fifth, not rais'd by the Oppoſers, but Admirers of OPERAS; and that is a Complaint of too great Simplicity or Sameneſs in thoſe Amuſements: The Whole being meer MUSICK, not diverſify'd with Grand CHORUSSES, DANCING, MACHINERY, and all the other Theatrical Embelliſhments, which are look'd upon as the very Limbs of the Body of an OPERA, which it not only allows, but demands, and ſo eſſential are they to its Nature, that the Neglect of them ſhews us at beſt but a lame, imperfect Figure But I ſhall ſpeak more fully to this Point, in the Eſſay appropriated to *Choruſſes*, where I ſhall obſerve how far theſe auxiliary Ornaments are to be made uſe of in an OPERA: Therefore I

ſhall

shall now proceed to consider these Objections in a new Light, and as there may be some just Grounds for finding Fault, yet let us not rashly cut down the Tree we should only prune: 'Tis more praise-worthy to improve than to destroy, nay, if we look upon our Love of MUSICK as an incurable Folly, let us then find out some Lenitives to moderate the Malignity of the Disease we can't entirely eradicate.

I hope none of my courteous Readers will be surpriz'd, if I declare that I am so far charm'd with our present OPERAS, though perform'd in *Italian*, that I look upon them as compleat Entertainments in their way, that is, to the last Degree perfect, as to the Article of MUSICK, which is the only Point they aim at

BUT as I am sensible, that their being perform'd in a foreign Tongue disgusts many of my Countrymen, who (tho' great *Philarmonicks*) yet being *True Britons*, and staunch *Protestants*, to shew their Love to their Country, and their Zeal for their Religion, are prepossess'd against Singing as well as Praying in an unknown Dialect: I propose to remove this ill-grounded Suggestion, and help the Academy in this Scene of Distress, by dividing the Argument. As the Dir——ors of the OPERA can never hope for a Set of Singers, Natives of this Island, equal to what we are supply'd with from Abroad (as long as our Laws in Relation to Emasculation confine that small Ceremony to the Bodies of our Brutes,) if they would but allow some extraordinary Events either historical or traditionary (which wholly regard our selves) to be translated into *Italian*, I'll engage for my Countrymen they'll resign the Language for the History, that being undoubtedly

edly originally our own, and the *English* Page always leading in the Opera Books, we gain the disputed Punctilio, and bring off our Honour safe, which is dearer to every *True Briton* than Life.

To set this Affair in a true Light, I beg leave to illustrate this Essay with some of our most noted domestick *Fables*, which must please an *English* Audience, and at the same time make a beautiful Appearance on the Stage. These shall be principally borrow'd from a Subject which can boast an inexhaustible Fund of Models for Theatrical Entertainments, particularly OPERAS; *viz. Knight-Errantry*, which has in all Ages produc'd so many valuable Volumes of Romances, Memoirs, Novels and Ballads, either written or oral.

A late eminent ingenious Author propos'd to the then Master of the OPERA-STAGE, *Whittington and his Cat*, and went so far in the Design, as to procure a Puss or two, who could pur tolerably in Time and Tune: But the Inconveniencies arising from the Number of Vermin requisite to be destroy'd, in order to keep up to the Truth of the Story, blasted that Project.

MANY worthy Patriots amongst us (through the Prejudice of their Infant-Education) would doat upon the Representation of *Valentine and Orson*, but the Scene thro' every memorable Event of that wonderful History being entirely foreign, I cannot approve of its Admission, though I must own the H——y-M——t can never hope to shew the World two finer Bears than they can produce at present, which would be no small Addition to a Musical *Dramma*.

THE Generality of this Nation would likewise imbibe a Fondness for the *Seven Champions of Christen-*

Christendom, even from their Nursery; but the Ac———my not being able to furnish so many Heroes at a Time, we must drop that Design: Though I must say, our own St. *George*'s Part would equip us with Characters and Incidents for a very beautiful *Dramma*, in which the whole History of the G———r might be properly and naturally introduc'd, with a little Episode thrown in about the O———r of the T———le, then tack to to their Tails a large Troop of the K———ts of the B———h, with their Es———res, by way of a Grand Chorus: And this Scene would be truly great, and worthy a *Brittish* Audience.

BUT I fear we should find some Difficulty in meeting with a proper Dragon, unless the *Af———n* Company could procure us a sucking one, just out of the Nest, to be brought up tame, and skilful Masters to instruct it in the Rudiments of MUSICK, or that *Doctor Faustus* could be prevail'd upon to part with his artificial one, which really roars out a good tuneable Bass: Then if Sign^r B———*chi* would condescend to sing the Part of St. *George*'s *Horse*, with S———*no* upon his Back, and Sign^r *Pal———ni* allow himself to be clapp'd into the Dragon's Belly: I believe this Plan would surprize us not only with a noble Scene of Recitative, but furnish us with an Opportunity of throwing in the newest and finest *Duet* that ever was heard, *viz.* betwixt the *Horse* and the *Dragon*.

'TIS true, I here digress from my original Design of only celebrating old *English* Occurrences, for St. *George*, though our Patron Saint, was by Birth a *Cappadocian*, as this particular Scene of his Life was laid in *Egypt*, whose King's Daughter he freed from that terrible Monster. But as my mentioning a Dragon may excite the

Curiosity

Curiosity of many *Connoisseurs* to see such a Creature fly or tread the Stage, and hear him sing, I think we need not go from Home for a Fable, whose Authority is undisputed, and which can furnish out as noble a Monster Scene, as if we had gone to *China* for the Story.

MOST of our Countrymen, who are deeply read in the old *Brittish* Ballads, (which have been so curiously and carefully collected lately by a judicious Antiquary, with learned Observations and Annotations, by which means many remarkable Transactions are preserv'd in those Singsong *Annals*, which History has neglected) will readily imagine, that I hint at the noted Combat betwixt *Moor* of *Moor-hall*, and the Dragon of *Wantcliff*, which for the Beauty of Fable, Variety of Incidents, a Quantity of the Marvellous, and a glorious Catastrophe, may vie with any Story, ancient or modern.

INDEED this *Dramma* will admit but of two principal Characters, *viz.* 'Squire *Moor* and the *Dragon* But here is the most proper Occasion imaginable of introducing a magnificent Chorus in every Act, a Stage-Decoration so esteem'd by all the Ancients and Learned Moderns, that they thought all Theatrical Entertainments imperfect without one, as I shall farther explain in a separate *Essay*.

IN the first Act you have a Chorus of Men, Women, and Children, whose Bread and Butter, Milk-Pottage or Relations the Dragon had devour'd, accompany'd by a suitable Noise of Sobs, Sighs and Groans on proper Instruments, which must have a fine Effect, as to moving Pity These Lamentations rousing up the dormant Spirit of *Moor*, he declares for the Combat, which naturally ushers in the second Act a Chorus of

warlike

warlike Instruments on his Part, preparative to the Battle, join'd to a compleat Roar on the Part of the Dragon, which must exhibit Terror to a vast Degree: Then the third Act beginning with the Combat, concludes nobly with the Dragon's Death, and a grand Chorus of the whole Country, where Sounds of Triumph and Joy, mix'd with Bells, Bon-fires and Country-Dances, perform'd by Country-Squires, Shepherds, Milk-Maids, and a Saint or two introduc'd by a Machine, one suppos'd to have given *Moor* a Breast-Plate and Head-Piece, another more than humane Courage, to atchieve so wonderful an Exploit: Thus the Whole ends agreeably, and sends every Person of the Audience Home well pleased: In this little Story all the Passions are finely express'd.

Robbin Hood and *Little John* cannot fail of charming the *Brittish* Nation, being undoubtedly a Domestick Matter of Fact, but as no Singer in *Europe* can top the Part of *Little John* but Ber——dt, we must suspend that Performance till his Return, to bless our Eyes.

The *London 'Prentice* would infallibly gain the Hearts of the City, besides the valuable Incident of a *Lion-Scene*, as the *Abbot* of *Canterbury* would procure the Favour of the Clergy, and then the whole Audience (in Imitation of that polite, agreeable Custom practis'd at *Paris*) might join the Stage, every body beating Time, and singing, *Derry down, down, down,* &c.

Tom Thumb would be a beautiful Foundation to build a pretty little Pastoral on, his Length too being adequate to that of a Summer's Evening, the *Belles* and *Beaus* might arrive Time enough from either Park, and enjoy the whole of his Affair: Nay, it would admit of some very new Scenes, as surprizing as true: Witness the Accident of the Pudding, which would be something as uncommon as ever appear'd on any Stage, not excepting even a *Dutch* Tragedy --- N. B. Cu——ni *in Breeches would make a delightful* Tom Thumb.

SHOULD this Project of mine succeed, *Chevy-Chace* will be demanded by every *South* and *North* B——*n*. I confess the Beginning is very Theatrical, and will admit of a good Number of *French Horns*, which have been lately receiv'd at the H——y-M——t with tolerable Success: But I fear its bloody Catastrophe will not so well answer our Purpose: For though we have had some very handsome noisy Skirmishes on that Stage, and where both Generals and common Soldiers have merited an old *Roman* Triumph, yet I cannot say, that I ever knew any of the *Virtuosi* concern'd in those Engagements, reduc'd to so low a Pitch, as either to fight or sing on their Stumps, nor would they, I believe, be fond of the Operation.

I know, the severe deep-read *Criticks* will object to the Simplicity of these Subjects, and the Lowness of most of the Characters, our present OPERAS being generally form'd upon Plans of the greatest Events, and most celebrated Parts of History: To this I answer, that we are not oblig'd to be always ty'd down to Affairs of that vast Moment, some Stories of an inferior Rank allowing as proper Entertainments, as just Morality, and as tender Sentiments, as where we dwell entirely upon the Fates of Kings and Kingdoms. Let us instance that famous OPERA, where *Patient Grissel* appear'd in her proper Character, to the entire Satisfaction of several Audiences, as polite as crowded: Nay, some of the

best

best Tragedies belonging to the *English* Stage, are founded entirely upon the Distress of low Life, and the Misfortunes of private Families.

THUS *Dryden* allows, *That though the Persons represented in* OPERAS *are generally Gods, Goddesses, and Heroes, who are suppos'd to be their peculiar Care Yet this hinders not, but that meaner Persons may sometimes gracefully be introduc'd, especially, if by Reason of their Innocence, those happy Mortals were suppos'd to have had a more familiar Intercourse with superior Beings; and therefore Shepherds might reasonably be admitted, as of all Callings the most innocent, the most happy, and who, by reason of their almost idle Employment, had most Leisure to make Verses, and to be in Love; without which Passion no* OPERA *can possibly subsist.* This Concession is all I plead for, to make good my Assertion.

BUT at once to silence all Cavils of this Nature (without tiring my Readers, by pointing out any more proper Fables, or anticipating their Pleasure in finding them out for them,) I beg Leave to produce but one Example more, to stregthen my Argument, and to knock down all Opponents: This is an *English* Story, entirely calculated for the present Set of Singers, and capable of giving us a vast deal of the *Pathetick*, the *Wonderful*, and the *Terrible*, the distinguishing Characteristicks of MUSICK, as well as POERTY; nor will any of my Readers, I hope, seem startled, when I set full before their Eyes, *The Children in the Wood.*

AS to the Drammatical Distribution of the several Characters in this beautiful Fable, I fear we must implore the Assistance of Mr. H———ger, who has always graciously condescended to act any Part in Life, which could amuse this Nation in a polite Way: His Countenance (though far different from his Nature) will best become the *Uncle's* cruel Part: And some of our present Composers have a few savage Songs ready compos'd, adapted to his Face and Character in this OPERA. As F——na's Shake and Graces qualify her to appear the first old Woman in *Europe*, I have mark'd her as Nurse to the two Children, S——no and B——di will make a couple of chopping Infants, and as they can equally act the Parts of Boys or Girls, the Ac——my shall determine which shall be Male, which Female: Then I have an original Painting in my Possession, which with a little of B——chi's Advice and Stitching, will equip them with such Hanging-Sleeve-Coats, Bibs and Aprons, as were worn in those Days, which will add a Lustre to the Propriety of Dress. B——chi and P——ini may be very happily introduc'd as two Hob-goblins, to frighten the *Uncle* out of his Wits: Nor would it be amiss, if we could prevail on A——a R——n to perform the Part of an old Maiden *Aunt*, a Character absolutely necessary in a Country Family, and she, in Conjunction with the lamentable D——ti, would move most feelingly in a Funeral Chorus. Which last Scene, if well manag'd, cannot fail shewing true Distress to a vast Height. Then to make the Affair appear more solemn, after the Manner of the Ancients, there might be hir'd from *Ireland* (where that Custom is still observed) a full Cry of *Burial-Howlers*. And to add still to the Grandeur of that Scene, the Ac———my might agree with their Joiner to dress them cheap, a magnificent Wooden Supper, according to that old *English* Custom. As for our little Warbler C——ni, though last mention'd, yet neither despis'd, nor forgot, we can here fit her with the

finest

finest Part, she ever shone in As her Size and Voice will furnish out a mighty pretty Bird, she shall sing the Part of the *Robin-Red-Breast*, which covers the dead Children with Leaves: She shall be usher'd in by a *Cock-Sparrow*, and allow'd two *Tom-Tits* to hold up her Tail. N B *The Composers of* Elpidia, *and some other late* OPERAS, *will be the proper Masters to set this* Dramma *to* MUSICK

As touching and, of Consequence, improving the Passions, is the highest Flight that Art, in conjunction with Nature, can soar, we see from the Plan of this simple neglected Story, to what a Pitch of Instruction the musical Stage may be screw'd, when all the *Utile Dulci* of POETRY may, even in an OPERA, be exhibited for the Benefit of Mankind.

THE furnishing our *Musick-Theatre* with Fables of this Kind will produce another Advantage, perhaps not yet discover'd by the Admirers of that Art, the Simplicity and Lowness of the Characters in general adapted to these Scenes in Life, will extinguish those Fire-brands of Dissention, and Heart-burning Animosities, which Grandeur, and natural Love of Empire, have kindled in the Breasts of several of our Performers, especially those of the Fair Sex, and for the future, prevent the Sparks inherent to the Jealousy of Power, from being blown up into such Flames.

WE are sensible this Thirst of Royal Sway had almost prov'd fatal to the Republick of *Sounds*; nor have we yet perfectly recover'd what we suffer'd and fear'd from those horrid Civil Wars. In these Stories I recommend, the principal Parts will be upon the Level: No Room for Contest; no Dispute who shall be Empress, Queen, or Princess; no Rivalship but in Love, when contending Nymphs and Shepherdesses strive and scold, and sing to gain S——no's Heart.

Not that I would entirely banish from the *Opera-Stage* Heroick Deeds, or Characters of the first Rank: Nor would I confine the *Dramma* to such alone: Our *English* History is prolifick of Ground-work for all Theatrical Entertainments. As our Nation can boast of Persons and Actions equal in Fame to any Part of Antiquity, so can we vie with their Golden Age, in *Sylvan* Scenes, and rural Innocence

This amusing Variety in the Choice of Subjects for our Operas, will allow a greater Latitude in Composition than we have yet known: It will employ all our Masters in their different Talents, and in course destroy that Schism which at present divides our Lovers of Musick, and turns even Harmony into Discord. The Dispute will not then be, who is the justest, or brightest Composer, or which the finest Operas, those of our own Growth, or those imported from *Italy*? Every Man would be set to Work, and strive to excel in his own Way H——l would furnish us with Airs expressive of the Rage of Tyrants, the Passions of Heroes, and the Distresses of Lovers in the Heroick Stile B——ni sooth us with sighing Shepherds, bleating Flocks, chirping Birds, and purling Streams in the *Pastoral* · And A——o give us good Dungeon Scenes, Marches for a Battel, or Minuets for a Ball, in the *Miserere*. H——l would warm us in Frost or Snow, by rousing every Passion with Notes proper to the Subject: Whilst B——ni would fan us, in the *Dog-Days*, with an *Italian* Breeze, and lull us asleep with gentle Whispers: Nay, the pretty Operas from t'other Side the Water, might serve to tickle us in the Time of *Christmas-Gambols,*

bols, or mortify us in the Time of *Lent*, so make us very merry, or very sad.

I have made my Remarks on this Head the more full, in hopes that the Hints advanced here, might of themselves accommodate our *Italian* OPERAS to the *British* Taste and Ears; and in some Measure, make a small Recompence for the Defects we find in them, or the Prejudices we have unthinkingly entertain'd against them, in the foregoing Objections: However, I shall lightly touch upon each of the other three, as I go along, so proceed orderly to the second, which would destroy the *Recitative*.

No Criticism upon our OPERAS has prevail'd more universally, nor more unjustly, than that upon the *Recitative*, yet so it happens, that the Generality of our Audiences have a secret distaste to it, and many, even of our Patrons of MUSICK, are shock'd with it: How to remedy this Want of Taste, or how to sacrifice our Recitative to Caprice, I know not. We must therefore find out some moderating Expedient to humour the first, for giving into the latter, would demolish the Design and Nature of an OPERA quite.

I have been inform'd of a Medium propos'd in this Affair by some true *English-men* (who bear a vast Respect for the last Age; and who would have as much of their Country appear in every thing, as possible) which is, to have the Recitative Part of every Character perform'd by an *English* Singer, or Actor, and then at an Air, his *Italian* Counter-part slip from behind his Robe, or jump out of his Pocket, and sing the Air. but the Contradictions and Absurdities of this Proposal are so notorious, that I think my self to blame in the bare mentioning of it.

THEREFORE to wave Things of this Nature, which are founded on Whim and Chimera, and at once to fix upon something new, pretty and probable, I must acquaint my Readers, that of fourscore and nineteen Expedients I started, I could lay my Finger but upon one to please my self, and that, if rightly understood, will have the desired Effect: My Project is, to have the Singers of the OPERA all thoroughly skill'd in DANCING, and so the whole of the Recitative danc'd, after the expressive Manner of the old *Pantomines*, and our modern *Grotesque Dances*. Every body must be sensible of the Force and Elegance of a Meaning-Dance; and as all Dances are to some Tune, the Musick need never cease, no more than in the accompanying the Recitative, so the OPERA will still appear all of a-piece. This will produce an agreeable Variety, and lead us insensibly into the Beauty of an *Antique Chorus*, which consisted both of DANCING and SINGING. But, in order to explain this Proposition in a more just and regular Method, let us but seriously reflect, that none of the Passions, either in PLAYS or OPERAS, can be agreeably express'd by the Voice, or at least not truly, without some emphatical Motions so order'd, as to support the Meaning by a significant Force, and which are judiciously adapted to every particular Subject and Passion: For as Recitative is not properly either direct MUSICK or SPEECH, but a tuneable Sort of a Medium betwixt both, which makes a juster Alliance betwixt the Words and the Voice: So all proper Actions, which give new Life and Vigour to SPEECH in the Explanation of our Thoughts, are a Kind of DANCING; and every Posture, Attitude, or Motion requisite to that Purpose, is but a different Step of the *Grand Dance*, and where there is a strict and beautiful

beautiful Union betwixt these two *Sister-Graces*, in the Manner here propos'd, the Expression of the Passions must appear in a more ravishing Point of View, than has been ever known in Modern OPERAS or PLAYS, or even to *Rome* and *Greece* themselves.

FOR Example, —— Should a Hero make Love to a Princess in Recitative, if he danc'd a little at the same time, I cannot suppose, that an easie Minuet-step, a sprightly Caper, or a strong Bound, would appear ungenteel, unactive, or unnatural, all Members would shew out in full Order and high Vigour, and might perhaps prove as recommendatory Graces with most fine Ladies, as a sweet Voice.

SHOULD an absolute Monarch, in a Rage, display unlimited Rule, I fancy, that thundering Kicks and Cuffs, those weighty Expressions of Anger by Legs and Arms, laid on in proper Time and Tune, would denote the Tyrant, and Arbitrary Power, in a greater Force of Reasoning, than any Words, or Notes, that ever Poet or Musician produc'd.

OR, if we may be allow'd to borrow a Beauty from the *French* Opera-Stage; what Phrases could be invented, to delineate the Fury of a Mad-man, with that Strength of Meaning, as when *Roland Furieux*, without Saying, or Singing, shews you Madness to the Life, in traversing the Stage with a thousand frantick Capers and Gestures, whilst the expressive Flourishes of a broad Back-sword, hack and hew to pieces an entire Sett of Scenes, as large as the *Bois de Boulogne*.

THE same Reasons will hold good in every Character in Life, there being as great a Variety and Latitude in DANCES, as in the Passions themselves: But I shall proceed no farther on this Head at present, being oblig'd to treat it more at large in the third *Essay*, where the Affair of DANCING in general, comes upon the *Carpet*. So I shall step on to the third Objection, *viz.* the High Prices we pay at an OPERA.

I have already acknowledg'd, that the Clamour rais'd against our OPERAS in this Objection, is very near as just, as it is general, and I have likewise made manifest, that as the Majority of our People of Fashion are willing to have such exquisite Entertainments at any rate, so it is impossible to remedy the Inconveniencies arising from the first Part of this Objection, by having the best Performers at a trifling Expence. Every body must be satisfy'd with the Reasons already given on that Point, but as to the second Part, the Price every Person of the Audience pays, there we may be readily eas'd, which will answer our Purpose to the full, as well. I will be bold to say, there is but one Method can be pursu'd in attaining this desir'd End, and I at the same time, with all humility aver, that the original Hint is not my own: For I have often heard it very publickly whisper'd, that some great People intended to have a larger *Opera-House* built, but what obstructed so noble and laudable a Design, I could never learn. Had it been carried on, and executed, according to the Plans of some THEATRES in *Italy*, which are capale of containing an Audience of several Thousands, the Advantages resulting from so great an Undertaking would prove infinite.

AN *Opera-House* so contriv'd as to allow a Number of Spectators, would admit of several Degrees of Seats, suited in their Prices to all Ranks of People, from the highest to the lowest Station of Life: And from an Audience so numerous, might be rais'd all Sums necessary to defray the greatest

greatest Expences, as the heaviest Taxes are made easy, by being made general.

SUCH large Sums coming in every *Opera Night*, would quickly enable the Directors of the H———y M———t to out-bid all *Europe* in the Salaries given to Performers, both Vocal and Instrumental; and fix the best Composers obedient to their Call. What Glory would redound to the *British* Nation, from so signal a Triumph! So far should we then be from grudging the necessary Expences of an OPERA, that we might afford to be profuse, to Extravagancy, in the most trifling Ornaments, and leave no Grounds for Complaint, that the Magnificence of our Musical Stage, as to Chorus, Scenes, Machines, and Dancing, is totally neglected.

How polish'd a People should we then prove? The very Envy of our neighbouring Nations! When not a Tinker or Cobler should miss an OPERA. The Prices being once reduc'd, no Man so profess'd a Foe to Musick, as not to turn Proselyte to so delicious an Entertainment —— Happy *Venice*! where every *Gondolier* can whistle his *Opera-Air*, and judge of *Harmony*! Could we but live to see such pleasant Times in *England*, I make no Doubt but OPERA-STOCK would soon out-sell the *Indian* or *South-Sea*. How great was our Misfortune, that the Foundation of a capacious, splendid *Opera-House* was not laid, the wonderful Year of Projection! Thence proceeds my Concern, the Want of a spacious Piece of Ground, and a suitable Fund to carry on so publick-spirited a Design, while People are running mad in subscribing to HISTORY, POETRY, ROMANCES, nay, SERMONS too, there's no Subscription propos'd for what out-weighs them all: But still I keep close a Project *in petto*, which can

can effectually do our Business, and lay no new Burden on the Rich or Poor.

But not to keep my Fellow-Citizens longer in Suspence, I propose the seizing the Revenues, Ground, and Buildings of one of our largest Hospitals, and by converting them into ready Money, raise a Structure worthy such an Entertainment and such Audiences: Besides, there will be an Annual Income sufficient to defray those necessary or accidental Charges we can't avoid, should a Deficiency at any Time happen.

This Proposal may sound very harsh at first to most charitable Ears, but I shall make it evident to all my unprejudic'd Readers, that though I would willingly help the Ac———my in their generous Labours to please Mankind, by seasonable Instructions how to render the OPERA as reasonable in its Prices, as it is delightful in the Performance, so that we may agreeably spend our Time, and save our Money, yet my Intentions are so far from defeating the well-meant Design of any pious Founder of such Edifices, that the just Execution of my Project will infallibly maintain a greater Number of the *Old* and *Infirm*, and yearly educate and dispose of more young and helpless Orphans, in a more regular Method, and after a genteeler Manner, than ever was practis'd in any such Foundation, either at Home or Abroad.

As to the Aged and Sickly Part of an Hospital, there are very few of them but might be of vast Service to the Ac———my, and according to their former Stations in Life, before they were reduced by Age, Diseases or Misfortunes, they should make their Appearance on the Stage: A decay'd Gentleman would furnish out a Captain of the Guards, a grave Senator, or silent Embassador.

In

in short, all Places of Honour, where their Parts require them to march gravely, look wisely, seem thoughtful and be mute, a stately Step, a graceful Bow, the Coat of Mail, or solemn Robe would become them, as the Scene requir'd it: Orderly Matrons, and unfortunate Widows might commence *Dames of Honour*, drop a Curtsy, flirt a Fan, shew their Bubbies, shine in Tinsel, and make F——na's and C——ni's Trains of *State-Virgins* compleat: Others not so qualify'd for the Grandeur of publick Shew, would serve as Necessary-Women to the Stage-Queens and Princesses behind the Scenes: Men of an inferior Rank should form Troops of Guards, a full Senate, Attendants to all Solemnities, in short, be ready on all Occasions, where a crowded Stage is requisite, to give an Air of Magnificence to that Part of the Performance, then they might clash Swords, beat Drums, move Scenes, snuff Candles, and each, according to his Talent, manage some Employment in the many that are necessary in a Theatre.

Thus People need not idle the latter Part of Life away, but do something, by Gratitude at least to merit a Support, the Day would be sufficient for them to eat, drink, and pray in: Nor would their Labour be more than a genteel Evening's Amusement

As for the friendless Infants belonging to this Hospital, in order to be sent into the World capable of getting their Bread, particular Regard should be shewn to them by the Managers of the Opera: Yearly out of them should be chosen a certain Number of Males and Females, (we being not allow'd to make use of the Neuter Gender) who in their tenderest Years should be instructed in the justest Notions of Harmony by Masters, and as it were moulded into a Musical

E

Form:

Form: Those who succeeded best in that Art, should, when perfect, be brought upon the Stage; and thus we might make the justest Trial of our native Voices; the others dispos'd of as usual, to proper Trades, according to their Governours Judgments: Then the Directors of the OPERA may lay a well-grounded Claim to the Title of an Ac——my, and we, after the Rules of some of our wisest Neighbours, mix even in our Amusements, something of manifest Advantage to the *Publick Good*.

THIS Project, like many of the utmost Importance, may chance to be approv'd, but never follow'd: I own my self at a Loss by any other Means to contrive an Abatement of the immoderate Expence these Entertainments occasion. This I have supported not by plausible Surmises, but the strongest Matters of Fact. As the Case stands, we must have good OPERAS, or none.— If none, how shall we spend our Time? If good—— we must pay for them.

I am now arriv'd at the fourth and last Objection; *viz.* the Absurdities and Irregularities which our Lords the *Criticks* smell out in the OPERAS. This is already so fully answer'd, and shewn in it self so ridiculous, that it shall give me very little Trouble here.

THEIR Criticisms are improper, and their Complaints groundless, therefore I think my self not oblig'd here, as in the others, to study a Redress of Grievances: The former Objections had but too much Weight in them, not to be thoroughly consider'd: Being sensible of their Defects, I made some Overtures in each, towards accommodating the Differences betwixt the Stage and the Audience. In this there is no Medium left, to build a Reconciliation on; their Demands are so monstrous, that giving them the

least

least Grains of Allowance, destroys the very Being of an OPERA, but all true Judges of this Entertainment have plac'd it out of their Jurisdiction: However, in hopes to please the froward Infants, and to amuse their sower'd Tempers during the Time of the OPERA, we give them Leave to note down in their Books ⸺ Such a Scene is highly unnatural, according to *Aristotle* ⸺ *Rapin* would damn that *Simile*, it has no Business there ⸺ If *Longinus* is to be credited, the Words of this Air are not the true *Sublime* ⸺ Perhaps the Sufferance of these little Liberties, might calm the boiling Ferment of their Blood, and sweeten Spleen it self into good Humour.

As OPERAS are divided into two principal Factions, the *Italian* and the *French*; *England*, some Parts of *Germany*, &c following the first, *Holland*, *Flanders*, &c. the latter, it may be expected, that having been very ample in my treating of one, some Notice should be taken of the other, at least by Way of Parallel. But though I have been often an Auditor, and sometimes a Performer in *French* MUSICK, I can neither describe, nor give any Man, that has not heard it, a tolerable Idea of it: 'Tis so much an Original, that it neither tallies with, nor imitates any other Sounds that ever were, antique or modern: 'Tis entirely their own Invention, and all of a Piece with itself: So I leave it with them, being foreign to my Design, and claiming no Place in an Essay upon *Harmony*

SOME clever Adepts in MUSICK will shew as unreasonable a Surprize as the former, that while I am discoursing on this Subject, I should pass over in Silence the pretty harmonious Appendixes to most of our publick Diversions, as the Farcical OPERAS and MASQUES often exhibited

hibited at both Play-Houses, the fine Performances of some *Italian* Airs, stole or borrow'd from the H———y-M———s, which so genteely embroider a plain Play, or that new Method of filling the Vacancies betwixt the Acts with the choicest Opera-Songs improv'd by the additional Excellencies of a hoarse Hoat-Boy, or a screaming little Flute, which, by the Strength of Imagination, we are to belive S———no and C———z———ni. But I beg of those Gentlemen to consider, that introducing such Rabble amongst the Company we now are in, is dressing in *Monmouth-Street* of a Birth-Day. I propos'd in these Essays giving orr publick Diversions some Physick, in order to better their Constitutions, but I intend, going through the Operation without prescribing Water-gruel. A Person of nice Judgment in Dress, may find it reasonable to rectify some small Disorders in a Lady's Hair, Mantua, or Hoop: Is it therefore necessary he should new-model her Kitchen-Maids Pinners into a *French* Head, her Lockram Handkerchief into a Tippet, or stiffen her dangling doily Tail into a fashionable Rump? No! parallel to this Case are our Act-tunes, Play-House Jigs, *Scotch* Songs, C———y's Ballads, and *Beggars Operas*. The Nakedness of one is cloath'd with Sounds, which they call MUSICK; as the Kitchen-Maid is with Gown and Petticoat, and fancies her self dress'd to go to *Court*.

I flatter my self, that by this Time, every thinking *Briton* is convinc'd, that an *Italian Opera* is an innocent and perfect Entertainment, and may be render'd as improving as agreeable: It may indeed be disorder'd in some Parts of its Constitution, but labours under no Disease that is incurable.

ESSAY

ESSAY II.

OF POETRY;

Particularly DRAMATICK.

The Decay of those Entertainments enquir'd into: Imputed to Poets, Actors, and Spectators: Their Mistakes set in a true Light, and some of the most probable Amendments to those Grievances proposed.

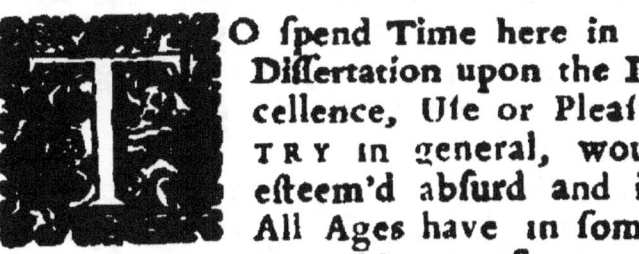O spend Time here in a pompous Dissertation upon the Dignity, Excellence, Use or Pleasure of POETRY in general, would be justly esteem'd absurd and impertinent. All Ages have in some extraordinary Manner shewn their Value for it; and all Men of true Wit and Learning have agreed in its being the noblest and most

most useful of the Polite Arts, nay, Barbarity it self has ever had its POETRY.

IT may be thought as trifling and improper to take Notice in this Place of the Contest betwixt the *Epick* and *Dramatick Poets* for Pre-eminence. My Study in POETRY confining me at present to the *Dramma* alone, I may be looked upon as too partial to my favourite Lucubrations, therefore shall only assert, That both are admirable in their different Views, divinely bright are the Virtues they plant in our Souls, and innocently ravishing, the Amusements they give us.

I must beg Leave tho' to throw in a trifling Hint by way of Observation, before I quit this Subject entirely, which is, that in all Nations where POETRY has the least Influence, the *Dramma* must be of more general Use than the *Epopœia*, as to the improving our Minds, the Reformation of Manners, and as an Academy of Politeness, and amongst others, for the two following Reasons.

IN the first Place, the best *Epick Poets* the World can boast of, are in the dead Languages, and either read or understood by a few *Literati*, or but indifferently translated into the living Languages, so can have but very little Influence on the present Age: On the other hand, *Drammatick Poets*, are seen, read and enter'd into by all Degrees of Stations or Understandings, nor are we oblig'd to copy entirely from the Ancients on that Head, since we can produce Originals that come up to, if not excel, the best of their Stage-Performances.

SECONDLY, the *Dramma* approaching so near Nature in Life and Action, every thing appears real; and of consequence is more apt to stir, awake, and improve the Passions, than those tedious Narrations, which most People read without being in the least agreeably mov'd: So that we may venture to affirm, that one Stage-Play, well acted, will have more Power over the politest Audience, in the Articles of Pleasure and Reformation, than all the *Epick Poems* that ever were wrote. Now if the Criticks will not allow the Shadow of a Parallel betwixt them in the Point of Merit, we may claim justly a Superiority in that of Use, and being undoubtedly more beneficial to Mankind.

IF *Aristotle* may be appealed to as a competent Judge, he decides very fairly in Favour of *Tragedy* against the *Epopœia*, he impartially examines to the Bottom, which is most excellent; candidly proposes every thing that can be advanced on the Side of the latter, but declares for the first, in shewing the infinite Advantages it has over its Rival: Which 'tis needless to enumerate here, since every body can easily turn to his *Poeticks* in that Language, antique or modern, which he's most Master of.

WITH us I hope the Stage will subsist, as long as we have the least Remains of Liberty, Virtue, or an elegant Taste, maugre *Prynn*'s Enthusiastick Nonsense, *Collier*'s ill-grounded, dogmatical Zeal, or *Bedford*'s and *Law*'s ignorantly pious Blunders: Nor shall Men, eminent for Sense and Morality, blush to patronize it, the Vicious and Foolish may rail, their Censures leave no Blemishes behind them.

SINCE then the Antiquity, Rise, Progress, or different Kinds of POETRY, need not be canvass'd here (those Subjects being so copiously handled by the greatest Geniusses, and most learned Pens of the past and present Times,) let us at once strike into, and proceed regularly in the beaten Path of our publick Diversions,

from

from which I have deviated a little; so change the Scene without quitting the Stage, by a small Hop from the *Opera* to the *Play-Houses*.

But first it will be highly proper, and prove a material Evidence in explaining the Merits of this Cause, to inquire into the Deference, and vast Regard paid by the *Ancients*, to their *Poets, Players* and *Theatres*.

In *Greece* the first were held almost sacred in their Persons, Professions and Works, particularly the Drammatick Writers: Their Name implied a Kind of Divinity attending their Productions, they being stil'd *Creators*. The Privileges and Immunities granted to them, were extraordinary and numerous: They were always esteem'd superior to the Professors of all other Kinds of Literature, Arts and Sciences: Often entrusted with the Management of the State or Army; still proving equal in Capacity or Courage, for Court or Camp; nor did they want but the last Adoration to make them, even in this Life, equal to their Gods. *Plato* himself wrote several Tragedies, and was protected by *Dion*, who at his private Expence furnish'd the *Chorus*.

As *Lycurgus* was proud of being a Patron, *Solon* was pleas'd to be reckon'd a Brother of the *Poetical Tribe*. *Alexander* could not sleep without *Homer* under his Pillow; whose Works may be justly stil'd a-kin to, or at least a beautiful Model for *Drammatick Writings*, there runs that Spirit of real Life and Action thro' the Whole. *Socrates* himself, in spite of his conspicuous Wisdom, and vast Power, was overcome by the more prevailing Wit of a *Comick Poet*. Nor could any thing calm the raging Tyranny of *Phalaris*, but *Stesichorus*'s Muse.

OF POETRY.

AT *Rome* POETRY was not cultivated with that Warmth, or follow'd with that Assiduity as in *Greece*, their Heroes (at least in the Beginning of their Empire) being more eminent for Arms than Arts, but at last, by the Countenance of some Great ones, and the surprizing Beauties of a few of their *Poets*, it began to flourish, and rose to a great Height, but still as far short of the *Grecian* in Splendor, as Merit.

HOWEVER, those excellent *Poets* they could boast, were particularly distinguish'd, and fondly cherish'd by their greatest Philosophers and Princes. The *Scipios* could scarcely live without their *Ennius* and *Terence* *Cæsar* favour'd, and was himself not the least of *Poets* *Augustus* and *Mæcenas* pretended to write, as well as patronize, and flew with Raptures from the Grandeur and Cares of Empire, to the beloved Bosoms of *Virgil* and *Horace*. *Seneca* preferr'd his Tragedies to all his other Philosophical Works, nor could the Severity of *Cato*'s *Stoicism* stifle his predominant Passion for POETRY Nay, *Nero* picqu'd himself more upon the Name of the best Poet, than the Fame of being follow'd as the first Man of the Universe, in all the other Gifts of Fortune: In *Empire* he could rather brook a Rival than in *Parnassus*, so sacrific'd *Lucan* to his Jealousy, for writing *better* Verses

IF the *Poets* were thus look'd upon by the Ancients with an Eye of Reverence, almost bordering upon divine Worship; we may be certain, that the Persons of their Players, and all Expences incident to their Theatres were not neglected: Their Actors were encourag'd and caress'd; were often Men of Rank and Figure in Life, Masters of all polite Parts of Learning, and of consequence perfect in the minutest Niceties of their

Profession,

Profession, and skill'd in the just Representation of all Characters the World could furnish the Stage with: Nor did some of their principal *Poets* blush to perform in their own Plays, tho' perhaps the first of the State either in a civil or military Capacity: Indeed I must own that their Players, generally speaking, behav'd up to the Virtues and Grandeur of their Stage Characters, in some Respects even in private Life; nor were the Names of *Actor* and *Actress* then synonomous Terms with *Vagabond* and *Strumpet*.

IF our Players complain, that there is no *Tully* to patronize them, we may more justly lament, that there is no *Roscius* for whom a *Cicero* might plead without blushing, nor an *Æsopus* worthy to be admitted into the most intimate Friendship of the *Wise* and the *Great*.

THE extraordinary Expences of their Theatres, particularly those of the Chorus (which were generally very large,) were always defray'd out of the publick Stock, not promiscuously, or upon a Level with other common State-Necessities, but a particular Fund was laid aside for that Purpose, committed to the Guardianship of some of the most eminent Citizens, not to be touch'd, but upon the Emergency of a Theatrical Deficiency, and held inviolable upon all other Occasions. *Demosthenes* was reduc'd to the nicest Turns of his Rhetorick and Oratory, in daring but to mention to the *Athenians* the medling with that *sacred Bank*, though Ruin almost inevitable star'd them full in the Face; nor had they any other Means left to ward off an approaching general Calamity: But those worthy and polite People preferr'd the inculcating Virtue, a genteel Behaviour, and elegant Taste, to the most extended Empire;

content

content rather to enslave their Bodies than Minds. The chief Magistrates had entirely the Inspection of the Theatres committed to their Care, and the richest of the Nobility either bore the Charge of the *Chorus*, in favour of some particular *Poet*, or that and all other Charges which the Poets and Players could not answer, were allow'd out of the publick Treasury: And so prodigious was the Grandeur and Magnificence of those Stages, in *Actors, Musicians, Dancers, Cloaths, Scenes*, and *Machines*, that, by the nicest Computation, a Set of Clouds only for a Comedy, cost the State as much, as a *Coronation* would at this Time in *England*.

WE must likewise observe, that no publick Edifices were so much taken Care of, or erected at that amazing Labour and Expence, as the Theatres, Amphitheatres, and other Buildings of that Nature, either amongst the *Grecians* or *Romans*; their Academies, Porticos, Schools, &c. were Baubles in comparison with them, and generally rais'd from some private Pocket, and indeed they were at most the Plants, the others the Trees in full Perfection. Nay, the very Temples of those superstitiously religious People, fell far short of their *Play-Houses* in the Articles of Beauty, Grandeur and Cost.

THE greatest Princes, most flourishing Republicks, and the wisest Men, thus interesting themselves so arduously in the Cause of POETRY, gave it that Spirit and Vigour we admire in the *Ancients*, and undoubtedly those prudent Nations never perceiv'd their Empire lessen'd, their Senses impair'd, or their Manners corrupted, by the hearty Encouragement given to that Mistress of all *Arts*. But, alas! on the other hand, both *Grecians* and *Romans*, with its Fall, saw every Thing

Thing that could be dear to a brave and wise People, trampled under foot; nor could they ever have been conquer'd, had not their POETRY first languish'd, and so stifled that Life it us'd to inspire. Their Conquerors were *Barbarians*, as void of Humanity, as Sciences, who boasted no Knowledge but Force, and thought Life and Power only given to destroy the rest of Mankind. —— How opposite these Maxims to the Rules of *Poetry* and Virtue! those inseparable Companions.

WERE I to dwell longer upon this melancholy Subject, I should almost perswade my self to be grave in earnest, therefore I shall quit it as soon as possible, and take a peep into our Playhouses, where every thing one sees, or hears, or imagines, will contribute to our Mirth —— or Indignation.

That our Modern Poets are very bad in the Drammatick Way —— is allowed: *That the Generality of our Players are ten times worse* —— is not deny'd: *And that the Majority of all Audiences know not whether a Play is good or bad* ——must be granted. Here then let us fairly state the Case, and consider to what Causes this Decay in *Drammatick Poetry*, this Lowness in Stageaction, and this Depravity of Taste in the present Age is owing.

As I have the Happiness to think generally out of the common Road; I fancy, I shall advance some Reasons, obvious to very few Criticks, yet when made publick, shall be granted by all: and without fixing the Fault altogether on Poets, Actors, or Audiences, I shall make manifest, in what Points they are all wrong, so interspersing some very new Remarks by way of Cure, I shall conclude this ESSAY.

To begin then with our Poets —— I do not here pretend to make any Comparison betwixt our past and present *Dramatick* Writers, or them, and the Antients, neither shall I undertake to praise, or censure any particular PLAYS, by pointing out some hidden Beauties, or neglected Faults. That is a Piece of Criticism, of too refin'd and abstruse a Nature, to be trusted to any one private Judgment: I shall only gently lay my Finger upon those Blots in their Conduct, which are notoriously wrong, tho' hitherto unobserv'd, and which have undoubtedly occasion'd that Inundation of execrable PLAYS, which has overwhelm'd both THEATRES and Press. These I reduce to four Heads. The first is, their mistaken Notions in Choice of Subjects for the Stage: The second, their strange Mismanagement in relation to the Effects of a *Stage-Play*, in giving us TRAGEDIES to make us laugh, and COMEDIES to make us cry. The third, their Ignorance, or total Neglect of the true Sublime: The fourth, their trusting to Narration, rather than Action, the most material Incidents of the *Drama*.

FIRST, then I think our Poets to blame in their Choice of improper Subjects for the Stage, and to their ill Judgment on that Head, is partly owing the bad State of both THEATRES, which are by that Means liable to the severest Censures of above three Parts in four of the People, who are afraid to visit either House: They have, in a Manner, confin'd the *Drama* to prophane *History*, and to the worst Topicks of Prophaness, Rage and Love, so that all our TRAGEDIES are fill'd with the flagrant Crimes and audacious Passions of *Grecian*, *Roman*, or *Turkish* Tyrants; and our COMEDIES very decently deck'd out with our own bold-face Follies and nasty Vices.

I know they'll answer, That if these Things are not drawn to the Life, and expos'd, even naked, that it will be impossible to give an Audience that Abhorrence (which they would have them to imbibe) for those destructive Sins, or ridiculous Affectations which TRAGEDY and COMEDY lash.

BUT to this I reply, That they paint their Follies so fair, and shew their Passions in such glaring Colours, that People are apt rather to grow fond, than afraid of them. The Knowledge of these bewitching Allurements banishes from the *Play-house* the greatest part of the Town, who dare not venture, or trust themselves amidst *Theatrical* Enchantments, and of Consequence, they are debarr'd all that Improvement and Instruction, which the Stage should promote, by recommending Virtue, and putting Vice out of Countenance. 'Tis true, prophane Stories might in some Measure answer that End, did not their heathenish Names frighten honest Christian People from coming near them.

THE Antients (who are said to have equall'd, if not excell'd us, both in TRAGEDY and COMEDY) thought no part of their Religion either too sacred, or solemn for the Stage. They introduc'd their greatest Misteries with Applause, nay, made their *Stage-Plays* the chief part of their Worship: So People could pray, and laugh, and cry, and improve at the same time. *Jupiter* mounted on his Eagle, us'd to throw his Thunder and Lightening about at a strange Rate. *Mercury* would speak *Prologues* and *Epilogues*, or dance on the high Ropes. *Mars* and *Venus* were often very merry behind the Curtain, while *Bacchus* entertain'd them with Drinking-Catches: *Apollo* flying cross the Stage in his blazing Machine, would tickle their Ears with his Lyre: *Pallas*

found

found to Arms, and *Diana* shew her full Moon, while the lesser Deities would sing and caper in Chorus, or snuff Candles.

THEN the Stage shone out in its full Splendor, and every Man thought it his Duty to promote the Interest of those Poets, or Players, who made it the Study of their Lives to convey so gently and insensibly into their Souls, a Love of Virtue, by the politest and most pleasing Amusements

I hope none of my candid Readers will so far mis-interpret what I have here innocently advanc'd, as to imagine that what I insinuate, is design'd in the least to burlesque even the heathen Religion: No!—— far from my Pen fly such impious Thoughts, as idly to reflect upon any thing that boasts the Shadow of Religion.

WHAT I infer from this Observation is, That if our Poets would judiciously choose from out the Old T———nt or Ap———ha the finest Historical Parts, and upon such substantial Foundations, and beautiful Incidents, form all their Theatrical Representations, and introduce them in a proper Manner, upon our Stages, the Gravity of the Subjects, and the Grandeur of such Scenes, would invite the Godly thither, and keep the wicked in awe, and, of Consequence, our THEATRES would be crowded with Audiences as religious as polite: Then no body daring to entertain an Objection to the *Play-house*. How far this Scheme might contribute to Numbers of People out of Harm's-way, (as Infants are first sent to School) and make a stricter Union betwixt Religion and Morality, (according to the Notions the World has of both) I leave the sober Part of Mankind to judge

I am sensible, some People will be very grave, and others as merry, upon meeting with this Proposal: The first will be shock'd at the Impiety of any Project which would bring a Sc——re Story on the Stage, and at once tax with Prophaneness, every Thought, which deviates from the narrow Road of their nonsensical Capacities, the others will ridicule me for advancing as new, what is so openly practis'd abroad in every christian Country; nor are we without frequent Instances of it here at Home, since the first Appearance of a Stage amongst us.

THE Churches in *Italy* and *Spain*, on all Festivals, are turn'd into THEATRES *pro tempore*, and there they exhibit some Sacred Story, by Way of a *Stage-Play*. In *France*, the same Custom prevails: Nay, their best Poets have founded their best PLAYS for the Stage, upon Divine Subjects. In *Germany* and *Holland* you seldom meet with any Theatrical Entertainments, but the Fable is entirely borrow'd from the Scripture. At Home, *Dryden* has given us the *Fall of Man*, and a *Saint Catharine*, which is next Door to the Sign of the *Bible*, and *Milton* his *Sampson Agonistes*, besides, several Authors of an inferior Rank, have built sorry Superstructures on that noble Foundation, and in the Infancy of our *Poetry*, the *Stage-Plays* then presented, were altogether Scriptural.

BUT some squeamish Consciences, as silly as zealous, will object, That we should not in so nice a Point follow the outlandish, heathenish Customs of Papists and Foreigners, and that those PLAYS, but now cited, tho' wrote at Home, yet never were acted —— I partly agree with them there: Thence proceeds my Complaint, I would have them acted, and more attempted in the same Stile, till they got entire Possession

of

of our THEATRES: Then those *Priest-Plays* of the Stage would lay all the *Bug-bears* and *Hob-goblins*, which terrify scrupulous People from coming thither: Then every body might frequent the *Play-Houses* with a Certainty of being improv'd on all Sides, without being look'd upon as Heathens. Then Tradesmen need not hinder their Wives and Prentices, Masters, their Servants, Tutors, their Pupils, nor the religious, their whole sanctify'd Families, from going to an Evening's Exercise.

SHOULD this Project of mine succeed, I make no Doubt of hearing a broad-brimm'd Hat, a starch'd Band and short Cloak, speak an *extempore Prologue* to a PLAY, with as much Form, Grimace and Devotion, as they would say a long Grace to a poach'd Egg.

IT is impossible to enumerate in this small Sketch, the infinite Advantages that must accrue from such a Design, well executed, to the Publick in General, and to the noble Art of *Dramatick Poetry* in particular.

Holland, (a Nation we may look upon amongst the wisest of our Neighbours, and to whom we are deeply indebted on several Scores) will sufficiently instruct us on that Head, if we are not too conceited to follow so prudent a Guide. The Subjects they choose for the Stage, are mostly Scriptural; nor do they ever meddle with any part of it, but with an Intent by some new Turn, or surprizing Thought, to heighten the Story, and improve their People, of which an Example or two may not be reckon'd digressive.

To begin therefore with an *Examen* of one of their most noted Pieces, according to the Rules of the Stage, which is the Sacrifice of I——c. The Subject, I own, seems barren, and promises very little; but the greater the Art of the Poet, to raise something noble and new, from so poor a Foundation.

Ab——m goes to sacrifice I——c, by shooting him thro' the Head with a Blunderbuss, an Angel popping from behind a Fuz-Bush, p——s in the Pan, On this the Gun misses Fire, so I——c escapes, and the Angel with a tolerable rough Compliment in the Low-dutch Dialect, closes the Scene.

HERE the Contrivance is very new, thro' the whole PLAY, and the Conduct very artful. The *Catastrophe* is, (as the *French* term it) to the last Degree *suprenant* and *merveilleux*, and gives the Audience all that can be imagin'd of an agreeable Astonishment, which is the chief End of Poetry. This Management shews what bright Sparks may be struck out of the rough Flint-stone of such a Subject, by an inventive Genius, and besides, rectifies a vulgar Error crept in amongst us, That Gun-powder is but a very modern Invention, a lucky Accident of t'other Day, when by this we are assur'd, that it might have been us'd by the Patriarchs before the Flood.

IT would be trifling and endless to enter into any more Particulars, in so copious a Manner of Criticism, let it suffice to give my Readers an Idea of their prodigious Talents in the Choice and Improvement of Subjects for the Stage. In short, I have seen the Witch of *Endor*, and *Samuel*'s Ghost, by the Help of well-dispos'd Squibs, f——t Fire at one another, for the space of half an hour, by Way of Salute, which imprinted the justest Notions of Terror on the Minds of an Audience: Nor could Pity be less predominant, when they consider'd the Uncertainty of this World's Grandeur, in seeing *Nebuchadnezzar* sow'd up in a Wolf's Skin, reduc'd from royal Dainties to a Handful of Grass.

How

How have I seen the *Dutch* amaz'd at the magnificent Decorations of *Bell* and the *Dragon*, introduc'd by way of OPERA, with vast Success! Nor were they less pleas'd with the Justice of Providence, in the several wonderful Escapes of *Tobit* and his *Dog*, thrown in as a merry Interlude.

BEING confin'd within narrow Bounds, I need not touch upon many more Instances, to shew what Advantage attends those PLAYS, which are taken from *Sacred History*, rather than *Prophane*. I choose to strengthen my Arguments on this Head from Abroad, knowing it would have the greater Influence at Home, especially coming recommended by their Taste, whose *Delicatesse* is unexceptionable.

IT may be reckon'd needless to point out those Parts which would furnish the properest Theatrical Foundations, but where can an undaunted Bravery of Soul, or the prodigious Effects of Faith, be better exemplify'd, than in *Shedrach*, *Meshach*, and *Abednego*'s being thrown into, and yet preserv'd from the Fiery Furnace? —— as *Daniel* was from the *Lion*'s *Den*.

WHERE do the Triumphs of Virtue, or the just Rewards of Lust, appear more conspicuous, than in *Susanna* and the two Elders? —— Where can true Fortitude, or invincible Piety, shine brighter, than in Heroick *Judith*'s Conquest over *Holofernes*? —— or Captivating Modesty, than in *Esther*'s over *Ahasuerus*? —— But to descend thus to some Circumstances, is to imagine there can be an End of Examples, where the Store is inexhaustible.

I cannot pass over in Silence, the Force that the Face of Religion has in *Stage-Entertainments*, urg'd from the most remarkable Instance the
World

World can produce, than which we cannot bring a more powerful Argument to clench the Nail of an Assertion, which is the surprizing Run of Success that attended the Farcical, Musical Dance of *Doctor Faustus*, at both Houses, which must be owing to that Religious, Moral, Poetick Justice, so finely interwoven thro' the whole Piece, particularly, in the wicked Conjurer's dismal End, by infernal *Fiends* at one House, and a terrible *Dragon* at the other. These lively Ideas of Hell deservedly drew the Town after them. The Criticks may assign what Cause they please, for what they term an Infatuation; but I insist upon it, I have only touch'd the true one. I am sorry the *Beggars Opera* has not either Religion, or Justice, to countenance its Run, and screen it from the Criticks.

THE second Mismanagement I charge upon our *Poets*, is their Ignorance in, or Neglect of the true Design and Nature of a *Stage-Play*; by presenting us with merry *Tragedies*, or sad *Comedies*. This Disease is in a Manner *Epidemick* amongst that Tribe; yet by the strictest Enquiry into the original Seeds of POETRY, I cannot fix upon a natural Reason, whence so general a Malignity can spring; of consequence, I must be pretty much at a Loss in proposing a Remedy.

I believe it often happens, that an old, or a young *Poet*, takes Pen, Ink and Paper,—— sits down to his Scrutore—— or perhaps a Table ——he finds it necessary to write a PLAY——he turns over God knows how many Volumes for a Story—— or he makes one, and then—— he writes a PLAY: The Dispute is, Must it be a *Tragedy* or *Comedy*? The Arguments of both Sides are weighty—— It cannot be decided, the Reasons

sons are so equal—— At last he wisely counts his Buttons—— or trusts to Cross and Pile —— As Fortune would have it, *Tragedy* wins the Day: You see in the Play-Bill and Title-Page, *TRAGEDY*, in large Red Letters, like a Saint in the *Calendar* Of Consequence, we must be Spectators and Readers of that Performance, in a Deluge of Tears Another writes a *Comedy* by the same Rules, and wonders, that an Excess of Mirth does not crack our Voices, and split our Sides: When, alas! the World does laugh at the Absurdities of the first, and is griev'd at the Stupidity of the other

THESE Gentlemen, sure, from their Infancy, have been only accustom'd to Cross-purposes, and would give Pleasure to the World by Contraries They never make the Passions their Study, and are utter Strangers to what is true Humour: Their POETRY has the same Effect upon an Audience, that the Quack's Medicines had on his Patients, he vomited one by a Purge, and purged another by a Vomit So with these *Poets*, 'tis laughing and crying still, let *Tragedy* or *Comedy* be the Cause.

AN honest old Woman (who, like *Moliere*'s House-keeper, judg'd from pure Nature) frankly own'd to her Neighbour, (who carry'd her to a *Comedy* to make her merry) that they might call it a *Comedy*, if they would, but, for her Part, she never had been more sleepy or melancholy at a Sermon

THERE is another Fault to be spoke to under this Head, as preposterous as the former, which is, the blending of Sorrow and Mirth so cunningly together, that a Man does not know whether to cry or laugh, without he could play *Heraclitus* and *Democritus* at the same time. These

Cubs of POETRY, that have never been lick'd into any true Form, can neither be call'd *Tragedies*, *Comedies*, nor *Tragi-Comedies*; they are no real Manufacture, but a Sort of Linsy-Woolsy Entertainment, where a Man of Sense is at a Loss how to settle his Looks, unless he could new coin his Face, and let one Side wear the Stamp of Grief, and t'other that of Joy: Nay, so sudden are the Changes from one to the other, that his right Eye must look grave, and the left smile at the same time, lest he should be surpriz'd into a wrong Behaviour before the Scene is half out.

I must own, most of our greatest *Poets* have been particularly to blame in this Point, and have given us PLAYS that are the very *Oglios* of POETRY, no Dish of a Piece with it self. In the most grave Affairs of State, you'll have a Dialogue betwixt a Privy-councellor and a Jack-pudding, in the Recital of the most passionate Distresses of Lovers, a pert Chamber-Maid will tell her Mistress a smutty Story; in the same Scene you'll have a Husband killing his beloved Wife, and a rampant Widow caterwauling for a Husband; or the Fates of Empires and Republicks toss'd up with the Humours of *Purgatory* and *Bedlam*. Thus in Matters of the greatest Moment to Mankind, in Virtue, Policy, or Love, the whole will be so larded with the lowest, most nauseous Farce, that a sensible Spectator is readier to puke, than pity the unfortunate *Hero*, or suffering *Fair*.

THIS Fault (though in it self so notorious and defenceless) has so far engross'd the *English Stage*, that, despairing of any Redress, I cannot mention it with common Patience.

THE third Charge I bring against our *Poets*, is, their not having a right Idea of, or at least
totally

OF POETRY. 59

totally neglecting the true *Sublime* in their Writings, nor will they be at the Trouble of turning their Thoughts towards what is new and surprizing. For these three thousand Years, they have been hobling on after one anothers Tails, in the same dull Pace, and beaten Track, and the same insipid Tale over and over again, and a hundred times repeated, has furnish'd the Stage, in all Ages and Languages, with what they call *New Entertainments*.

THE first *Poets* the World could boast, were Men of Genius, Spirit, and Invention. They left behind them a few very fine Go-carts, and a parcel of very strong Leading-strings, for the Use of *Infant-Poets*, and Arm'd Chairs, or Crutches, for the *Aged* and *Infirm*. The puny *Moderns* (who presume upon being call'd their Successors) think they are Heroes, if they can creep about with those necessary Machines, and that they do but scurvily: They are afraid to venture a Step out of them, lest they meet with a bloody Nose, or crack'd Skull, and are so pleas'd with being paultry Imitators, that they dare not attempt the Honour of being bold Originals.

But then the Ancient Poets had the wide World of Invention free before them, to range in, and every thing they said, must be new. This is readily granted, but not allow'd as an Excuse for our present Bards. If much has been said, how much more is left untouch'd! If Laziness, or Stupidity, did not hinder their Search, Fancy is unconfin'd, and, as a Poet is not ty'd down to Truth, there can be no End of agreeable Fiction.

THOSE old Fellows made a terrible Noise and Splutter about a Town call'd *Troy*, its King *Priam*, his Son *Paris*, and a *Grecian* Curtezan, call'd *Helen*. They talk'd so long of it, and nothing

thing else, that they deafened the Ears of the whole World with their Chatt'ring. We, forsooth must take up the Cudgels, and receive the Fray betwixt *Trojans* and *Grecians*, to the End of Time.

BUT, to render this Affair a little more familiar to my Readers, and explain the Merits of the Cause, before I appeal to their Judgments,

Let us suppose, that the Master of the Red-Lion-Inn *in the City of* Brentford, *has an unlucky Boy to his Son, whom we'll call* Paris: *This same Youth often plays the Truant, and one Day, under Pretence of visiting an Aunt, who sold Asparagus at* Battersea, *he crosses the Water, and having stole some Money out of the Bar-box, whips to the* Star and Garter *at* Mortlack, *in order to spend it He there gets acquainted with* Nelly, *the Landlord's Wife; she bargains with him to elope from her Husband, and he carries her home to* Brentford, *telling his Father, he had married a fine Woman, and a great Fortune. The Father believes, and protects them,* Menelaus *at the* Star and Garter, *misses his Wife, Fame informs him where she is; he demands her in Form, and is deny'd. Things carry'd thus far, he raises a Posse of his Friends, Neighbours and Constables; surrounds the* Red-Lion, *makes many brave Attacks, and at last, in the Space of ten Days after, being often repuls'd, he demolishes the* Red-Lion, *breaks old* Priam's *Head, makes* Paris *beg Pardon on his Knees, and brings back* Nelly's *crack'd Pipkin to* Mortlack *in Triumph. The Man has his Mare again, and all is well.*

IN fine, from a Story not one bit better or truer than this, have all our *Epick* and *Dramatick Poems* been borrow'd for these three thousand Years, and from this Body of a Tree have sprouted I know not how many Branches to amuse us One General was ten Years a wandering Home,
another

another was kill'd by his Wife, as soon as he came Home, a third was forc'd into a strange Country by contrary Winds, and built a City there, a fourth had a terrible Dispute with *Neptune* and *Eolus*, so was drown'd by the Way, and a fifth got safe to *Italy* (as they say) and laid a Foundation for another *Romance*.

BUT, in order to give our young *Poets* a juster Idea of what I mean, to enliven their Understandings, and rescue them from the pitiful Slavery of always treading in the direct Foot-steps of the Ancients, I shall give but one Instance of the Ingenuity, Fire and Strength of Expression, of a poor *French Stroler*.

THE Prince of a Tribe of *Dramacick Wanderers*, once fix'd the Seat of his Empire in the largest Barn of one of the *Hans-Towns*; His vast Equipage of tatter'd Scenes, various Instruments, tarnish'd Tinsel, and empty Band-boxes, delighted the Populace, and gave Wonder to the Magistrates. After a Week's necessary Preparation, he promis'd the City a most entertaining and magnificent PLAY, upon the Story of St. *Peter's* following our SAVIOUR into *Galilee*. The Play-Bills gave the Town Hopes of fine MACHINERY, gay SCENES, and exquisite MUSICK, surprizing DANCING, and all those additional Ornaments of the Stage, which are requir'd to coax a *High-Dutch Audience* into swallowing Wit.

THE long-expected Night comes, the House quickly fills, Crowds that could not enter, were so unfortunate as to be oblig'd to carry back their Money. Prodigious was the Expectation of the happy Mortals within, as great the Vexation of the Wretches excluded. At last, the wish'd for Minute comes, the Curtain flies up, and he who personated our SAVIOUR, appears with good St.

Peter at his Heels, whom, with an Air of Majesty, he commands to follow him into *Galilee*, then quits the Stage—— and St. *Peter* follows. From behind the Scenes, they immediately convey their Persons, with the Treasure of their Wit. So grand an Opening of a PLAY promising wonderful things to come, the Audience, with unspeakable Impatience, waited their Return to proceed with the Business of the Stage—— but all in vain—— Moment succeeds to Moment, no Tidings, no Appearance of our SAVIOUR, or St. *Peter*, to finish the PLAY. The Audience, enquiring into the Reasons of their Delay, were inform'd, that indeed they had taken Post-Horses, and were by that Time got out of the Territories of the said Town, in their Way to *Galilee*.

Now those Novices in polite Literature, who are ignorant of the true Art of *Dramatick Poetry*, will imagine, that this Audience was bit, as we emphatically express it; but I boldly maintain, that no Audience ever enjoy'd a Stage-Entertainment in a higher Degree of Perfection. To give a fine Surprize, and raise our Passions, then gently let them sink, is the greatest Height the *Drama* can arrive to; which certainly was their Case exactly: And if what was new, or out of the Way could please, they, sure, had Reason to be charm'd! And, in Vindication of that excellent Master of his Art, as Poet and Player, I presume to say, That the few Words he repeated, had more of the true *Sublime* in them, according to *Longinus*, than any one PLAY now in being. *That Simplicity of Expression, without a Poverty of Stile! That Grandeur of Elocution!* —— *yet void of Bombast. How delicate the Sentiments!* —— *yet free from the least Affectation.* This happy Conjunction of so many Beauties, has fix'd upon

it

'it the Mark of the true *Sublime*, according to the great Critick just mention'd; and, as such, I recommend it to all our young *Poets*, hoping that, for the future, they'll take Care to introduce, in all their Writings, that noble Simplicity, which is the Quintessence of Nature and Art, in POETRY or PROSE.

Fourthly, I accuse our *Dramatists* of a grand Mistake, which they are frequently guilty of, particularly in *Tragedy*. This is too far trusting the most essential Parts of their PLAYS, upon which the Main of the Plot turns, rather to tiresome Narration, than the Force of Action; in direct Opposition to a positive Maxim of *Horace*, that consummate Critick, and exquisite Poet; who says —— *Some Things are acted, others only told; but what we hear, moves less than what we see: Spectators only have their Eyes to trust; but Auditors must trust their Ears and you.*

BY this Conduct they deprive the Stage of one of its greatest Beauties, and, indeed, what we look upon as the most material Difference betwixt the *Epick* and *Dramatick Poetry*.

OUR Actors too must prove better Orators than we can boast at present, if they pretend to move an Audience as much, by telling them, such and such an Affair happen'd —— so and so —— at that and t'other Time —— As the Action it self will affect their Understandings, when faithfully represented before their Eyes, they'll expect we should suppose it all to be brought about in the *Green-Room*; but it might as well be transacted at *Grand Cairo*, or *Greenland*.

IF a *Poet* would have me to mourn his *Distress'd Widow*, let her appear upon the Stage, suitable to her Character, like the Picture of *Charity*, with an Infant at each Breast, one on her Back, and a Couple led: Then what Heart of *Adamant* could refrain from Tears, to see them weep?

IF from the Rage of a *Jealous Husband*, I am to guess at what he inwardly feels, let me first view him, brandishing his Wife's Heart on the Point of his Sword, red with the Blood of every Man that but spoke to her.

IF the justest Idea of an absolute Tyrant is to be imprinted on the Minds of the Spectators, shew us the Monster surrounded with Guards, Arms, Legs, Racks, Gibbets, and Axes, then we are sure, whenever he speaks, each Word pronounces Death and Terror.

I must confess, that as to the Articles of Stabbing, Poysoning, and Tortures, our *Poets* have play'd their Parts, and laid about them very handsomely; and several *Tragedies* have ow'd their Success to a Ruffian in an old Red Coat, a Carbuncle Face, and Black Perriwig; who is sure always to come off with Applause, especially in the Slaughter-Scene.

BUT I am principally concern'd, that some small Love-Affairs, are not transacted in so clear a Manner of Negotiation, and to the entire Satisfaction of an Audience, as I could wish: Indeed, in some PLAYS, the Affair of a Rape has been push'd a tolerable Length; nor has any thing but the critical Minute been hid from our longing Eyes; yet had they gone a little farther, then we might have seen a just Resentment of the Villainy in every Spectator's Eyes, each Hand prepar'd to assassinate the Ravisher.

I am sensible that this Defect in our PLAYS, is partly owing to the innate Modesty of our *Poets*, and partly to the excessively nice Stomachs and well-bred Rules of our own, and the *French* Criticks; for one of the most noted of them observes,

serves, that an excellent *Tragedy* of *Corneille*'s was damn'd to all Intents and Purposes, only for a Rape's being mention'd in it. The shocking Idea so disgusted those squeamish Knight-Errants, those very civil Heroes, that their fine-spun Notions of Love and Honour, could not digest the naughty Word.

BUT why should we plan out a Method of Behaviour to our selves in this Point, from their puny Appetites and weak Desires? We *English* scorn such trifling Kick-shaws; what is substantial, alone charms us, and, when we feed, it must be Knuckle-deep in a Sirloin. Let not then the Forms of their Romantick Love and Honour, regulate our Taste. We are convinc'd, that the more naturally things are represented on the Stage, the more shocking, or agreeable they prove, according to the Heinousness, or Innocence of the Fact. How can we shew a just Abhorrence of that Crime we sleep over, when 'tis told? Let the Representation be faithful, and every Passion is rous'd, the Sight blows up the Coals of Indignation, and Rivets a Detestation in our Souls. Thus the wise *Spartans* made their Slaves get drunk, that their Children might imbibe the truest Idea of, and fix'd Aversion for that beastly Vice.

BUT I only presume to speak my humble Opinion, in an Affair of so great Consequence: I submit my Thoughts on this Head, and all others, to a general Council of the Learned; not to any *Pope-Critick* who pretends to be infallible.

HAVING declar'd my principal Objections to the Conduct of the Masters of our POETRY, and, I think, in every Particular made good my Charge, I shall next attack, in Form, their Journeymen, in their Quarters; *viz.* the Managers and Actors of our *Play-Houses*, or, *vice versâ*, the

G 3 Actors

Actors and Managers, they being allow'd, by some unaccountable Blunder in the Politicks of that vast Empire, to be both, and permitted to sit as Judges, when they are at most, but a Party concern'd.

So many petty Kings in one Kingdom occasion a great Confusion and Distractions in the State: Each Monarch studies only to enrich himself, nor is the publick Welfare or Pleasure taken Notice of, but where their private separate Interests require it. To this *Aristocracy* then are owing several of the following Misfortunes, which have occasion'd the Decay of the *Dramatick Art*, as will be manifest to every unbiass'd Reader, without pointing to Particulars.

My Complaints against the Managers of our *Play-Houses*, are near as numerous as against the *Poets*: For, to their Mismanagement I impute the Scandal the Stage and their Profession lies under, by their mistaken Choice of *Poets*, *Plays* and *Players*, and their almost total Neglect of those Decorations which are essentially necessary to the Beauty and Life of the Stage.

If our *Poets* are to blame in their Choice of Subjects for the *Theatre*, the Managers are as much out in their Judgment of the PLAYS, when brought to their fiery Trial. They don't consider a PLAY as to its Merit, the Reputation it would bring to their Art, or the Pleasure, or Instruction it would give the Town, but what Expences must we be at, to fit it for the Stage? What Time must we lose, to study the Parts? and what Money will it bring in, to answer our Pains and Expences?

We may proceed with those *Stock-Plays* we are perfect in, or revive those which have lain dormant

mant half an Age: They'll be new to the Town, and save us the Trouble of getting by Rote, more Parts than we can remember, and anticipate the Charge of Cloaths, Scenes, and the *Poet*'s third Night.

THUS argue *Laziness, Ignorance* and *Avarice*: This is the Care they take of encouraging POETRY, and obliging the Town. Their Behaviour is recent in every Memory, when both Companies were united under their Banner. The Spectators, Poets and Actors of those Days, can but in Death forget it. We seldom then had an OPERA to entertain us, and our MUSICK was in a tolerable bad Way: PLAY we had none, but what, and when they pleas'd to give us one: So even our Men of Sense, and Ladies of Fashion, were forc'd to run for Amusement to the *Puppet-Show* and *Bear-Garden*. Either the underling Actors were dignify'd with the principal Characters, or, if the *Heads* condescended to favour the Town, they but trifled, yawn'd and slept three Hours away. They grudg'd the smallest Expence to invite, or amuse Company, they were sensible they had no other House to go to, a new Scene, or suit of Cloaths, a new Dance, or Piece of MUSICK, were as rare as a Comet; and when they blaz'd forth, the Prices were rais'd, and the Town pay'd the Piper. Thus they enrich'd themselves, starv'd their Players, and fool'd our Nobility and Gentry.

SINCE the Establishment of the two *Theatres*, our Usage has been kinder, and their Behaviour modester; and 'tis absolutely proper, that two Houses should always subsist, not that Wit thrives better than before, they affecting only to encourage the Heel, and not the Head: But

the

the Dread of a powerful Rival may keep both in Awe, though neither is to be trusted.

IF a Poet appears at their critical Tribunal, he is judg'd in the general Way of the World. *What is his Name, his Character and Fortune?—— Is he a Whig or Tory?—— What great Men countenance him?—— Is he known, or supported at* WILL's?—— *Does he frequent* BUTTON's?—— *What says the Lion's Face to him there?—— or the rest of the witty Wooden Heads?—— What thinks* Co—ly *of the Affair?—— Will the Gentleman allow his* PLAY *to be alter'd, and resign the Profits of his third Night, for the Name of a Poet?*

THIS they call sitting as Judges upon the Body of a PLAY, in order to see Poetick Justice impartially distributed, for the Credit, Pleasure and Improvement of the Nation. Thus Gentlemen are to be treated, who (however they succeed) design their Labours to delight and instruct Mankind by those Upstarts in Manners, as well as Fortune, and who are as great Strangers to Sense, as to Gentility; who have as little Knowledge in judging of such an Affair, as they have Right to manage a *Theatre*, nor can any thing but the grossest and most general Infatuation, account for either.

IF one of their own Fraternity is deliver'd of a Bastard, however ridiculous, vile, or misshapen the Changling is, it must be publickly christen'd, finely dress'd, and put to Nurse at the publick Charge: But had Men of Wit and Reputation, above all Bribery, and every Way unprejudic'd, canvass'd the PLAYS, with a Power to receive or refuse what has gone thro' their Hands, many valuable Entertainments would be rescued from Obscurity, and a vast Quantity of execrable Trash be buried in Oblivion. But it is needless to dwell any longer on so disagreeable a Subject, since,

in

in order to make their own Dross pass at Home, the Gold they have refus'd, is allow'd Sterling in another Kingdom.

WERE the Managers of our *Theatres* as sollicitous about the true Use of the Stage to the World, and the Dignity of their Profession, as they are about filling their Pockets, in order to enable them to W—re, and D—nk, and G—me, as if they had as much Right to those Vices, as the first Men of Quality in the Kingdom, they would then give all due Encouragement to the Poets, to stick close to sacred Subjects, and by once making such a *Dramatick* Law, they might, with a well-bred Confidence, refuse all PLAYS built on prophane Foundation.

THEN our Stage would rise in Grandeur and Reputation, equal to the Plans they follow'd; and perhaps, might be permitted, by our Superiours, to entertain us prudently, and gravely, even on *Sundays* and *Holidays* And instead of our *Play-Houses* being silenc'd on *Wednesdays* and *Fridays* in *Lent*, and other *Fasts* and *Festivals*, they might be open'd to our Edification, as well as Amusement.

ALL civiliz'd Nations in *Europe* allow PLAYS and OPERAS on *Sunday Nights*, but the *Dutch* and we, or some other insignificant, petty States, below our Notice, yet our conscientious Neighbours just mention'd, approve of private and publick Gaming in Assemblies, Coffee-houses, &c. on those Evenings, when Divine Service is over. Now the numerous Mischiefs arising from that Liberty to all civil Societies, are so scandalously notorious, that the most innocent Game cannot be brought upon the Parallel with the most faulty Stage-Entertainment we ever knew.

MORE-

MOREOVER, we should consider, that above two Parts in three of any Audience, can find out no manner of Way so agreeably instructive, and virtuously amusing, as a PLAY, to kill Time, and Time will be as uneasy to them on a *Sunday Evening* as any other.

BESIDES, all our Tradesmen, and others of an inferior Rank, (who are oblig'd to labour hard six Days of the Week, and are by their Callings depriv'd of such Diversions) may have then an Opportunity of improving, in a moral and polite Way, as well as their Betters: For, let our Divines preach up what Doctrines they please, *Sundays* and *Holidays* being, as the *Presbyterian* Parson call'd them, *Idle days*; People of that Rank will then unbend their Minds from the Cares of the World, and hunt out Amusements of some Sort or other: Therefore let us give them those which may prove pleasing, harmless and instructive.

THERE are but few of our meanest Mechanicks now, that will condescend to spend those Evenings only over a Psalm, a Slice of cold Beef and Carrot, so grunt, lovingly, Arm in Arm to Bed: The Taste, even of the Dregs of the People, is at present more refin'd, and we that toil for the publick Good, ought to give it suitable Encouragement: For, as Mr *Dennis* wisely observes, in his *Remarks* upon Mr. *Collier*'s *Thundering Essay* against the Stage—— "Nor will the "People of this Age be satisfy'd, to be always en-"tertain'd with Prayers and Sermons, but require "other Diversions."

IT is evident, indeed, that if the higher Powers should take this Proposal of mine into Consideration, and shelter it under the Wings of Authority, our Taverns and Bawdy-houses would

be

be confiderable Sufferers in the Manufactures of Wine and Flesh, which the vast Trade of that Day calls for, it being their weekly Market: But whither Wh——ing and Dr——ness, or seeing a PLAY, is most offensive to Religion or Morality, I leave the pious and virtuous Part of Mankind to judge. I think it appears very plain, that Nature requires a gentle raising of the Spirits, after the Fatigue of that Day, and the generality of People are agreed to have it one way or t'other.

WE all are sensible, that this Affair of innocent Recreations, was not only allow'd, but encourag'd, in the Days of a most religious King, and zealous Metropolitan. They knew that the Genius of the Nation demanded this Relief on such Occasions: For that reason, the *Book of Sports* after Divine Service was publish'd by Royal Authority, to prevent their running into greater Excesses.

BUT, if the pure Simplicity of undebauch'd Nature can have any Weight with us, I need only appeal to the unaffected Innocence and rural Customs of the *Welsh*, who never fail spending in this laudable Manner, their *Sunday Evenings*. The honest Parson, after Preaching to, and Catechising his Parish, with a Cup of Ale gives them a Tune on the Fiddle, while they lovingly dance after their Pastor. The Physician of the Soul acting in this, like the Physician of the Body, cloathing the black Pill of Religion with the golden Garment of Mirth

THE next Error in Management of the Masters of our *Play-houses* is visible, in a wrong Disposition, or Choice of proper Actors for the Stage.

HERE are a Company of Players enter'd as the King's Servants, who (as *Hamlet* has it) are

fit

fit either for *Tragedy, Comedy, History, Pastoral, Pastorical-Comical-Historical-Pastoral, Tragical-Historical.* This Sett of Gentlemen and Ladies are to go thro' all PLAYS, and all Characters, in as many different Shapes, as the World and THEATRE can vary them.

THE same Man must one Day keep justly up to the Grandeur of a Monarch, the next, personate as exactly the miserable Beggar. Now a Tyrant defying the gods, and breathing Destruction to Mankind, anon a whining Lover, expiring for a Frown. In one PLAY he must put on the ridiculous Fop, in another a slovenly Justice of Peace, or Courtier, or Cit, or Statesman, or Captain of the Militia; just as his Lot is that Evening.

THE Women too must pass thro' the same Variety of Characters. The romping Country Hoyden to Night, must shine out the fine Lady of the PLAY to Morrow. One Day as starch'd as a formal City Matron, the next, as flippant as a Court Cocquet in *Tragedy*. A proud ambitious Queen dwindles in *Comedy*, to a Pert, Jilting Chamber-maid, and she who yesterday was the gentlest, best natur'd Creature alive, this Evening must have Jealousy flaming in her Eyes, and Revenge brooding in her Heart.

I think, the Faults we find in our best and oldest Actors, and the little Hopes we have of any tolerable springing up, are owing to this odd Jumble of Characters in the same Person, and obliging a Man to change his Air, Voice, Face and Motions, as often and easily as he might a Vizor-Masque. In that Particular, the Antients had the Advantage of us, that Disguise to a Man's Countenance, by an Alteration of Speech, very much favouring the Deceit.

BUT

BUT in acting to Perfection, as well as in Writing, a Genius is requir'd, and it is impossible for one Person truly to form himself to so many different Parts. Therefore, where Nature has furnish'd any Man with that happy Talent, he should stick to that Character he's most adapted to, for in throwing himself out of his natural Biass, he'll run wide of all the rest he aims at. Where an Actor is born with a Notion of any Part in Life, of which we may form a proper Stage-Character, and studies by Art (which must have its Part in the Affair) to model himself entirely to it, there he'll be perfect, and may represent some others tolerably, but they must appear forc'd and affected: But one Robe can sit easy on him, and that which sits not easy, cannot please. I believe, this general Rule will admit of as few Exceptions as any that we know.

SOME wonderful Adepts in Criticism, and Sticklers for the present Management of our THEATRES, will very civilly and cunningly demand, *What's to be done in this Case? The Masters of a Play-house, cannot pretend to keep a different Actor for every different Part.* I grant it, not for every different Part, but for every general Character, at least, they may: Nay, I insist upon it, to do the Town and the Stage Justice on that Head, several ought to be kept to represent the same general Character. One Man may be very capable of representing a King, or Hero, as describ'd in such a Play, that may be highly unfit to enter into those Parts, as their Pictures are drawn in another. An Actor may shine in the Parts of *Don Sebastian*, or *Mark Anthony*, and be hiss'd in those of *Maximin*, or *Bajazet*. Thus widely too may differ the Humours of old Men in *Comedy*, and an admirable *Foresight* fit

H   out

out a scurvy *Don Cholerick Snap Shorto de Testy*. Nature delights in Variety, and is not content to divide the World into Heroes, Cowards, wise Men, Fools, Divines, or Atheists, but makes every Individual differ in some Particularity from all the rest of that Species, and every Ideot upon Earth has some Folly cleaving to him, a Secret to the rest of the Herd.

As a negligent blind-fold Choice of Actors for the Stage, is the Source from whence spring these Evils so justly complain'd of, I can think of no Redress, but cautioning the Managers of our *Play-houses*, to choose for the future, prudently and circumspectly, which can only be brought about, by a careful Visitation of the most publick, or generally frequented Places of this METROPOLIS; where they may readily spy out People born to represent, in a natural and easy Way, every Character that Life can shew, or the Stage demand: Those who may be entirely of a-piece with the Parts they are to appear in; and whose Stations in the World may not scorn moderate Proposals.

As the Accidents in Life of the conspicuous Part of the World, furnish the Stage with Characters, by a natural Representation of, and exposing their most ridiculous Follies, or dangerous Passions: So, in the lowest Scenes of Life, we may, by a curious View, discover an Imitation or Resemblance of the Behaviour of their Betters; from whom we may borrow Persons, cut out by Nature, to appear justly in all Branches of the Theatrical Business.

THE *Dutch* (whom I am oblig'd to name so often, with Regret to my Countrymen, in the Articles of Politeness and Penetration) allow a considerable Pension to some Men, eminent for

their

their great Sagacity, who are constant Surveyors of all publick Meetings, and Crowds. They carefully inspect the very Refuse of low Life, in order to cull out proper Persons to supply all *Dramatical* Characters. This Project has succeeded to Admiration, for their Discernment is such, that they read immediately in every Countenance, or judge nicely from some Particularity of Behaviour, what every Man is most capable of, by exerting his Top-talent.

They'll fix upon a Statesman, from a Tailor's threading his Needle, and discover an invincible Hero, in the Shoulders of a brawny Drayman. A Cobler's easy Whistle will distinguish the fine Gentleman, as the Management of his Awl will point out a General. A surly Skipper never fails in furnishing a charming Tyrant, as the Hen-peck'd Husband makes the most submissive Lover. If they are in distress for an able Lawyer, the Fish-market supplies them, and they borrow all their Beaus from the Baker's Flower-tub. Nay, I have known them very happily guess at a Judge in the Care of a Kennel-sweeper, and catch at a Critick, in the Dexterity of a Hang-man.

Their little Theatrical World is in the same Manner supply'd with female Characters; and the Queen, the fine Lady, the Prude, the Coquet, the Jilt, the Termagant, are occasionly pick'd out from amongst broken Tradesmen's Wives, gay Sempstresses, demure Widows, Boors Daughters, City Gossips, and bawling Oister-women

They all return next Morning to their several Trades, and unlike our Actors and Actresses, lay aside their borrow'd Dignities with the *Playhouse* dress. The Publick are entertain'd at an easy Rate; nor are they forc'd into an idle, useless Life, for they work by Day to maintain their Families, and by Night to divert their Neighbours.

It will not be improper to observe here, that in several Towns in *Holland*, the Revenues of the THEATRE are wholly appropriated to the Maintenance of some Hospitals, as the Stews at *Rome*, keep the Head of the Church in Pocket-money. This Oeconomy tallies exactly with my Project, advanc'd in the preceeding ESSAY, relating to the *Opera-house*.

But, to Instance a few Domestick Examples. Can any reasonable Man suppose, that the late Worshipful Sir *Ja——s B——ker*, Knight, was design'd by Heaven to be only a Cypher in Life, the Scorn of Wise-men, the But of Ridicule to Fools, or a Banter upon all the Dignities of the Great. To what End then serv'd his Air of Wisdom? his Philosophical Countenance, and Solemnity of Address? —— No! —— he was born to be an Actor. As Fortune favour'd him with no Station adequate to his Merit, he should have been seiz'd by the Stage, and at least have appear'd, in Imagination, to himself, and the World, what he ought to have been in Reality. In his being excluded the THEATRES, the Town was depriv'd of a sedate Privy-Counsellor, a solemn Ambassadour, and an awful Doge of *Venice*.

No body can imagine that ——*P——ne*, Esq; was sent into Life, only to pace twenty times a Day round the Mall, regardless of the Crowds of Beaus and Belles, to write, in transitory Chalk those valuable Scraps of Politicks which engage the admiring Eyes of all Passengers. How consummate a Statesman! How profound a Politician here is lost! One, who may have Cunning enough

OF POETRY.

enough to set Fools together by the Ears, and Prudence to screen himself from the Scrutinies of the wisest: But his Merits being neglected by the World, yet what a Figure might he make in the Business of the Stage, it's Miniature?

ARE we to believe that C—t H——r's terrible Countenance was chizzell'd out by Nature, only to preside at a *Masquerade*, frighten Wh---res of Rank into decent Behaviour, or grace a Board of O——a D——rs? Impossible! That just Copy of *Gorgon*, was only made to fit the Shoulders of a First-rate Tyrant. How is the Stage cheated of a *Maximin*, Persecution in every Feature! —— The very Figure of *Dionysius*! Nay, *Phalaris* himself! For who can look at him, without expecting the brazen Bull to follow? But thus contrary to the Designs of Nature, Mortals often are put to a wrong Use. For want of a capable Actor, no such Part is attempted, we are disappointed in our Pleasures, and he, in the End of his Creation.

LET us next inspect Taverns, Coffee-houses, and Gaming tables. How many *Tragick* Heroes are there to be met with! Fellows! —— who are only proper to express those Passions to the Life, which are never vented but in Words, and evaporate into Air. Those Drums of the Creation, sent into the World to make a Noise, and be beat upon. Your *Mohuns*, *Harts*, *Bettertons*, and *Booths*, are but Apes of them; for they are the Men, who, like *Maximin*, can brave all the Gods, rage like *Hotspur*, and rave like *Othello*. On the Stage, those Bellows of Conversation might stretch their Lungs for the publick Good, which are now the Bane of all Civil Society, and a Nusance to all Ears within reach of their Throats.

ESSAY II.

LET us venture farther, and visit the Churches, Drawing-rooms, and Front-boxes. How many shall we find there that out-pitch, a Bar's length, any Character a Poetical Fancy ever form'd?

'TIS true, the Stage is look'd upon as a magnifying Glass, and allow'd to shew Vices, and Follies, full blown. Every Thing ought to be represented there, larger than the Life, the readier to distaste the Beholders, and that the smallest Error being made plain on the Surface, no part of wrong Behaviour should escape their Eyes unregarded:

YET, on the Stage of Life, we every Day meet with those that are as ridiculously affected as *Lord Foppington*, as stupidly vicious as *Lord Brute*; as fawning as *Lord Plausible*; as impertinent as *Novel*, as impotently fond as *Limberham*, as treacherous as *Maskwell*, as superstitious as *Foresight*, as subtil as *Volpone*, as humoursome as *Morose*, as silly as *Sir Martin*, as hypocritical as *Tartuff*, and as jealous as *Fondle-Wife*.

WERE it proper to find Fault with the other Sex, any Man that was resolv'd to spy Blemishes in them, and examin'd their Behaviour in the Middle of an OPERA, or a Sermon, or pry'd into their Conduct in an Assembly, or Closet, might find the most glaring Female Characters that ever Poet drew, very tenderly touch'd, and all the *Olivias*, *Lætitias*, *Belindas*, *Lucretias*, *Isabellas*, *Marias* COMEDY has given us, are but Foils to the more brilliant Follies the Town every Day throws in our Way.

NOW, as by all Political Constitutions, every body ought, in their several Stations, to be in some respect conducive to the publick Good, I would have an Embargo laid upon the Persons of all those Gentlemen and Ladies, who have so

natural

natural a Turn to those small Foibles, and their Bodies seiz'd for the Use of the Stage, that as they boldly appear in open Defiance of the Reformation intended, they may shine out there to some purpose, and hinder others from falling into the same Errors.

I look upon this innate Propensity to what is ridiculous, as a Distemper, and pity it as a Species of civiliz'd Madness. Therefore, let their Births and Fortunes be ever so great, I would allow them the Liberty of displaying their Parts in the most publick Manner, that at once they may divert and improve their fellow-Subjects, and humour their own Frenzy: Perhaps, we may easier conquer the Disease, by giving Way to, than opposing it.

FROM what I have here urg'd on this Head, I think the Necessity of furnishing the Stage with Actors, after this Manner, must at first sight appear plain to every Frequenter of a *Play-house*, nor can there be any other Method of advancing a just Supply, in Propriety, Number, and Expedition. But, as the Obstinate and Self-conceited, are not easily convinc'd of the Truth, if there are any such, let them but consider W——ks as a Heroe, B——th as a fine Gentleman, M——ls as a Lover, C——er an old General, D---y N---ss a Tyrant, O——ld a Prude, P——er a Cocquet, and B——ker an Empress, which Disposition of Characters we commonly meet with. Then let them say, we have no reason of Complaint. 'Tis true, there are but a few good Actors for numberless Parts, but, as I have propos'd a Remedy, no body will pity their Indisposition, if they refuse a Cure.

IF I might touch upon Things, P---C---or E---- this Affair may admit of several new
Hints

Hints for the Service of the Publick, nor wou'd it prove the worst Rule in the Choice of our ---- and our ----- and the ----- and them ------- and those -------- and that ----- by these prudent and political Maxims, the Nation just recommended, successfully regulate their S ---- and their S -----, but I am of Opinion, this Point will be more fully and pertinently spoke to in the ESSAY upon MASQUERADES.

I come now to the third Article of high Crimes and Misdemeanors charg'd upon our Theatrical Managers; which is made manifest in their strange Negligence of, and prodigious Oeconomy in the Decorations of the Stage, which are so visibly essential both to *Tragedy* and *Comedy,* and consist of SCENERY, MACHINERY, HABITS, ATTENDANCE, MUSICK and DANCING

IT is morally impossible for any POET, or Master of a *Play-House,* to be too expensive in the Beauty or Grandeur of their SCENES and MACHINES: The more just and surprizing they appear, the sooner will the Spectator be led insensibly into imagining every thing real, and, of consequence, prove the easier perswaded of the Instruction intended. Besides, they are absolutely necessary in all Parts of a PLAY, where the Plot requires the Intervention of some supernatural Power, in order to conquer Difficulties, and solve Misteries: For, what is a God, or a Devil, or a Conjurer, ⎯⎯ without Moving Clouds, Blazing Chariots, Flying Dragons, and Enchanted Castles? ⎯⎯ Airy Sprites, Terrestrial Hob-goblins, and Infernal Demons, must, at a Word, descend, rise, and vanish These things, justly introduc'd, strike an Awe upon the Audience; and, while they are amaz'd and delighted, they are instructed. This gives the STAGE a

Character

OF POETRY.

Character with the World, and POETS and ACTORS are esteem'd Demi-gods. Thus, when People are prepossess'd in Favour of their Power, they dare not but embrace their Doctrines.

ABBOT *Hedelin* observes, *That the Ornaments of the Stage, so sensibly delight us, by a Kind of witty Magick, as to raise from the Dead Heroes of past Ages. They present, as it were to our Eyes, a new Heaven and Earth, while we are so agreeably deceiv'd, as to imagine every thing present Even People of Understanding take them for Enchantments, and are pleas'd with the Dexterity of the Artists, and the neat Execution of so many Contrivances. For this End the Ancients bestow'd the richest Decorations upon their* THEATRES: *The Heavens would open for their gods to descend, and converse with Men, the Air would be fill'd with Thunder, Lightening and Storms, the Sea would shew Tempests, Ship-wrecks, and Sea-fights, the Earth would produce Gardens, Forests, Desarts, Palaces and Temples, out of its Bosom would rise Furies, Demons, and all the Prodigies of their fabulous Hell, and the* POETS *never fail'd to fill their* PLAYS *with such Incidents as requir'd those magnificent Decorations*

THE Habits of the Actors likewise have a prodigious Influence on the Minds of an Audience. We see daily, in the great World, a vast Deference shewn to the Figure of a Suit of Cloaths, and how regularly Degrees of Respect rise, from the Gold and Silver Button and Button-hole, to Lace and Embroidery How nicely are the Distances betwixt Cloth, Velvet, and Brocade, observ'd? Much more in the THEATRE should this Distinction prevail, where our Senses are to be touch'd, pleas'd, and taken by Surprize, and where every Spectator, indeed, is to receive an Impression of the Character of the Person from his
Dress,

Dress; and the first Ideas are generally most lasting.

TRAGEDY borrows vast Advantages from the additional Ornaments of Feathers and high Heels, and it is impossible, but that two Foot and a Half of Plume and Buskin must go a great Length, in giving an Audience a just Notion of a Hero. That great Appearance gives an Air of Grandeur to every thing he says, or does. The best *Grecian* POETS, who brought TRAGEDY to its Perfection, first gave Birth to this Invention: They found it of Service, and all other Nations continued it. In *Rome*, commenc'd once a famous Dispute betwixt two eminent *Tragedians*, which best represented *Agamemnon*; he that step'd loftily, and on tip-toes, or, he who appear'd pensive, as if concern'd for the Safety of his People, but the tall Man carry'd it. These useful Allies to the *Drama*, take more with the Generality of People, than the brightest Thoughts, or justest Expressions; and, I defy any of our best tragick Bards, so readily to give an Audience a true Idea of a Queen, by the noblest Sentiments, or finest Language, as the Wardrobe-Keeper can, by half a Dozen lac'd Pages, and as many Yards of embroider'd Tail, and, indeed, there should be something particularly adapted to the Look and Dress of every ACTOR, which should, at first View, speak his Character, before he opens his Mouth, and, as the Frown shews the King, the Stride, the Hero, the thoughtful Air, the Statesman, and the silly Smile, the Fop, so do the Robe, the Truncheon, the Bundle of Papers, and Clock'd Stockings.

THE Appearance of a Retinue suitable to every distinct Character of the *Drama*, (which should make

make a Figure on the Stage) is another Point of very great Consequence, and ought to be principally regarded. What is a Tyrant without his Guards? or a Princess, without her Maids of Honour? A General, without a Troop of Officers? Or, a first Minister, without a Levee of Spies and Dependants? A Lawyer, without a Flock of Clients? Or, a Beau, without a Train of Lacquies?

A just Number of Attendants gives an Air of Dignity to, and distinguishes the proper Superiority of each Character, besides, when the Stage is crowded, the Greatness of the Shew casts a Mist, as it were, over the Eyes of the Spectators, and makes the thinnest Plot appear full of Business. Keep the Stage fill'd thus, you'll instill Life and Spirit into the dullest PLAY, the Passions will never flag, nor the Action cool.

I have known a *Tragedy* succeed, by the irresistible Force of a Squadron of *Turkish Turbans* and *Scimiters*, and, another owe the whole of its Merit to the graceful Procession of a *Mufti*, and a Tribe of Priests. A POET who fights cunning, will judiciously throw into every Act a Triumph, a Wedding, a Funeral, a Christening, a Feast, or some such Spectacle, which must be manag'd by a Multitude. Thus, by a well-dispos'd Succession of Crowds in every Scene, he lies, as it were, safe under Cover from all Criticism.

AND, indeed, I am inclinable to believe, that this was the chief Design of the Ancients, in establishing and encouraging, at so prodigious an Expence, their CHORUS: For by this Means, the Stage could never be empty, which prov'd of infinite Service to their POETS, and contributed vastly to the Satisfaction of the People.

THE

THE *French* Critick just mention'd, (whose Authority, in Stage-Affairs, is undoubted) says, *That the most magnificent Part of the Representations of the Ancients consisted, in their seldom suffering an Actor to come upon the Stage alone*, and remarks, *That if a Prince, Princess, or any other Person of eminent Quality appear'd, they were follow'd by a large Retinue, sometimes Soldiers, sometimes Courtiers, but always those who were proper Attendants to the Ground-work of that Scene. A rich Citizen would not enter without many Servants, and even a publick Courtezan scorn'd to make her Appearance, but surrounded with Maids, and, in short, every Body was well accompany'd, without some particular Reason requir'd their being alone* For, they did not understand that *Hibernicism,* so judiciously us'd by our modern POETS, of an Actor's making a *Soliloquy* in the middle of a Crowd.

As to MUSICK and DANCING, I cannot object a Deficiency in those Articles to our Stage Directors: They cannot well be more expensive in those Entertainments, without it were possible to bring about the compleat Re-establishment of the old CHORUS: Therefore, if I blame them on that Head, it is, because they are rather extravagant than sparing, especially in the latter, which deprives us of Decorations more essential to the *Drama* But of this we shall talk amply in the next ESSAY

I am at last arriv'd at the finishing Stroke of this ESSAY, which was to consider, To what Causes is owing the vitious Taste of the Town, and how far the Decay of *Dramatick Poetry* is owing to Spectators, or Readers of it But this Affair is of that Consequence to the Relish and Encouragement of every thing polite, its Faults are

are so notorious, and Amendments so necessary, that I shall reserve the further Consideration of it, till I come to the ESSAY upon AUDIENCES in general, where I have so many Orders of People to speak to in a different Way, so many mistaken Judgments to set right; so many Kinds of Criticks to call Names, and so much more to that Purpose, and all, that I must beg of my Readers to suspend their Curiosity, in Relation to themselves, till the Fifth ESSAY, when I intend to play the Devil with them all.

ESSAY III.
OF DANCING,
Religious and Dramatical.

An Historical Account of the Mimes *and* Pantomimes *of the Ancients; with a short Parallel betwixt them and our modern* Arlequins *and* Scaramouches; *and a learned Criticism on our present* Grotesque Dances *To which are added, Some Reflections upon* Dancing, *of a publick and private Nature; with a Side-step towards* Tumblers, Posture-Masters, *and* Rope-Dancers.

S no Man can deny the vast Veneration the Antients, on all Occasions, profess'd for Dancing, I need not be too copious on that Head, or lay too weighty a Stress of Arguments, where there is but a small Foundation for Dispute. To be prolix, in tracing it to the remotest Ages of Antiquity, would be amusing the World with trifling

trifling Flourishes, and cutting Capers to very little Purpose, my principal Aim being to point out its Beauties, and make manifest some Steps in it of the utmost Importance to the Publick, not yet discover'd.

BUT, in order to prosecute this laudable Design regularly, and give compleat Satisfaction to all my Readers, learned and illiterate, by improving one, and shewing the others my Reading, I must beg Leave to throw in some small Hints, necessary to clear up its Original, and manifest the Purity of the Spring from whence so beautiful a Stream does flow.

BOTH sacred and profane History talk much in Favour of DANCING. All Ages have shewn their Esteem for it, from the Beginning of Time to this Day: And, to a DANCE and a SONG, in Honour of *Bacchus*, we owe the Rise of all *Stage-Entertainments*; and, of consequence, all that Instruction and Delight the World has from time to time receiv'd, either from TRAGEDY, COMEDY, or OPERA.

NAY, should we view DANCING in a private, as well as publick Light, it would appear to us as healthful in one, as agreeable in the other. But having confin'd my self within the Circle of the Town-Diversions, I shall not, at present, touch any farther upon that Subject, than in observing, That I look upon a DANCING-MASTER as a very useful Member in a Commonwealth: Nor can I well avoid making a small Excursion, towards the End of this ESSAY, in recommending some new Movements absolutely essential to the most material Points of private, as well as publick Life.

BUT, to proceed methodically —I just hinted before, that the God *Bacchus*, having first brought the Art of planting of Grapes into *Greece* (for which I heartily thank him) *Icarius* (to whom he imparted the Secret) finding a Goat too free with his Grapes, sacrific'd the Beast to the Honour of that Deity; at the same time giving an Entertainment of MUSICK and DANCING. This Solemnity pleas'd, and grew into an annual Custom, every Year adding something new to the first Plan; and the POETS intermedling with the Affair, first added an ACTOR; another *Two*; the next *Three*; till by degrees, and new-modelling, it was so far improv'd, that at last it ended in a regular TRAGEDY, and that which was only design'd as a Sacrifice, became a finish'd STAGE-PLAY.

THUS the THEATRES rose by, and borrow'd DANCING from the Temples, and what was at first a softly Hymn, by way of Chorus, in a blind ridiculous Religion, gave Birth to the noblest Amusement, and most instructive Entertainment, that the politest Nations of the World could ever boast.

BUT we are not to suppose that DANCING was confin'd to this Part of their Worship alone: No, the World grew so fond of Religious Agility, that the Festivals of each particular Deity show'd away with a different DANCE. *Ceres*, *Venus*, *Priapus*, and the whole Rag-man-roll of Gods and Goddesses, invented various Gestures and Motions appropriated to their several Rites. *Bacchus*, indeed, had his Misteries, in a more especial Manner, celebrated by DANCING, as may be gather'd from the wild Rants and frolicksome Capers the *Bacchanal Priests* made use of, during their mad Performances and Enthusiastick Solemnities.

BUT

OF POETRY.

BUT, whilst we are poking into Antiquity (were it proper to carry this Affair higher, than either mentioning it as a Part of a publick religious Ceremony, or a private elegant Entertainment) we might instance, from several of the most antient POETS, Places, where the Gods themselves are introduc'd dancing. In *Pindar*, *Apollo* is called, by Way of Excellence, The DANCER.

IN *Homer*, he plays upon his Harp, and dances at the same time. Nay, *Jupiter* himself, in the Fragment of an old *Greek* Poem (the Author of which is uncertain) is usher'd in as the Father of gods and Men, in a Minuet-Step.

WE learn, from the Right Reverend Bishop Potter's *Antiquities of* Greece, *That from the most antient Times,* MUSICK *and* DANCING *were the principal Diversions at all Entertainments, and that, in every Step of private Life,* DANCING *was particularly esteem'd an Accomplishment becoming all Persons of Honour and Wisdom* Epaminondas (who always was look'd upon as the Chief of the *Grecian* Heroes) is celebrated for being a fine DANCER, and playing very genteely on the Flute.

'TIS true, the same profound Author gives us to understand, *That the* Romans *look'd upon these Amusements as trivial, and not worthy to be mention'd, though in* Greece, *they were thought very commendable.* In answer to this ill-grounded Assertion, I must observe, That his Authorities are only cited from a very few old, morose Orators and Historians, who, of consequence, must blame what they are unfit for, or did not comprehend. To their narrow-soul'd Opinions, we object the Practice of all the politest *Romans*, who beheld DANCING with a suitable Regard and favourable Eye, both in their Religious Worship, and Civil Amusements. The most esteem-

I 3 ed

ed Tribe of their Priests were call'd *Salii*, from *Saliendo*, Dancing: Nay, they were founded by *Numa* himself, the *Roman Licurgus*, and to their Care was entrusted the famous Target which drop'd from Heaven, upon the safe keeping of which, the Fate of their Empire depended. At their yearly Procession (which was one of the most splendid Sights of *Old Rome*) they travers'd all the Streets with nimble Motions, prodigious Agility, and handsome Turns of the Body, as we are inform'd by several wise Authors.

As to their well-judg'd Amusements in private Life, even *Brutus*, *Catiline*, *Julius Cæsar*, *Mark Anthony*, &c. some of their most distinguish'd great ones, were preferr'd to their Fellow-Citizens, more for their DANCING, than any noted Martial Exploit.

BUT how can we reckon the Art of DANCING to be despis'd, either by the Religious, Military, or polite Men of *Rome*? when the first made use of it, more or less, in all the Misteries of their Religion, which is already made sufficiently plain: The second, by its Assistance, qualify'd themselves for all Feats of War, as is evident by the *Saltatio Pyrrhica*, and *Trojæ Ludus*, which were only military DANCING-BOUTS. And, for the third, I may venture to affirm, That no Nation ever look'd upon a Man as polite, that could not dance.

THE Institution and Progress of the *Trojæ-Ludus* is known to every School-Boy, and the Description of it under their little Leader *Ascanius*, at the Games for *Anchises*'s Death, so very full and beautiful, in the inimitable Lines of *Virgil*, that as every body has him in *Latin* or *English*, I need say nothing more of it here, only that it was always perform'd on Horseback, as the *Pyrrhica Salta-*
tio

tio was a-Foot: The Original of which is not quite so clear. The Accounts given us of it by Historians, Criticks, and Commentators, all widely differing from, and contradicting one another. Some ascribe its Foundation to *Minerva*'s leading up a Warlike-like DANCE, after the Conquest of the Giants by the Gods: Others hold its Rise to be from the DANCES of the *Corybantes*, who took Care of young *Jupiter*, and, in their mad Fits, danc'd about, clashing their Spears against their Shields, to drown the Infants Cries, that *Saturn* might not find him out, and eat him. These, indeed, have an Eye to the Affair it self; but account not in the least for its Name, therefore the most probable Conjecture is, That it had its Name and Steps from *Pyrrhus*, Son to *Achilles*, who instituted these warlike Motions to the Honour of his Father, at his Funeral Games: And what adds to its Probability is, the exact Description we find of the *Pyrrhick* DANCE in *Homer*, perfectly delineated upon the Shield of *Achilles*, in the Account he gives us of the Armour made for him by *Vulcan*. From whence we may reasonably suppose, he borrow'd the Design.

BUT what are all these trifling DANCES to those celebrated ones of *Old Greece!* where, at all the solemn Games, such as the *Olympick, Nemæan, Elæan, Pythian*, &c. those Prizes of Honour were gain'd by the Strength, Agility, or Swiftness of the Body: Where the Victors were esteem'd superior to the Conquerors of the World, and their immortal Fame founded upon the lasting Basis of a well regulated DANCE.

HOWEVER plausible and just this Account of the first publick Appearance of DANCING, may seem to every thinking, or unthinking Reader,

I will

ESSAY III.

I will boldly maintain, that (after canvassing all the Poets, Criticks, Historians, &c. either of this, or former Ages, on that Head) I take this noble Art to be of a much older Date than any of them have allow'd it. I could give undeniable Authorities for this, from sacred History, as, *Miriam* the Prophetess, and her Damsels, going out with *Timbrels* and with *Dances*. The Daughters of *Shiloh* went every Year to dance, only for their Diversion. *David* himself danc'd before the Ark, and *Herodias* danc'd *John* the *Baptist*'s Head off, &c. But to wave all Instances of this Nature, lest we disoblige any Body by a seeming Offence, I shall only cite what Conjectures or Proofs I think are for my Purpose, from profane History, and support my Arguments by honest Heathen Quotations.

CERTAINLY, DANCING is much antienter than any Author, *Grecian* or *Roman*, makes out. If we judge by any Light they give us into that Affair, 'tis already prov'd, That it was first us'd in Religious Worship, at least publickly. Now as *Rome* had its Religion, Morals, Laws, and every Thing polite or useful, from *Old Greece*, on the other Hand, *Greece* was as much indebted, for all these valuable Blessings, to *Old Egypt*. At least, for the principal Part, however the whole may be disputed.

NOR will this appear a bare Conjecture, but a well-grounded Assertion, when we reflect, that all former Ages and different Parts of the known World, made DANCING a principal Ingredient in a Religious Hodge-Podge: And as *Egypt* is the oldest Nation we can well give an Account of, undoubtedly from thence the first *Grecian* Sages brought their Divine, Civil and polite Learning; as on the other hand, the *Romans* borrow'd

all

all from them. And as it is notorious, that these three pious, wise, genteel Nations danc'd over the largest Share of their Prayers, so it is easy to account for the first Institution and Progress of RELIGIOUS DANCING

BUT to bring this Point nearer home than the first Establishment of Religious Dances in *Greece*, even down to the Beginning of the *Mimes* and *Pantomimes*, which was long after. I say, these dumb Representations of proper Fables by Motions, Gestures, Attitudes, *&c.* must be entirely taken from the old *Egyptians*, as any curious Antiquary may readily discover, in the near Resemblance betwixt these Twin-Brothers, *viz.* The *Hieroglyphicks* of one, and *Dances* of the other; or indeed, (to speak more properly) what is every Step in these *Dances*, but a significant *Hieroglyphical* Expression?

SINCE DANCING then, either *Theatrical*, (as it is commonly introduc'd on the *Stage* without any particular Meaning) or *Dramatical* (when we have a Story properly *danc'd*, so as to form a perfect Entertainment to be understood) is what I am now principally to speak to. I think it will not be impertinent here to take a more particular View of their first Rise in *Greece*, either before the *Chorus* was found out, or as they were introduc'd as Parts of the *Chorus*, after the Invention of that Supplement to a *Stage-Entertainment*, when we may consider DANCING in the Infancy of its Merit, so trace it down to those Days when the *Mimes* and *Pantomimes* came so much into Vogue, that they were admir'd by the greatest Princes, Poets, and Philosophers, both *Grecian* and *Roman*. When we may look upon DANCING in general to stand tip-toe on the very Pinnacle of Perfection.

FOR

ESSAY III.

FOR several Ages the Profession of DANCING remain'd in a quiet, unpolish'd State, contriving a friendly Alliance betwixt the *Altar* and the *Stage*, and proving a very humble Servant to both, till some old *Greek* (whose Brains lay in his Heels) thought there might be something more made of DANCING, than just pleasing the Eye; wisely judging, That if *Dancers* could arrive at speaking to the Mind without Words, Mankind might be instructed without the Trouble of Speech. But who first chalk'd out the Steps for a dumb *Tragedy* or *Comedy*, I could never yet discover; only I imagine, he must be very expert in the *Egyptian* Hieroglyphicks. Having once got firm Footing in *Greece*, it long flourish'd there before it was transplanted to *Rome*, where that Art likewise throve wonderfully for several Centuries.

BEFORE I proceed any farther, some of my Readers may be inquisitive to find out a Distinction betwixt the *Mimes* and *Pantomimes*, as they may happen to be mention'd separately, or together. As I do not suppose those curious Persons to be any Conjurers in Criticism, the most plain and satisfactory Account I can give them, in so material a Point, is to set full before them the Difference betwixt his Grace of Y——k, and his Grace of C——ry; one being Pr——te of E——nd, the other of all E——nd.

THE most rational then, and succinct Method I can pursue, in explaining the Rise and Progress of the *Mimes* and *Pantomimes*, take as follows. The old *Grecian* COMEDY being restrain'd of its Licentiousness, in abusing nominally Persons of the highest Stations and brightest Characters, the Stage was oblig'd to have recourse to feign'd Stories, which were confin'd to the meanest Events in low Life, after the Manner of our
Modern

Modern COMEDIES: But long before this they had lost their *Chorus* of MUSICK and DANCING, either because they could not, in those Representations, preserve a *Chorus* with any Decency; or, that the Magistrates refus'd being at the Trouble or Expence of a *Chorus* for COMEDY, which Reason indeed seems best grounded.

THUS the old COMEDY and its *Chorus* being laid aside, the new COMEDY was receiv'd, with what we call Interludes of SINGING and DANCING, in a Way of *Mimickry* and *Buffoonery*, in Place of the *Chorus*, as being more of a-piece with *Comick-Poetry*, and more answerable to its Nature.

FROM these Plants then I fancy, (for there is no more in it) the *Mimes* and *Pantomimes* in *Greece* sprung up, from whence they were usher'd into *Rome* with vast Applause.

IT is certain, they were of very old standing in *Greece*, being mention'd by *Aristotle*, nay, by *Eschylus* himself. They were held so much in Esteem, that they were introduc'd at all publick Shews, and private Feasts, and were every where receiv'd with Encomiums suitable to their distinguish'd Merit. *Plutarch* calls them *Dumb Poems*; as, *vice versâ*, he does POETRY, a *Speaking-dance*. So just was their Expression of every Passion, that the least Motion of Head, Arm, or Foot, had so far its due Weight with the Audience, that nothing (which could be made intelligible by Words) was left imperfect, or the Sense lost in their Action. *Aristotle* (who was the justest and most learn'd Critick in POETRY, as well as one of the First-rate Philosophers) so much admir'd their Mimick Art, that he call'd one of them a divine Dancer, for having so well danc'd a whole *Tragedy* of *Eschylus*'s, call'd, *The seven before*

fore Thebes: Which alone is sufficient to stifle the ridiculous Notions of some pretended Dablers in Antiquity who would insinuate, That the two first of this Tribe that were famous, were *Pylades* and *Bathyllus*, who came from *Greece* to *Rome* in the Time of *Augustus*, when it is rather more than probable, that this Art (which had been so long cultivated amongst the *Grecians*, with the greatest Care and Success) was with their Empire rather in its Decline, before its first Appearance in *Italy*.

NOT but *Pylades* and *Bathyllus* were both eminent, in their Way, to a vast Degree, one being as noted for imitating the *Tragick*, as the other the *Comick* Passions. *Seneca* mentions them with great Respect, and from the Consideration of their different Excellencies, lays it down as an infallible Maxim, That no Man should undertake to profess any Science, but what he is design'd by Nature to excel in. Which I think fully corroborates my Project mention'd in the precedent ESSAY, where I advanc'd some Rules for better supplying the Stage with proper Actors, and will, I hope, bear as great Weight in a following ESSAY, when I shall produce some Hints very New (yet undeniably useful and solid) for trying and qualifying all People for those Employments Nature has fitted them for.

THERE is another Argument which strengthens the imagin'd Antiquity of the *Pantomimes*, which arises from my past Reflections upon the *Pyrrhick* and *Trojan* DANCES, which were partly of this Kind: And, as they were introduc'd in the earliest Accounts we have of those two celebrated Nations, 'tis reasonable to believe, that the *Mimes* had an Eye to their Performances, both in their Original and Progress.

SOME

SOME People may here object (and not without Cause) to the wanton Gestures, and lascivious Behaviour of the *Mimes* in general, which were Incendiaries to vitious Love, Provocatives to all Beastliness, and Shocks to modest Eyes. Part of this Charge I allow, and will not defend it, what was blameable in them, I give up, but must desire my Reader's Patience in observing two Things. This Accusation, in the first Place, touches not the *Grecian Pantomimes*. This Art was allow'd no such Excess amongst the *Greeks*; tho' it was held there in the highest Esteem. Those polite and prudent People encourag'd no Diversions, but what could stand the Test of Virtue as well as Pleasure, and tho' some of their Amusements might only aim at an agreeable Ingenuity, yet they were never suffer'd to look a-squint at Vice. In the second Place, we learn from this, that the *Mimick Art* soon degenerated with the *Romans* The *Grecian* Masters being gone, and no skilful Successors to support their Stage, People were oblig'd to take up with the Refuse of their Society, who, in order to carry on their Trade, (by the Inclinations of the Generality of their Spectators, and the Countenance of some lustful Emperours) grew so impure in their Actions, and nauseous in their Obscenities, that even corrupted *Rome* it self was asham'd to be pleas'd with a Diversion so notoriously scandalous, and fairly laid them aside.

BUT, before I intirely leave this Subject, I cannot avoid taking Notice of some absurd Accounts handed down to us by very grave, learned Authors in Relation to the *Mimes*, particularly Mr *Kennet* in his *Roman Antiquities* Who says, that *Scaliger* defines *Mimickry* to be a POEM imitating any sort of Actions, so as to make them appear ridiculous. This Definition, I am sure, is highly imperfect, ridiculous, and wide of the Mark: For, every School-boy knows, that in the true Art of the *Mimes*, there never was any Speech made use of, as is already sufficiently prov'd from the Authors, both *Grecian* and *Roman*, above cited. Indeed, there were a Set of Farce Writers and Actors, who, by Way of Interlude, either betwixt the Acts, or at the End of a Play, rehears'd several odd Pieces of POETRY, but how they came by the Name of *Mimes*, I cannot comprehend: For, I take *Mimickry* to be a just Explanation of all Actions of Life, by Motions alone without Words. This Definition may not be according to Mood and Figure; but 'tis just and true: For, in that consisted the Merit of the *Pantomimes*.

Mr. *Kennet* himself owns, that the Original of what he calls the *Mimi*, was owing to a Set of Actors, who after the *Chorus* went off the Stage, diverted the Audience with apish Postures, and antick Dances: This indeed was a Part of *Mimickry*, but the poorest: For *Laberius* and *Tublius*, (whom he stiles the two famous *Pantomimi*) with their imperfect odd *Drama*, were Farce Writers, and Farce Actors, noted indeed in their Way; and the first of them (tho' of the *Equestrian Order*) was oblig'd by *Cæsar* to act in one of his Farces: But, neither that Part of his *Prologue* cited, or what *Horace* mentions of him in the tenth *Satire* of his first Book, insinuate in the least his being one of the *Mimi*. it being undeniable, that the two first that visited *Rome* in that Character, were *Pylades* and *Batlyllus*, before spoken of, and fully.

BUT what a Right Reverend Author means by a total Neglect of the *Mimi*, tho' so very particular

cular in the other Antiquities of *Greece*, I cannot account for: This I am sure of, that he treats of many Customs at large, of less moment in general to Mankind, and in particular to the learned World: nor is there one of their miscellany Customs there treated of, but is a Trifle in comparison to a thorough Knowledge of the *Pantomime* Art.

HAVING been very plain and particular on this Head, as far as it relates to the *Antients*, it will not be improper now to consider how far the *Moderns* have imitated them in this Art; so make a sort of Connexion betwixt those Times and the present Age, in the Case before us.

I believe, that from some faint Notions of these dumb *Orators*, imprinted on the Minds of the late *Greeks*, or some remaining Tracks left of their former Foot-steps, the Custom arose of having *Mutes* in the *Grand Signior's Seraglio*, and which is so strictly observ'd in all the Palaces of the Tyrants of the *East*. For, they being no Blabbers, Secrets of the greatest Moment are alway entrusted with them. They are the most officious and handy, as well as silent Servants; and as they do not disturb one with their impertinent Voices, so they cannot tell Tales out of School; which Perfections would highly recommend them to the generality of our fine Ladies: And on the other Side, I fancy most *British* Husbands would not be displeas'd, if the mute Article was by some Means or other introduc'd in Matrimonial Life.

WHAT very much confirms my Belief in this Point of the *Mutes* being related to the *Mimes*, is, that to this Day they often act little Pieces in the *Mimick* Way to divert the *Grand Signior*;

which is indeed the only Theatrical *Entertainment* the *Turks* have any Notion of.

As the *Sultan* has furnish'd the Privacies of his Court from the Remains of the old *Mimes*, so has the *Italians* supply'd their *Comick* Stages with Actors from their Relicks in *Rome*. For from their Ashes (*Phœnix-like*) have sprung up our Modern *Arlequins*, *Scaramouches* and *Punchinello's*, which must be apparent to all who are conversant with the History of one Set, and the Performances of the other.

I must own, that the best *Italian* COMEDY is a tolerable Imitation of the old *Pantomimes*, only a little *Gothicis'd*, most of the other *Antique* Arts have in a great measure retriev'd their pristine Glory: *Painting*, *Sculpture*, and *Architecture*, have for these three last Centuries flourish'd prodigiously: And, as I have already observ'd, I am inclinable to think, that the present State of our MUSICK by far exceeds any thing of that Kind, ever known to *Greece* or *Rome*: Only POETRY, and this its dumb younger Sister, fly a low pitch, in comparison with the high Flights of their Ancestors.

IF any Nation can be brought to a juster Understanding or Performance of the old *Mimickry*, than we have in Modern Times met with; it must undoubtedly be attempted after the Manner of the *Italian* COMEDY: That is, by preserving what is just and beautiful in the *Antick* Action, but rejecting their ridiculous Innovations in bad, low Dialogues; and worse vocal MUSICK.

THIS Affair is of greater Moment to Mankind than may appear at first View, and should be manag'd with Sense and Discretion, not by a Set of ignorant, strolling Scoundrels (such as for some Years past have infected both Sides of the *Hay-Market* with their nonsensical *Jargon*, and *Jack-pudding* Action;) but by a chosen Society of learned *Antiquaries* and penetrating *Virtuosi*; who may gather from old *Urns*, *Vales*, *Statues*, *Bustos*, *Bass-Relieves*, *Intaglias*, *Cameas*, and *Monumental Inscriptions*, an intire Set of *Vizor-masks*, *Features*, *Grimaces*, *Steps*, *Motions*, *Attitudes*, significant *Postures*, and learn'd *Directions*, in order to instruct a young *Group* of *Mimicks*, in all that was peculiar to, or us'd by the antient *Pantomimes*. Then these Gentlemen, by the necessary Assistance of some *Tumblers*, *Posture-masters*, and *Rope-dancers*, might produce a Set of *Actors* to amaze the World, who might by the strongest and finest Turns of *Argument*, enforce all Precepts of *Religion*, and *Morality*, by their dumb *Eloquence*, and silent *Rhetorick*.

As for those poor Wretches, known here by the Title of the *Italian-Comedians*; I shall not at present meddle any farther with their absurd Performances, till I come to mention, them as pretending to the Form of a Theatre.

THE true *Italian* COMEDY, is neither perfect *Farce* nor old *Mimickry*, for, tho' they often make use of very proper and emphatical Motions, and really manage Arms, Legs, and Heads to very good purpose, yet their wretched Stuff of *Farce* quite destroys the Merit of their Action, and is an Obstacle to their Improvement, so in aiming at both, are in effect neither. The nearest Resemblance they bear to any part of the *Antique Stage*, is that Set of *Farce-Performers*, call'd by Mr. *Kennet*, the *Mimi*.

I acknowledge I have often met Abroad with very clever Fellows upon the *Italian Stage*, in every respect design'd by Nature to make excellent

lent *Mimicks*; could they have been content to make the use of all Members but their Tongues. For, according to an establish'd Rule of the old *Pantomimes*, they may open their Mouths, but must never speak.

THE nearest then of all Modern Inventions to the Primitive *Mimick Art*, are some *Grotesque* DANCES, which have been lately very happily introduc'd upon the *English* Stage, with Applause almost equal to their Merit; they being a Glory to our Nation, an Ornament to our THEATRES, and the Test of Politeness in our present *Gou*. They have, indeed, in the compass of a few Years arriv'd to that Perfection, and in some Respects so far kept up to the Severity of the Rules, and Justness of the Measures of the *Antique Mimes*, that they may boldly demand a Continuance of the Success they have met with (especially those perform'd at *Lincoln's-Inn Fields*,) could they be prevail'd upon to stick to their DANCING, and banish their *Songsters*: But it is impossible to make them sensible, that their Vocal MUSICK is as inconsistent with the Main of their *Entertainments*, as the *Comick Poetry* of the *Italians* with a just Imitation of the old *Mimes*. Thus by an ill-judg'd Jumble, and wrong blending of two Arts in one Piece, both the true *Italian* COMEDY, and our *Grotesque Dramatical* DANCES, have miss'd their Point, they form Alliances which will ruin them, and by joining execrable POETRY and vile MUSICK to beautiful Scenes of just *Grotesque* DANCING, the Perfection of one is lost in the Stupidity of the other, and instead of a single, compleat *Entertainment*, they will be both reduc'd to the low State of *Buffoonery*, tho' they aim at soaring to the most exalted Pitch of true *Mimickry*. And, indeed,

indeed, our Theatrical DANCING, in thus mixing *Scenery*, *Machinery*, and *Musick*, Vocal and Instrumental, with their Steps, comes nearer to the Nature of an old *Grecian Chorus*, than that of their Reprefentations, or Interludes by *Pantomimes*, which will appear evident to all Capacities in the next ESSAY, where I shall examine all Particulars relating to a *Chorus*.

As for those humorous DANCES exhibited at *Drury-lane*, I have not yet discover'd, whether they are defign'd as a *Burlefque* upon the other House, or themselves. But, as their *Mimes* are arriv'd at the *Ne-plus-ultra* of Badness in that Way, if they cannot improve, I think 'tis high time they should leave off, since they cannot do worse. I must observe one Thing, tho' in their Favour, which is, that their Defigns answer more to the Spirit of the old *Mimes*, they keeping up intirely to the Life and Beauty of Action, however lame in the Execution: not clogging their *Entertainments* with those monstrous Loads of harmonious Rubbish, we are tired with at the other House. One would swear, that both THEATRES were afraid of doing too well, or giving Pleasure too exquisite to their Audiences, therefore are sure to throw in some Allay; one is not content to act well, unless they are allow'd to dance ill at the same time, the other charms us with their DANCES, therefore are at some Pains and Expence to squawl and scrape us out of our Senses.

BUT, in order to make a just Application of all that has been said on this Head, and not to find out Difeafes without propofing Remedies, let us at once come to the most material Point, and confider what is to be encourag'd, and what amended in this Noble Art, and how far such an Amusement may be render'd of the utmost Consequence to the Republick of Letters.

In our present visible Decay of all Sense, especially *Poetick*, and of all Poetry, particularly *Dramatick*; the Art of DANCING should again wholly ingross the Stage, as it did formerly in its Infancy: For, since we can no longer boast the Shadow of those Beauties, for whose Sakes we banish'd it thence; why should any one now object to its Restoration? If we consider this Art of *Mimickry* thoroughly, either in its former flourishing State, or in the Addition of some late Improvements; I believe, every impartial Judge will allow, that it may be prodigiously advanc'd in this Age, not only to its pristine Height, but, perhaps, (if taken in a right Light) more to the Advantage of Mankind in general, than has been yet known from any publick Amusement. And, since Nonsense has so long usurp'd the Provinces of Tongue and Pen, we may chance to improve, by dumb Wit: And, since Head-pieces are at a Loss in giving us proper Documents, we may look for Instruction from Arms and Legs.

I am sensible, that some Book-learn'd Criticks, or formal, ignorant Humourists, will immediately reproach me with the vast Progress these Stage DANCES have already made amongst us, and that any farther Encouragement given them, would prove the utter Ruin of that small, expiring Spirit of Poetry left. To this I readily answer, That *Dramatick* Poetry is at present at so low an Ebb of Merit, that 'tis neither worth minding, nor retrieving, nor can its Place be better supply'd, than by that instructive Art, which was the Admiration even of the greatest Poets, when the Stage was in its full-blown Flower of Perfection.

BUT, what would those very wise Gentlemen say, should I screw my Argument a Note higher, and maintain, that Poetry it self may be brought to a greater Pitch of Instruction and Delight by these DANCES, than by the Works of any Poet now living, and in one Night's *Entertainment*, we may skim the Cream of all the different Kinds of that Noble Art. But, in order to fortify my Assertions by some Examples, let us only suppose one of my old Friend *Bays*'s Grand DANCES.

ENTER first, a strapping two-handed Fellow, with a bright Shield, a broad Sword, and a suitable Plume of Feathers, moving exactly to a Trumpet-tune, frowning and laying about him as if the Devil was in him. Won't he give us a just Idea of the Fire and Grandeur of *Heroick Poetry* in general? Then, if he falls in Love with all the Women, kills all the Men he meets, and at last stabs or poisons himself, this will have a particular Regard to that part of it, call'd *Dramatick*, as twelve or twenty-four very high Capers, and Military Flourishes, with a just Pause at the End of each, will to the *Epick*.

If a Giant and Dwarf hop about Hand in Hand; the long Stride of one, and short Step of the other, figure out to the meanest Capacity the Beauties of *Pindarique Poems*. Should the tall Fellow sometimes stare, foam and gallop full drive, as if possess'd with a Fury, anon, all of a sudden stand stock still, as if quite out of Breath; while the little Shaver is playing some genteel Tricks, toying, singing, smiling, by Starts, they thus point out to us the unequal Enthusiasm of the great *Ode*, and Pleasantry of the small *One*, with the Variety of the *Lyrick*.

AN Upholder's Retinue moving gravely round a Coffin, attended by some Bedlamite Lovers, cursing, crying, blessing, laughing, sighing, as if their Hearts would break, the different Postures of this mad, whimsical, melancholy *Group*, will justly comprehend all Sorts of *Elegiack* Complaints.

AN open, sincere Countenance, generally dress'd in Frowns, with a Looking-glass in one Hand, and the Balance of Justice in the other, explains to us the necessary Truths of bold *Satire*: as a Vizard Mask, Dark Lanthorn, and frequent Whispers, do its Counter-part, a private *Lampoon*.

A Set of Hay-makers, a sprightly Jig, rural Love, with a River-God or two, and as many Wood *Nymphs*, denote the natural Simplicity, and Innocence of *Pastoral*.

A *Pigmy*, with a diminutive, but very keen Dagger, cutting and pricking every body as high as he can reach, gives us at once the Sting in the Tail of an *Epigram*.

THE *Heroic-comick*, may be distinguish'd by a purple Robe and Sceptre, with a *Satyr's* Hoofs and Horns, as its Half-brother *Burlesque* (who's generally more Knave than Fool) may by a *Jack-pudding's* Coat over a Philosopher's Garment.

THUS the *Anacreontick* may be describ'd by a Train of jolly Lads, and blooming Lasses, led by *Bacchus* and *Venus*, playing, drinking, loving, moving in the easiest Manner, to the softest MUSICK: As the Modern Imitation of them, the *Philippick*, and the Improvement upon the *Philippick*, call'd the *Lilliputian*, may, by some Infants, that just can go and speak, shining in their innocent PLAYS, catching Butter-flies,
blowing

OF DANCING.

blowing Bubbles, tossing Balls: *Witty Master! Pretty Miss!*

THEN if a Dancer would in a more particular Manner chalk out some private Subjects, it may be easily brought about in the following Method:

By a pale Complexion, dirty Shirt, uncomb'd Wig, and distracted Step, the Love-sick Songster is known, as a tolerable deal of Lace and Fringe, clock'd Stockings, and a Minuet Step, are certain Signs of genteel Poetry, the Wit of the *Beau-monde*, or, as *Waller* has it, *soft Words, with nothing in them*, &c. A blind Man with an *Antique* Robe, and Modern Brocade Wastecoat, a Sceptre in his Hand, and Buskins on his Legs, who loves the roughest Roads, treads loftily, but seldom stumbles, is an exact Emblem of *Blank Verse.* As a Morris-dancer, adorn'd with Garlands of Flowers, fetter'd with silken Cords, and deck'd all round with Bells, does *Rhime.* And so a fruitful Genius, may proceed *ad Infinitum.*

Now could our Eye at one View take in all these, jumbled together in a Grand Dance, at the same time we should enjoy the Quintessence of all Kinds of POETRY, as significantly explain'd to us as the Nature of an Eclipse was by the *Hays* in the *Rehearsal.* The Success of which Dance, and Justness of the Representation, shew to what Perfection such Entertainments may be brought in natural, and all other Sorts of Philosophy.

I am perswaded, that DANCING is the only Method of making all Parts of the Mathematicks to be easily comprehended by the dullest Capacities, nor can I think of any Means so proper of rendering familiar to a young Lad's Understanding any Problem of *Euclid*, as dancing it over to him. Sir *I---c N----n* often own'd to me, he was entirely of my Opinion. Mr *R---ly*, Dr. *Ha---ly*, and the rest of our principal Mathematicians, will come readily into it, if they once consider the various Natures of Motions absolute, and relative, regular and irregular, of Bodies mix'd and simple, elastick and volatile, with all the rest of the necessary Jargon, in the proper Terms of Art: And would those Gentlemen be at a little Pains with some of the bad Clock-work Machines belonging to both *Play-Houses*, I am confident no Lecture or tedious Harangue, spun out by a trifling Superfluity of Words, could give so much Satisfaction to an Audience, or so true Notions of the Elements of Things, as a *Mathematical Dance*.

I need not proceed to set off every other particular Art in this Light, any Man that is Master of a ready Head and Heel, will quickly reduce, from Speculation to Practice, all Branches of any other Science, in the same Manner I propose As these Grotesque Dances have met with a favourable Reception from all true Judges of Wit and Politeness, even where there was but little of the *Utile* mix'd with the *Dulci* What might we not expect from Entertainments upon the fore-mention'd Plans, especially at the *New House*, under the Direction, and conducted by *J----n R----b*, Esq, who is Master of an unparallel'd Genius to excel in that Way: And I will venture to proclaim him the the greatest Poet, Philosopher, and Mathematician now in Being, if he pleases to exert his nimble Talents according to the Schemes I have here laid down for throwing these Arts into proper Motion and Figure.

I fear it might be highly resented by several of my kind Readers, if, in an ESSAY upon

Theatrical

OF DANCING.

Theatrical Dancing, no honourable Mention should be made of *Tumblers*, *Posture-Masters*, and *Rope-Dancers*, therefore I shall not wholly neglect, nor dwell too long upon that Subject. The two first we look upon as humble Creepers in DANCING, as the last are generally High-flyers. They all have their Merits in their different Stations. *Tumbling* and *Postures* require as great Agility and Dexterity, and their various Tricks may appear as pleasing to the Eye, as the brave Attempts of *Rope-Dancing*. But this last is more surprizing and hazardous, giving the Spectator a sort of painful Pleasure, and, indeed, a naturally steady Head, and bold Heart, are more requisite in this mysterious Science, than that mean Cunning, supple Limbs, seemingly dislocated Joints, flexible Hams, and artificial bending any Way, which is all the two first can boast of.

'Tis true, these low Movers have infinitely of late, got the Advantage over the High-flyers, yet the last, with the Generality of People, are still in great Esteem, and live in Hopes of one Day or another having Liberty again to divert both Court, Town and Country. And though for some Years past the laudable Art of ROPE-DANCING has been held in great Contempt in the refin'd Neighbourhood of St *James's*, yet, I can't say, but of late they have got Ground remarkably, by the fine Performances of Signior *Violante* and his Lady, who have given vast Content to all Ranks of People, and flatter the High-flyers with a Prospect of being once more in Request. A Time may come, when their Antagonists shall be oblig'd to resign the Power they gain'd by *Postures*, *Grimace* and *Agility*. And if they care not to dance on, they may swing in a Rope, and quaver their Toes in the Air, though

L now

now they're confin'd to *Terra Firma* I say, this is not improbable, especially since Signior *Violante* has taken Possession of the highest Part of the Steeple of the K——g's own Parish-Church, in order to shew his Skill to Multitudes of admiring Spectators. 'Tis true, the chief *Posture-Master* of that Parish had a Stop put to his shewing any more there, but we expect Orders from a higher Power to permit him to perform.

BEFORE I take my Leave of *Stage-Dancing*, it will not be thought impertinent, if I remind my Readers here of what I advanc'd in my first ESSAY, about the Recitative of an OPERA being danc'd: I believe they'll all enter more readily into that Project, now that the Nature and Beauty of DANCING is more fully explain'd.

THE Use that may be made of these *Theatrical Grotesque Dances* is, I hope, by this Time so obvious to every thinking *Briton*, and the Advantages accruing from them so demonstrable, that I shall not any longer insist upon their extraordinary Merit, but apply some new Steps in DANCING to private Life, which may be of the utmost Consequence to the *Publick Good*.

I desire that our present worthy Set of *Dancing-Masters* would not be displeas'd, if I propose erecting several publick Schools in this *Metropolis*, and other great Towns of this Island, in order to instruct all our Youth in speaking *Dances*, or a *Dancing Speech*. They are themselves yet ignorant of that mysterious Part of DANCING; but as they could qualify themselves for such a laudable Work, they should preferably to others be encourag'd, in the mean time we should have skilful Masters brought from *Turkey*, *Persia*, &c. protected by the Government, and paid at the Publick Expence. THE

OF DANCING.

THE Benefits arising from this Art to the Majority of a trading Nation, may be easily made manifest from the ready and quiet Dispatch of Business in this and all great Cities; for a Nod, a Shrug, a wry Face; the Motion of a Leg or Arm, right or left; nay, the Disposition of a different Finger (according to the old Custom of speaking with our Fingers) will, without the Appearance of any Hurry, or the shocking Noise of stunning Voices, facilitate, to Admiration, the most expeditious Manner of Commerce amongst the busy Part of Mankind: Not so much as a Humm will be heard in the *Royal Exchange*, but the whole Crowd will appear as serene as a *Quaker's Meeting*, when the Spirit works not on the Flesh. Then we might see an *European* calmly dancing a Bargain with an *Asiatick*, a *Bristol* Merchant drawing a Bill on *Scanderoon* with one smart Caper; a *Jew* bowing himself into the Favour of a *Christian*; and one of the Pure ones, without the Expence even of *Yea* or *Nay*, outwit a *Chancery* Sollicitor with a clean Hop. In such a Medley of foreign Tongues, as must necessarily attend the Trade of such a Town as *London*, where you meet all Nations of the known World in a Compass of an Acre of Ground, what can we expect but *Babel* it self, in the transacting of Business. Now this Hint of mine, rightly improv'd, would enable every one to manage his Affairs, without being skill'd in the Mother-Tongue of him he deals with: And I am certain, that it is next to a Demonstration (if I may be allow'd the *Paradox*) that the only Method of attaining an universal Language, is to be *Dumb* A Toss of the Head, a Wink of an Eye, or Shrug of the Shoulders, will distinguish whether you deal in *South-Sea*, *India*, or *Bank-*

Stock, an Arm or Leg will tell whether you are a Buyer or Seller. And as to Numbers, every Child knows, we may reckon to Millions by our Fingers in the readiest Manner of Accompts, and to the greatest Exactness in Arithmetick. Besides, every different Movement at once proclaims the Man's Country you would deal with. If you see a Gentleman move slowly along in a grave Sarabrand Step, as if he was afraid to dislocate his Bones, or fall a-pieces, you, at once, know him to be a *Spaniard*. If you see another cut fifty Capers in the making one Bow, always gay, always in Motion, and never out of Countenance, you're certain he's a *Frenchman*. This last tho' must be allow'd the Liberty of his Tongue, in some few particular Monosyllables, or he's undone for ever. The *English* (those *Tragi-Comedians* of the World) with one merry Leg, and one sad, are known to all Nations upon Earth by a grave Jig peculiar to themselves. The *Germans* are as noted for their long Stride, Turky-Cock Strut, and dancing in the Ox-Stile, as the *Low-Dutch* are for their aukward Imitation of the *French, a-la-Clumsie*. Thus, without observing even the Countenances of People (which might be of great Advantage in this Affair) or any Part or Kind of Speech, every Man's Birth and Business is made manifest by his Country-Steps.

SOMETHING, in the Nature of these DANCES, was begun and carry'd on in the Way of Trade, about the Year *Seventeen Hundred and Twenty*, but the Masters of those Times and *Dancing-Schools* (tho' otherwise vast Proficients in their Calling) made their Scholars dance so long, and cut Capers so high, that all *Europe* grew quite sick of their Method in Business.

I can-

OF DANCING.

I cannot help obferving here, that as the firſt Inſtitution of DANCING was religious, ſo there is no Part of publick or private Life, to which it would prove more ſerviceable or becoming, in the way of dumb Oratory, than to the P——pit: It appears already, by the modeſt and well-judg'd Endeavours of a young Gentleman (who is as juſt an Actor, as a profound Scholar) to be a Science in all Reſpects highly proper in and worthy of that Place and Function.

No Words, without proper Motions, can have any tolerable Effect, as to inculcating ſound Doctrine with a ſuitable Vehemence: And if any Pr——ſt labours under the Infirmity of a bad Elocution, a ſtammering Utterance, or any kind of Impediment in Speech, every Member of his Body may aſſiſt in edifying his Congregation; and his Ser———n be fluently and elegantly deliver'd by Signs and Tokens, and Movements, and all that; what ſignifies it, whether he ſpeaks or no, ſo he is underſtood to the Purpoſe. Nor would it be amiſs, were all our Pu———ts made of a commodious Largeneſs, and then our Par---ns might have Space ſufficient to ſhew us, that we muſt be content with a Sort of a rough, hobling *Courant*, to get to H——n, or, that if we don't take ſpecial Care, we may ſlide in a fine eaſy Minuet-Step (before we are aware) to the D---l: In ſhort, one might * * * * * * and ſo * * * * * and thus * * * * * and * * * * * * and then * * * * * * * but more of this * * * * * another Time * * * * * as my Project thrives in its Infancy.

It may be naturally expected, by the Majority of my Readers, that, in a general Diſcourſe upon DANCING, the *French* Nation ſhould make a greater Figure, eſpecially as I have

thought

thought fit to touch upon other Countries, both antique and modern in this ESSAY. But being oblig'd, by several material and unavoidable Hints, to stretch this Subject to its utmost Extent, and no principal Part that they excel in being neglected, I thought it proper to toss their Merit, on that Head, by the Lump into the Scale: Besides, were I to enter into a formal Detail of the Beauties of DANCING, and a *Frenchman* at the same time, new Matter would, every Moment, flow in so copiously, that I should never know when to make an End.

I hope, (tho' I have promis'd not to meddle but with the *Publick Entertainments*) that what I have advanc'd in relation to some Parts of private Life, will not be look'd upon as altogether absurd; but that I shall be pardon'd for such seasonable Digressions, without the Trouble of digressing any farther, in order to excuse my self. So conclude very pertinently with that wise Assertion of *Epicurus*, "That the whole Frame, Con-
"trivance, and Structure of this Globe, is but an
"orderly Movement, by Atoms justly dispos'd for
"that End. Opposite to which, was that confus'd
"Jumble of jarring Atoms during the Reign of
"*Chaos*, before this World was tun'd by the Mu-
"SICK of the Spheres, into a regular DANCE

ESSAY

ESSAY IV.

OF CHORUSSES,

Antique and Modern; in great Esteem with the ANTIENTS; *neglected by the present Age. Of their Use and Beauty in all* STAGE-ENTERTAINMENTS. *To which are added, Some Reflections upon the English* CHORUS *of* CAT-CALLS.

AN ESSAY, explaining the Nature, Use and Beauty of a Grand CHORUS, as practis'd by the Antients, may be thought very impertinent at this Time of Day, being entirely banish'd the *Play-House*, and only the Name preserv'd in the *Opera*. This shall not deter me from introducing it amongst our publick Diversions, though laid aside,

aside, either with an Intent to shew the World what Notion Antiquity had of it, or by describing it exactly, leave a just Plan, in case any generous, poetical Patriot, should attempt re-establishing it in our THEATRES.

THE Antients look'd upon the CHORUS, *As a Troop of Actors, representing a Number of those Persons, who were, or probably might be, present at the Time of the Representation of a particular Fable: They interfer'd with the Business of the Stage, either by Side-Speeches, or in Dialogue with the Characters of the* DRAMA, *or sung and danc'd, to mark the Intervals of the Acts.*

BUT if we consider a CHORUS historically, we must take it in three different VIEWS: *First,* As it was the Whole of a *Stage-Entertainment*; *Next,* As it was brought in as an Interlude only, or Appendix to TRAGEDY and COMEDY; *Lastly,* As it was totally lost in *Greece* and *Rome*, and but the Shadow of it left remaining with the Moderns. But however they have neglected or despis'd the reviving what was so essential to the very Life and Being of a STAGE; yet I have that Deference for the Judgment of the Antients, who thought it even necessary, that I have set apart this whole ESSAY, to give my Countrymen (who do not dip into Antiquity to search for such Things) an Idea of its Beauty and Grandeur.

I observ'd, in my last ESSAY upon DANCING, that the Original of all *Theatrical Entertainments* was entirely owing to a merry Sacrifice, instituted to the Honour of the jolly God *Bacchus*: It consisted equally of SINGING and DANCING in a rude unpolish'd Way, and was the Whole of what we have since call'd, a CHORUS, as far as such a Performance was made up of MUSICK, Vocal or Instrumental, and DANCE.

The

OF CHORUSSES.

The POETS, taking the Hint, thought this Affair capable of Improvement, so threw in one Actor after another so fast, that in about fourscore Years the *Drama* was fram'd into regular TRAGEDY and COMEDY, and, from this wild Beginning, sprang the politest STAGES of *Greece*. Thus we see, at first, the Whole was but a CHORUS. Tho the POETS had made this Alteration in this rough *Entertainment*, they had too great a Deference for the old Plan, not to retain some Part of it, at least in Memory of their common Parent. So preserv'd entirely the MUSICK and DANCING of the OLD CHORUS, but exhibited after a juster and more beautiful Manner, and embellish'd it with all the Magnificence of *Scenes*, *Cloaths* and *Machines*, that Thought could invent, or Art supply. Nay, to push the Matter still farther, they oblig'd the CHORUS to enter into the Business it self of every PLAY: Thus it became not an additional only, but an essential Part of all *Stage-Representations*, and the Use of it look'd upon at least as necessary, as the Ornament.

IN this Station the CHORUS remain'd undisturb'd, from the Establishment, to the Ruin of the *Grecian Stage*. The Office of the CHORUS was to *Sing* and *Dance* in Notes and Measures, either of a Piece with the PLAY then represented in general, or some particular occasional Part; they frequently convers'd with the Characters on the *Stage*, especially the chief of them, call'd the *Coryphæus*, maintain'd the Dialogue, when there was but one Person of the *Drama* present, the Antients not allowing of *Soliloquies*, or but rarely, and it was very common for them to fill up any little requisite Vacancy by some Conversation amongst themselves *a propos* to the Affair in hand.

THUS

Thus the CHORUS being generally upon the Stage, and except, in some few Examples, continuing there during the whole Representation, they were always ready to ask or answer Questions, and moralize betwixt the *Scenes*, and by this means never suffer'd the Plot to cool, or the Business of the *Stage* to fall: Then their SINGING and DANCING betwixt the *Acts*, not only explain'd to the Audience the just Interspaces, but their SONGS and DANCES being allied to the Subject of the PLAY, kept the *Fable* entire; at the same time they gave the Spectators the most exquisite Delight, and added an Air of Magnificence and Surprize to the *Stage* and *Audience*.

THE CHORUS being fix'd upon this solid Basis, was found so beneficial and diverting, that it could not be lost but in the total Destruction of the THEATRE. COMEDY, indeed, was obliged to part with its CHORUS in a short Time after its Institution; but TRAGEDY preserv'd it to the very last. This Conduct, in relation to the different Kinds of *Dramatick Poetry*, was unavoidable; and the Reasons for proceeding in this Manner have been given in a former ESSAY.

THE *Romans* first alter'd the Office and Behaviour of the CHORUS, and, with that Empire, it by degrees dwindled, till it sunk to nothing. Their Successors, the Moderns, found it fallen to the Earth, they kept it down, and seem not inclinable to be at any Expence or Trouble to raise from Obscurity, and almost Oblivion, the noblest Ornament of the *Stage*.

I must take Notice tho', before I go on any farther, that from all my Observations upon the *Dramatick Poetry* of the *Romans*, and Reflections upon all their Writers of any Kind, I have no
Grounds

Grounds to believe, that with them the CHORUS ever appear'd in that Lustre, or Credit, as at *Athens*, but was in all Respects carry'd on in a meaner Method of Cost and Design: The *Grecian* CHORUS as much exceeding it, as their *Dramatick Poets* did those of *Rome*.

IT is not a difficult Task to account for the Ruin of the CHORUS amongst the *Antients*. The *Grecians* lost it with their Stage, and the *Romans* with their Empire: All fine Arts being look'd upon as Foes to Barbarity, in civilizing, not depopulating the World. We cannot suppose, that the *Goths*, *Huns*, *Vandals* and *Lombards* had them much in Esteem: But it will not prove so easy to give a good and sensible Reason, why, with the Restoration of all fine Arts, and polite Amusements, the *Chorus* too should not recover its pristine Glory.

IN *Comedy* a CHORUS has been found useless, even by the *Grecians* themselves, therefore justly laid aside: And, I so far despair of ever seeing it brought upon the Stage in *Tragedy*, or a Possibility of succeeding in it, tho' attempted (there lie so many unsurmountable Rubs in the Way, as the Stage is manag'd with us) that I would be content, it should resign all Pretensions to an Interest in the *Play-house*, was it but judiciously introduc'd in our OPERAS. I am sensible, that three Parts in four of the genteel Audiences, which crowd all Performances at the H—y—m——t, will immediately squall out, Pray when had we an OPERA without a CHORUS? To these I positively answer, That we never had an OPERA with one: The Name may be spelt the same way, but the Present is as unlike the Past, as a modern *Italian* differs from an old *Greek*. What we palm upon the World now,

cannot

cannot boast of being the Ghost of an *Antique* CHORUS.

BUT to bring this Dispute nearer a Conclusion, by setting it in a juster Point of View, let us inquire more particularly into the Nature of an old CHORUS, the Use the *Antients* made of it, and their prudent Management of it, in the vast Variety of CHORUSES agreed to every Subject, which Considerations join'd to our Remarks upon the Behaviour of the Moderns in that Way, may lay down some Rules, and advance some Reasons for its Revival here.

IN order to compass this End, I shall briefly recapitulate some Points already spoke to, so throw the Whole into a more regular and easy Method of being understood.

THE Duty of the Ancient CHORUS, consisted of two Parts: In the first, they spoke with the other Characters in the Business of the Play, and then appear'd as Actors concern'd in the Intrigues of the *Drama* then represented. In the second, they mark'd the Intervals of the *Acts* by MUSICK, Vocal and Instrumental, and DANCE, or perhaps sung in the *Acts* some Things relating to the Subject then brought upon the Stage.

THE Characters of the Persons which made up the CHORUS of different PLAYS, were as various as the Fables could be, on which they were founded, or, as the teeming Imaginations, and whimsical Fancies of Poets could make them. Tho' the *Antients* absolutely tied themselves down to this Rule, that the CHORUS was suppos'd to be a Company of those Persons, who might most probably be present on that individual Place, where the Scene of the PLAY, then in Representation, lay.

THUS

OF CHORUSSES.

THUS in the *Hecuba* of *Euripides*, the CHORUS consisted of *Trojan* Women, Captives, as she her self then was, and in his *Cyclops* of *Satires*, no others daring to stay near the Den of *Polyphemus*.

IN the *Antigone* of *Sophocles*, the CHORUS was made up of old Men, sent for to Council by *Creon*. And in his *Ajax*, of Seamen, who came to offer their Service to their Prince, on hearing of his Distraction.

IN the *Prometheus* of *Æschylus*, the Nymphs of the Ocean furnish'd a CHORUS, he being chain'd to a Rock in the Sea, and no other living Creature near him: And, in the *Seven before Thebes*, the young Women of the Town.

THUS we may observe, how strictly they confin'd themselves to what was proper on this Head, but still the Latitude in the Characters of the CHORUS, was as large as in Subjects, and in *Comedy* generally very entertaining. Of which I shall instance but a few Examples, since the Province of *Comedy* quickly was oblig'd to resign its Pretensions to a CHORUS.

Aristophanes, particularly of all the *Comick* Poets, was the most ingenious in the Whim and Contrivance of his CHORUS, tho' still with a nice Regard to Propriety. In one Play he gives us a CHORUS of Clouds, in order to ridicule the *Sophisms* of *Socrates*. In another, one of Birds; to which some *Athenians* prattle about building several Castles in the Air. In a third, he introduces a Nest of Wasps, to hinder an humoreus old Fellow from going abroad, which they perform'd, by stinging him home to some Tune: Nay, he once entertain'd his Audience with a musical CHORUS of Frogs, while *Bacchus* is passing *Styx* to visit *Pluto*. This some People may look upon, as carrying the Jest too far, and what was very unbecoming the Dignity and Gravity of any *Stage-plays*: But, still we may observe in all these Fancies, tho' of a very odd Turn, that they have an Eye to what is proper to the Subject in Hand.

From these few Citations, we may learn the Nature of an *Antique* CHORUS, both in *Tragedy* and *Comedy*, and they'll serve to shew us what Liberties their Poets took in that Part of their Plays, from whence we may gather, that even those design'd meerly for Mirth, were not against the Rules of their Art

For Example, Let us but suppose the Scene of an OPERA, laid in *H--l--nd*, or Hell, What can be more proper than a CHORUS of Frogs, yet the Probability is preserv'd, for that is the Harmony to be expected in those Regions.

The Consequences I would naturally draw from the Authority of these Quotations, will be contain'd in a small Compass: For I allow any unprejudic'd Person to determine, what wonderful Effects a well-judg'd CHORUS might produce in an *Italian* OPERA, where the Variety of Subjects I have propos'd in my first ESSAY, would allow that vast Latitude in the Choice of proper Persons to form a CHORUS, as would equal, if not surpass, the *Grecian* Stage, in Humour and Grandeur.

This will be more apparent, if we consider, that in forming our OPERAS upon the Plans of *English* Fables, either in the heroick or familiar Stile, we take in the utmost Extent of the *Antique* CHORUS, either as it related to *Tragedy* or *Comedy*, and, according to the Nature of each particular Story, make use of the Grandeur and Severity of one, or the Novelty and Pleasantry

of

of the other, while both may be attended with Variety and Magnificence in a different Taste.

THIS CHORUS should consist of MUSICK, Vocal and Instrumental, differing from what makes up the Body of each Act, but yet expressive of the Subject then on the Stage: Next of DANCING, and Sounds proper to accompany those Motions: Then no Cost should be spar'd in the proper Decoration of Scenery, Machinery and Habits, that the Spectators may be pleas'd and amaz'd. Thus the CHORUS need not break in upon the main Thread of the Design, by appearing in any Part of an ACT, but be rather conducive to the carrying it on, by being introduc'd as an Interlude, to fill up the Vacancies betwixt the *Acts*, which are now pass'd over in dull Chit-chat, or in our duller Gaping and Staring at one another, so never suffer the Business of the Stage to drop, amuse the Audience with an agreeable Variety, and preserve the Entertainment, from the Beginning to End, all of a-piece, and the Whole might be finish'd by a Grand CHORUS, or a *Tout-ensemble* of Voices, Instruments, Dancers, &c.

Now, if we reflect upon the Novelty and Variety of the *Antients* in their CHORUSSES, even when they had the greatest Regard to the strictest Rules of Poetry, what Liberties might we not allow to OPERAS, which are not confin'd to the Probable, but can call Gods, and Devils, and Machines upon the Stage (as fast as a Juggler does his Balls) where they may prophecy, or dance, solve Difficulties, or sing a Song, assist a Hero, or kiss a Shepherdess, thus unravel the most intricate Plots in a trice, by a very natural Catastrophe, and as easily as *Alexander* unty'd the *Gordian-Knot*.

By this Management, the OPERA will be established upon a lasting Foundation, without injuring the *Play-houses*, or their Manufactures. *Tragedy* shall be allow'd to make the most of its Terror and Pity, and *Comedy* of its Wit and Mirth: whilst the OPERAS shall subsist and flourish, by the absolute Power of the *Marvellous*, the *Etonnant*, and all that.

WAS our Musical THEATRE but once grac'd with such a CHORUS as is here specify'd, what Groves of Musical Warblers! what Troops of dancing Deities would ravish us! What rising Mountains, sinking Valleys, enamel'd Meads, and winding Streams, would appear in perspective, with enchanted Palaces and Gardens to surprize us! A new Creation should arise at the Prompter's Whistle, and Nature's Self be lost in what seem'd but natural: Then would Tapestry Figures and Joint-stools cut Capers to improve our Understanding, Jet caus and Cascades pour out Instruction; and flying Dragons, and walking Statues, demonstrate the great Truths of R——n, by amazing us.

ALL such Spectacles and Decorations were allow'd to be a Part of the *Antique* CHORUS, and by all Judges of the *Opera-stage*, are look'd upon as essential to it: So in this happy Conjunction, here propos'd, every Being, natural or supernatural, is order'd to obey its Commands. I am perswaded, that any Man, who has just Notions of what is surprizing, wonderful, metaphysical, and all that, will readily comprehend, what Pleasure and Profit must result from this Design.

WE dare not be positive, that the *Greeks* or *Romans* were so polite, as to have any Taste for an entire Musical Entertainment, consisting of

Recita

Recitative and Airs, like our OPERAS: But, this we may be assur'd of, had those prudent, genteel Nations, once harbour'd an Idea of such a Stage Diversion, they would not have forgot its most essential Part, a proper CHORUS.

A superior Genius ought to preside in the Conduct of these Affairs, lest we be mistaken in the End propos'd, and have our Performances turn'd into Ridicule, when we expect they should be admir'd. This was the very Case in an OPERA once exhibited at the H----y---m---t, a CHORUS of wild Sparrows was let fly behind the Scenes, but they were never heard (the Undertakers being out in their Choice of a Singing-bird) nor seen, but in their Effects, upon the Ladies Heads. Now, had the Wise-acres planted some tuneful Flageolets behind the Scenes, and let several artificial Nightingales appear hopping to and fro in the Grove, Art there, by imitating, would have out-done Nature. This Example may suffice to give the Managers of these Entertainments a Caution, not to be deceiv'd into things unnatural, by trusting to Nature too far.

OF all the Moderns, the *French* alone have enter'd a little into the Design of an antique CHORUS: They are but Copiers, 'tis true, and if the Resemblance be faint, and the Colouring and Features want the Spirit and Life of the Original, yet they are as like, as a *Frenchman* of this Age can be to a Citizen of *Sparta*. Their MUSICK I have not touch'd upon in any regular Method of Criticism, but I cannot help thinking their CHORUSSES the most harmonious, most beautiful, and most magnificent Part of their OPERAS, every Act there ends with a Grand CHORUS adapted to the Business of that Scene, which concludes each particular Act. Sometimes you have a Stage fill'd with quavering Nymphs and capering Shepherds, animated by the sweet Notes of *Flut-douxes* and rural *Bag-pipes*, anon a Troop of Blood-thirsty Warriors, with clashing Arms and sounding Trumpets, give you the Fury of a *Battle* in Air and Motion: And now the idle Gods and Goddesses chant and foot it away with celestial Steps and Graces, the very MUSICK of the Spheres ravishing the mortal Ears of the Audience, who kindly join the Stage, till the whole House appears a Heathen Paradise

THEY have likewise made some small Attempts towards introducing an antique CHORUS into their *Tragedies*, *Comedies*, and *Ballets*, but with Success answerable to such wretched Stuff: Though Abbot *Hedelin* laid them down the justest and most beautiful Rules for their Instruction Though Cardinal *Richlieu* encourag'd such an Enterprize, and tho' afterwards *Racine*, *Moliere*, and *Baptist Lully* were principally concern'd in the Management of the Whole, they could not perfect so great a Work, whether for Want of a suitable Genius, or a Fund sufficient to defray so vast an Expence, I will not determine

IN Fine, a CHORUS rightly introduc'd in an OPERA, must give the World the *NE PLUS ULTRA* of MUSICK; and, I think it manifest, that by the wilful and careless Omission of it on the present *Italian Stage*, we lose the Perfection of *Harmony*, and never allow our Composers an Opportunity of exerting their highest Talents, and displaying the Greatness of a Genius, by shewing what the Force of MUSICK can produce

WE may have an Idea of this from some Parts of our CHURCH-MUSICK, which though generally very bad, yet demonstrates, that those full

OF CHORUSSES.

full Parts of MUSICK, either in CHURCH or THEATRE, shew the Quintessence of Art in the Composer, and must give equal Delight to an Audience.

THAT pitiful Farce of Sounds, that less than the Shadow of what it represents, which passes upon us at the Conclusion of our OPERAS for a Grand CHORUS, is a *Burlesque* upon the Name, Design and Grandeur of the Thing, one may have as much, and as good for a Half-penny from a friendly Alliance of *Ballad-Singers* at *Pye-Corner*, or *Fleet-Bridge*. That which should be the Life, the Soul of the collective Body of MUSICK, DANCING, and MACHINERY, poorly drops into a few scurvy Scrapes, and Bows, and Curtseys from our Singers, and their Tinsel Attendant Snuff-Candles and Oyster-Girls, and the All of *Harmony* dwindles into a few sorry canting Notes, fit only to accompany a *Wapping Crowdero* And this is to be esteem'd the finishing Stroke, to close one of the noblest Entertainments, that Art, in Conjunction with Nature, can produce, to charm Mankind

I freely acknowledge, that the *English* Dramatick OPERAS of the last Age, by far exceeded our *Italian* in that Point, for every Act concluded with a Piece of MUSICK, DANCING and SCENERY, consonant to the Affairs then in Agitation; conducted, in some Respects, after the Manner of the Antients, or rather, in the Stile of the *French*, whose Fashions then prevailed in every thing polite. And as our Theatrical Managers were sensible, that we had a very mechanical Genius, they contriv'd so their little ornamental Incidents, as to humour that *Gou*, when *Elbow-Chairs* danc'd, *Flower-pots* sung, *Ghosts* walk'd, and *Devils* flew to divert us.

THERE

THERE is one thing more I must observe, to the Shame of the Masters of our THEATRES in general; which is, that the only just Remains of a true CHORUS appear in the artful Management of our *Puppet-Shews*, and, indeed, the entire Performance of these small, itinerant, wooden Actors, is a kind of Grand CHORUS in Miniature; especially their Prompter answers exactly to the Character and Business of the *Coryphæus* with the Antients, whose Office it is, to explain to the Audience, the most intricate Parts of what they see and hear, or to tell what is to come, to make wise Reflexions on what is past, or what may be, to enter into moral Dialogues pertinent to the Subject with his little Play-Fellows, nay, he generally talks as much to the Purpose as any of them; his Behaviour (with the Humours of *Punch*, and the MUSICK, DANCING and MACHINES, which are beautifully and prudently scatter'd up and down thro' the Whole) exactly discharges the Duty of an antique CHORUS.

To apply more particularly to our selves (by way of drawing towards a Conclusion) the Sum of what has been urg'd on this Head; let us but consider a CHORUS either in a critical, a political, or an ornamental Capacity, and judge how far it effects our Interest in all.

As far as Criticism is concern'd in this Affair, I think we are safe, as to the Judgment, Use and Beauty of a CHORUS: The whole Tenour of this ESSAY, and several undeniable Arguments dispers'd here and there in the others, with the general Consent of all the Antients, and the Approbation of the most Learned amongst the Moderns, have determin'd in our Favour, and confirmed the Necessity of it in every Particular.

But

But as the Manner of reasoning on this Head will not have its due Weight with the Generality of People, 'tis needless to insist any farther on that, but to speak to their Understanding, Interest and Pleasure, in the two other Points

IN sound Policy, I am certain, every *True Briton* ought to give the greatest Encouragement imaginable to a Grand CHORUS, the unavoidable and vast Expences which necessarily attend the Grandeur of such an Undertaking, must of course, bring along with them infinite Advantages to a trading People, in the Disposal of all Manufactures, Foreign and Domestick: Besides, the full Employment it will give to Hundreds of our Poor, who otherwise must steal or starve. Nor will it be amiss, if I here remind my Readers of my Project of establishing a *Musical Academy* in one of our Largest HOSPITALS; for were a CHORUS, proper to their Stage, once settled, no *Beggar* need walk *London* Streets; so great would be the Demand, for Crowds of Attendants to fill the spacious STAGE, and, on this Foundation alone, more *Aged, Infirm*, and *reduc'd Persons* (besides *Orphans*, and all real Objects of Charity) might be supported, than in all the Hospitals belonging to this City and its Liberties.

HOWEVER, other Diversions may be design'd only to affect the Ear or Eye, those of the Stage speak to the Mind, in order to improve us; but such is the Depravity of human Nature, that if we are not pleas'd, we will not be instructed, therefore all the additional Ornaments to *Stage-Entertainments* are highly necessary to entice us in, else we should never sit out a tedious Lecture of Morality This the Antients prudently considered, and artfully threw in those agreeable, amazing

zing Spectacles, and Decorations of all Kinds, which were Parts of their CHORUS, thus luring them cunningly into a Reformation of Manners.

THEY were sensible, that the Majority of all Audiences would never appear in a THEATRE were they not more charm'd with the Beauty of the SCENES, the Surprize of the MACHINERY, the Magnificence of the HABITS, and Variety of MUSICK and DANCING, than with the fine Language, the noble Sentiments, the Precepts, and divine Lessons contain'd in a TRAGEDY or COMEDY: Therefore the Poets, the Inventors, and the Magistrates, the Encouragers of the CHORUS, spar'd no Labour nor Expence to draw Numbers of People of all Ranks to their PLAYS, spite of themselves: For knowing that the Generality of Mankind are, naturally speaking, in a State of Infancy the greatest Part of their Lives, they were oblig'd to perswade them to swallow the black Potion of *Instruction*, by promising the Sugar-Plumb of *Delight*.

I have now, as briefly as possible, trac'd every Foot-step of a CHORUS, in its Rise, Progress and Declension with the Antients, and shewn how far the Moderns are mistaken in their Notions of that Part of a *Stage-Entertainment*, explain'd its infinite Use and Beauty, and proposed the most reasonable Method of attaining to it with the most moderate Expence: But there still remains to be spoken to, a CHORUS altogether of *British* Growth, a genuine Plant of this Isle: I mean a CONSORT of CAT-CALLS, which so often makes a vast *Eclat* in our THEATRES.

I confess, this Affair does not properly belong to the STAGE, the usual Station of a CHORUS in all former Ages, nor does the Performance of it in the least depend upon the Characters of any *Drama* represented, or any Person belonging to it, as an additional *Actor, Singer* or *Dancer*, but wholly regards the Behaviour of the Audience, when they have a Fancy to turn Performers instead of Spectators: Yet, as it alway makes its Appearance by way of a full CHORUS, I thought it could no where be introduc'd with that Justice, as in this ESSAY, therefore choose to tack this Domestick Invention to its Tail.

I fear, that in my historical Enquiries after the Origine of this polite Instrument, I shall have no Foundation to build upon, but Conjecture; so my Readers must be satisfied with Guess-Work. However, I shall omit nothing in the Way of Reading, or Intelligence from other Hands, that can give me any Light into its Antiquity or Merit.

BY its Etymology, it should be of *British* Extraction, for I have turn'd over a Thousand Volumes of *French* Cricks, and *Low-Dutch* Commentators, yet met with no single Hint that touch'd upon its Invention or Use; so lost my Time and Labour.

I was mightily puzzel'd to find out something in Antiquity, upon which I could ground the most trifling Surmise relating to its Birth, but my Search made me no wiser: Nor was there any thing answer'd in the least to my Purpose; excepting the CHORUS *of Frogs* in a Comedy of *Aristophanes*, before-mention'd, from whence I imagine, some of our modern Cricks (whose only Merit lies in a blind Admiration of the Antients) stole the Conceit, and fix'd this Instrument upon a Level with that MUSICK: And as the Business of the OLD CHORUS was to ask Questions of, or make Responses to, any Person of the *Drama, ma,* during the Reprefentation, or jointly, by SINGING and DANCING, to make the Intervals of the Acts: So I have perceiv'd, that the Performers on CAT-CALLS, are employ'd fingly in the Time of Action, or in a Body betwixt the Acts, the Obfervation of which Rule looks with an Eye towards the CHORUS of the Antients, in the Inftitution of theirs.

UPON mature Confideration, the Criticks, for several weighty Reafons, muft have been the Inventors of this Inftrument, either as a Signal to gather their Forces together, when difpers'd about the Houfe, or when to fall on, and when to make an orderly Retreat, it has exactly the fame Compafs of Notes with a Hunting-horn, and is us'd for much the fame Purpofe, either to throw a Pack on, or call them from their Prey. And fome Mafters, who have carefully ftudy'd Compofition on the CAT-CALL, will immediately tell you the Fate of every PLAY or OPERA, where its Sounds are heard: They diftinguifh with the greateft Eafe, whether the poor Hare of a *Poet* or *Compofer,* is only to be merrily run down, by way of pure Diverfion; or kill'd outright, for the Benefit of the critical Kennel.

N. B. *I am now practifing very hard, to qualify me for a Judge in this Performance.*

I am enclinable to think, that the Criticks rather hope to intimidate the Poets by this Noife, as the ftrongeft Lungs have often the beft of an Argument, by filencing an Opponent: 'Tis certain a CAT-CALL frequently has this Effect upon the Poets to a wonderful Degree, though generally very bold Rogues, which may proceed from fome fecret Antipathy in Nature, not yet accounted for by Philofophers, as the Crowing of a Cock frightens a Lion: Perhaps POETRY inspires

inspires her Disciples with an Aversion to a *Cat*, the solemn Demureness of one not being agreeable to the Wit and Life of the other: So the *Criticks* fight cunning, like the Gentleman who, in a Duel, drove his Antagonist out of the Field, by popping a Kitten in his Face, whenever he came near him, knowing he could not stand the Sight of that Creature

IF those profound Naturalists, the Gentlemen of the R——l S——y, can smell out any thing in the wonderful Antipathies of contrary Qualities, which will in the least countenance this Assertion of mine, we may be very positive, that the *Criticks*, in their Searches into Mysteries, had before discover'd the *Arcanum*, and borrow'd the Hint of a CAT-CALL, from the nightly Serenades of those Love-sick Creatures upon the Tops of Houses And, if we were nicely to make our Remarks upon the Life and Conversation of several young Noblemen and Gentlemen, who are particularly fond of that Instrument, we should discover, that they are much given to Catterwauling.

A very ingenious, but whimsical *Virtuoso* of my Acquaintance, strenuously avows, and insists upon it, That the CAT-CALL is one of the most antient Instruments we read of. Some People may urge, That what he advances is at best but a witty Supposition, but I'm of Opinion, that he has both an historical and poetical Foundation to ground his Argument on, and, if it is not absolutely Matter of Fact, I'm convinc'd, that it is a very pretty and just Presumption. His Manner of making it appear runs thus--- He says, " The CAT-CALL was the Instrument play'd " on by *Pan*, in his Contention with *Apollo*, for " the Prize in the Art of MUSICK *Ovid* very
" properly

"properly calls it the shrill Pipe. *Midas* being
"constituted Umpire in this Cause, very wisely
"gave the Palm to *Pan*'s harsh Notes, but be-
"ing justly honour'd with Asses Ears, for his
"rash and ignorant Judgment, he ever after
"made use of that Pipe to silence all Harmony,
"then left it as a Legacy to his lawful Succes-
"sors of the Family of the *Long-Ears* (*alias Cri-
"ticks*) who, upon all Occasions, make use of
"it to demolish POETRY and MUSICK, of
"both which Arts, *Apollo* is Patron."

I can't tell whether the *Criticks* will allow this to be sound Doctrine, but they'll find many Tenets worse supported in *Thomas Aquinas*.

I shall quote out of *Gesner*, in his History of four-footed Beasts, one Passage, which bears some small Resemblance to the Affair in Hand. He gives a very remarkable Account of two Creatures in *Ethiopia*, who are at continual Enmity, the first participates of the Natures of our Hares and Foxes, being as timerous as one, and witty as the other, without its Malice, by reason of a particular good Nature inherent to this Creature, and a Disposition to several little entertaining Gambols: It is a Favourite with, and protected by all the Beasts, but that which is its profess'd Foe; which, by the Description, I take to be a Sort of wild Cat, or Cat-a-mountain, a Species of small Tygers. This lives in a continued Pursuit of the other, and wherever it meets them, they are devour'd as lawful Prey, unless rescued by some of the other Beasts. If this makes nothing to my Purpose, in relation to the Cat call, yet it exactly describes the Nature and Behaviour of *Poets* and *Criticks*.

THIS is all I could gather to satisfy my Readers, as to the Invention of this Musical Machine. As to its proper Use and Application, 'tis too well known, to be enlarg'd on here, but I intend to publish in a little Time, by Subscription, a very large Folio, with all the Rules necessary to make a compleat Performer on this Instrument, with Directions how, when, where, and why any Gentleman should play on it single, or in Concert, with a just Scale of Notes, and Variety of Airs in all the Keys, and adapted to all Occasions, for the Use of those who do not compose *Extempore*

HAVING in this ESSAY impartially stated the Essence, Use, and Loss of a CHORUS, I leave every Man to make what Reflections, and draw what Inferences he thinks most pertinent to the Subject. I only beg Leave to conclude with my humble Opinion, that a CHORUS is allowable in a *Comedy*, proper in a *Tragedy*, and necessary in an OPERA.

ESSAY V.

OF AUDIENCES;

The several Orders of SPECTATORS *that form an* ENGLISH AUDIENCE. *Their Behaviour in the* THEATRES *consider'd. Their Manner of judging, in Publick and Private, set in a true Light: With a particular Account of the whole Race of* CRITICKS.

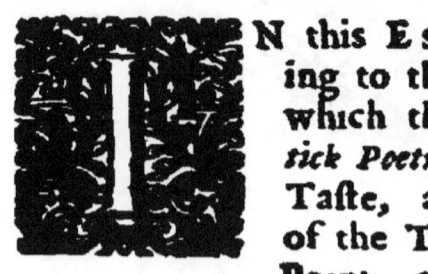N this ESSAY, I propose speaking to that Part of the second, in which the Decay of our *Dramatick Poetry* was imputed to the bad Taste, and little Encouragement of the Town for that Art. This Point, and several others as material, I reduce to one general Head, *An Audience*; which may be justly look'd upon as the

Primum

Primum Mobile of all Diversions; by whose Generosity they are supported, and by whose Smiles, or Frowns, they flourish or languish.

My Panegyricks shall be very modest, and my Censures very gentle, as to the Beauties or Blemishes in the Behaviour of this formidable and numerous Body: I shall set the Glass of Truth full before them, by which their Errors will readily reflect upon themselves, and from whence they may draw some natural Inferences, the easier to reform them: And, in order to bespeak the Favour of my courteous Readers (who, I suppose, will generally prove the Majority of an AUDIENCE at *Opera*, or *Play-House*) I declare, with the Air of a free-born *British* Subject, that as it is Truth I choose for my Guide, to lead me steadily through this Labyrinth of Errors, I am unconcern'd whether they treat me as a too severe Satyrist, a scandalous Lampooner, or insipid Trifler, being alike insensible to the Threats or Favours of the *Many*, so they do me Justice, and pay for my Book before they read it.

Tho' the fundamental Matters of an OPERA or PLAY, as to the Business of the Stage, are very different, and as such have been separately consider'd, yet I shall not make use of that Method in relation to their SPECTATORS, the Behaviour of an Audience at either, being much upon the same Footing, and equally notorious; so I shall jumble them together, thro' every Article of this ESSAY, in order to save my Reader some Time, and my self some Paper

But though I throw the two AUDIENCES into the same Point of View, as to the Regulation, of my approving or censuring their Conduct, yet I must beg my Readers to take one essential Difference along with them, and closely observe it whenever they are mention'd. The Inhabitants of the Boxes at the *Play-House*, make up Pit and Box at the *Opera*. The Pit at the *Play-House* is the first Gallery in the *Opera*. The first Gallery and middle Part of the upper Gallery in the *Play-House*, have no Representatives in the *Opera*, there are but few of that Country who care to part with a Crown for a Song. As for the Gentry at each End of the Upper Gallery in the *Play-House*, they enjoy that entire Region to themselves at the *Opera*, with Space to range, and Liberty to make as much Noise as they please, which grieves me not a little, nor shall I part with them unreprimanded: I wish my Pen, at every Stroke, was a Cat-of-nine-tails for their Sakes, and our own, that their Manners might be mended, and our Diversions not interrupted, but I shall talk with them by and by, when I have finish'd with their Masters.

FIRST, then, I shall strive to bring the several Degrees that compose a regular AUDIENCE, to bear upon the Parallel with the four principal Orders of Architecture. Under the *Dorick* and *Ionick*, I comprehend the Pit and first Galleries, I looking upon them as the most plain, solid and substantial Basis of an AUDIENCE, intermix'd with some People polite, and of good Fashion, who resemble the *Ionick* · Then the *Dorick*, allowing of some Asses or Goats Heads in the Cornish, by way of Ornament, that refers to the critical Part of that Order, the Boxes being some Steps higher, and altogether form'd in a genteeler and more elegant Taste than the former, I fix them as my *Corinthian*, that Order being very beautiful, and design'd much for Shew: Then the Upper Galleries answer exactly to the *Composite*, and that Order differing from the

Corinthian

Corinthian chiefly in the Capitol, I judge it thus: That Part which is the modestest, I borrow from the *Ionick* in the Pit, the other is entirely *Corinthian*, either as they belong to that Order in the Boxes, or as their Capitols are generally cast in that Brass.

THE Pit then in the *Play-Houses*, and first Gallery in the *Opera*, are supported either by some of our most substantial, plain, sober Tradesmen, their Wives and Children, in the *Dorick* Stile; or by Officers of the Army, Members of Parliament, and Gentlemen of good Character and plentiful Fortunes, in the *Ionick*, with a few Criticks, who are divided betwixt the two.

I have not much to say to the Quality from *Cheapside*, *Ludgate-Hill*, *Covent-Garden*, or the *Strand*, as to their erring in Point of Judgment, but a great deal as to their Behaviour in the THEATRES. They are generally so very impatient to gain the Centre of the Pit, or the first Row of the Gallery, that they hurry from Dinner with Spouse under one Arm, and the Remnants of an unfinish'd Meal, in a colour'd Handkerchief, under the other. As the Plot of the *Play* begins to thicken, their Appetites grow sharp, having not been sufficiently stuffed at Noon; then their greatest Concern is, how they may be satisfied with Decency and Oeconomy, that no curious Neighbour may discover their Treasure, and long for a Morsel. Thus restrain'd by the orderly Management of their portable Larder, it is impossible for them to have any Regard to the Business of the STAGE, but by that Time the Poet begins to unravel his Design by an *Artful Catastrophe*, which strikes an attentive Silence upon the sensible Part of the AUDIENCE, their natural Cloak-Bags are fill'd for a Journey, they

stretch,

ESSAY V.

stretch, and cry —— *Lord!* —— *when will these tiresome People have done?* —— *I wish we had a Dance, and were a-bed.*

I have had the ill Fortune to sit three Hours in such an elegant Neighbourhood often, and have seen the manly Concern due to the Weakness of human Nature in *Mark Anthony's* Fall, neglected for the Leg of a cold Pullet, or a *Naples* Bisket; and *Monimia's* Distress (which should draw Tears from every generous, or virtuous Eye) drowned in a Glass of Sack; as if the Diversion or Instruction of a PLAY was only to be taken in at the Mouth, while the Eyes, Ears or Soul, were entirely foreign to the Affair in hand; or as if the *Play-House* was rather a Twelve-penny Ordinary, than the noblest Entertainment which Nature, in conjunction with Art, can produce.

THE young Plants of this Tribe (who hire their Swords at some neighbouring Cutler's, in order to appear as Gentlemen there) are too apt to imitate the exterior Signs of a smart, rakish Gentility, and affect Airs wholly appropriated to the other End of the Town: They take Ill Manners to be Sense, Rudeness, an easy Politeness, and that nothing is so fashionable as to be noisy. But I caution them for the future, to leave off talking Bawdy to the Orange-Women, romping over People's Backs from Seat to Seat, and shewing the Keenness or Pleasantry of their Wit, by making the Women that sit next them *blush*.

THE female Part of this Band are generally of the Family of the Notables, and think it highly incumbent on them, whenever they go abroad, to shew themselves as stirring as in their own Kitchen, and as loud as in their own Bed, lest they should forfeit the Character of a clever House-wife. They are so very courteous, they get immediately

mediately acquainted with you, without Ceremony offer you a Pippin half roasted with the Warmth of a large Hip, and at once communicate to you the Secrets of the whole Family In Civility you are oblig'd to listen to *Susan's Intrigue with their 'Prentice* Tom, *how* Ralph, *their eldest Son, was a hopeful Boy as ever the Sun shone on, only he had the Rickets; and how poor* Molly *look'd wonderous pale, and eat every earthly thing.* This Alarum ceases not but with the PLAY, you must bear it, and lose the innocent Griefs of poor *Desdemona*, in the tedious Tale of *Dame such-a-one's tenth Child's breeding its Teeth*, and be deprived of the agreeably anxious Expectation depending upon the Discovery of *Othello*'s Handkerchief, for the dirty History of an unfortunate *Double-Clout*. I can use no other Reprimand to their Sex, but to entreat them, for the future, to gossip it at Home, or a Neighbour's House, and not disturb all who sit near them, at any publick Diversion, by the Recital of their private Affairs. By coming to a PLAY, they lose their Money, and turn common Nusances: If they do it in order to see and be seen, that laudable Curiosity should be confin'd to their going to Church.

THE second Division of these two Orders, consists of Gentlemen of sober Behaviour, good Nature, and plentiful Fortunes, mix'd with others in handsome Posts, Civil and Military. To these Gentlemen I can scarcely make an Objection, either in Point of Judgment, or Behaviour. Were they alone to sit as Umpires on any Performance, design'd as a publick Amusement, the Author might hope for Applause, proceeding from good Sense, and Criticism from good Nature, their Fortunes, Education and Generosity, set them above judging with Envy, Ignorance, or ill Manners

ners: If there is a Shadow of a Fault, it is in their censuring too favourably some Things they know are not perfectly right.

As to their Behaviour in the *Play-house*, it is altogether made up of Decency and good Humour, they are so unwilling to offend, that they never shew their Displeasure by the least Noise, unless some of the younger Sort, who are but just out of Leading-strings, get into Wit's Corner, or make an Elopement into the Side-Boxes: They having a natural Tendency to a Rattle, sometimes are fond of Playing upon that Instrument, which should never be seen but in the Hands of a Pedant, or Fool.

The poor Criticks, who are partly compos'd of these two Orders, must satisfy their Ignorance and Spleen, they spunge upon their Bellies fo. half a Crown, and we must allow them, in Return, to shew their ill Nature to the Authors of new Plays, and Actors of old; they come prepar'd to find Fault, and must be indulg'd, or they could not sleep. This Favour I must beg of them, that when they are out of Humour at any *Entertainment* (which always happens, when they are not the Authors) that their Censure may be as quiet as their Applause, which is always express'd in Silence, and not to hinder those who would be diverted, because they are resolv'd to be displeas'd. It is not necessary to take any farther Notice of them, till I come to the Rise, Progress, and present State of *Criticism*.

By a gentle Ascent, I soon arrive at the Station of the *Corinthian* Order, which includes the Pit and Boxes at the OPERA, and Front and Side-boxes at the *Play-houses*, with some inconsiderable Straglers behind the Scenes, and the

Flying-

Flying-squadron, who scorn to be settled any where.

We look upon the Natives of this Region, as so many small Divinities, the Ladies, from the Lustre of their Jewels, and the Power of their Eyes; the Men, from the Fame of their Places, Titles and Fortunes. Honour therefore calls upon them, to behave and judge in that polite, sedate Manner, that every Look, or Word of theirs, may be an infallible Rule for other Parts of the Audience to walk by: But the Regularity of their Conduct is so little answerable to this Maxim, that if their Behaviour is not altogether so loudly offensive, as what we suffer from those of a meaner Rank, yet they are, to the Full, as regardless of the Business of the Stage.

During the Time of the Representation, the Ladies are so employ'd in finding out all their Acquaintance, Male and Female, lest a Bow, or Curtsy should escape them, criticising on Fashions in Dress, whispering cross the Benches, with significant Nods, and Hints of Civil Scandal of this, and that, and t'other Body;—they scarcely know whether they are at Opera or Play.

While the Belles are ogling the Beaus, and the Beaus admiring themselves, the Affairs of real Moment (which should have seduc'd them there) are entirely neglected.

The Gentlemen are so taken up with their own Intrigues, or watching those of their Neighbours, that they never mind them on the Stage. A small Sketch of smutty Conversation is preferable with them to any Scene in the *Plain-Dealer*, tho' but with an Orange Wench: Nor is there one of them, but would rather boast a Smile from

from the reigning Toaſt, than liſten to the mourning *Belvidera*.

The Ladies tattle too much to one another to heed *Comedy*, it is too much of a-piece with their daily Life; then they are ſo buſy in ſecuring an Old Lover, or gaining a New, that all their Attention is ſeiz'd, before it can reach the Stage. Domeſtick Griefs from unlucky Cards and Dice, give ſuch real Pangs to other Hearts, that poor *Jaffeir* mounts the Scaffold unregarded, for what are *Cleopatra*'s Misfortunes to an ill Run at *Quadrille*, or *Baſſet* ! tho' all the World was loſt for Love.

If by ſome unavoidable Incidents in the Fable of Play or Opera, a *Stage-Entertainment* is lengthened with a few Additional Speeches or Airs, a quarter of an Hour beyond the uſual Time —— they ſtretch, —— they yawn, —— they die! Lard! —— we can be ſatisfied at an eaſier Rate, theſe horrid Poets and Actors think one never has enough for ones Money !—— When will the Curtain drop! —— And what pray may occaſion this ſtrange Uneaſineſs! —— An aſſembly at my Lady *Hazard*'s —— a Drawing-room-Night—a new Gown to be ſhewn there, —— or an Appointment at Mrs. * * * *or at Madam * * * * * or at my Lady * * * * * *. And it is certain, that could they with Decency decamp, as ſoon as the Ceremonies of being ſeen, pointed at, and bow'd to, were finiſhed, they would, without Heſitation, quit the Houſe before the End of the ſhorteſt firſt Act.

Upon ſumming up the Evidence, in the Caſe of the Conduct of the Boxes in this Particular, and from my own private Remarks, I vow, I think they are a'together as heedleſs of a Play,

or

or OPERA, as a Sermon,——which is a burning Shame!

I have taken more Notice of the Behaviour of the fair Sex in this Place, than the Men, because I shall speak to the latter in other Terms, when Judges and Criticks come in Form before me.

I cannot pass over in Silence, a Species of Animals belonging to this Order, whom I look upon as the *Hermaphrodites* of the Theatre, being neither Auditors nor Actors perfectly, and imperfectly both, I mean those Gentlemen who pass their Evenings behind the Scenes, and who are so busy in neglecting the *Entertainment*, that they obstruct the View of the AUDIENCE in the just Discernment of the Representation; and are a prodigious Hindrance to the Actors, in the Exactness of the Performance, the Beauty of which often depends upon a small Nicety.

I confess my self at a Loss, when I would account for the Reasons, which induce Gentlemen thus to lose their Money and Time, unless they think that their Complexions or Cloaths may appear to the best Advantage, by the Glare of a Stage Light, and that the Spectators cannot observe a bad Face, aukward Body, or crooked Leg, while their Eyes are dazzled with the Lustre of Powder, Brocade and Embroidery: Whatever are their Motives, I wish they would confine themselves to the Green Room, or the Actresses Shifts, and not occasion so many Confusions, by obstructing proper Enters and Exits, when Tupees and Feathers make up part of a *Turkish* Emperour's Train, and a fring'd Wastcoat or clock'd Stockings, are taken for the Dress of a *Grecian* or *Roman* Heroe.

THIS is not to be understood, as any Reflection upon that Part of an AUDIENCE, who are cramm'd behind the Scenes of a Benefit-Night: The Stage being for that Time for the Use of the House, and no body coming with a Design to be amus'd, there can be no Offence.

As I labour in climbing the steep Hill of *Parnassus*, I must call in at the first Gallery in the *Play-house*, to which nothing in the *Opera-house* answers: They are partly of the *Dorick* Order, or rather one more simple and heavy, so we'll imagine them the *Tuscan* in a wrong Scituation

As to Judgment, they seldom err, where pure Nature is the Test, if they are mistaken in Point of Art, it is thro' Ignorance, they judge according to their Knowledge, and are Strangers to Partiality or Prejudice, unless some malicious Wits take Shelter amongst them, in order to hiss *Incog* in some obscure Corner, or that some Party-stroke hits pat with, or opposes their political Principles. They generally come with an Intent to see the PLAY, and of consequence laugh heartily, and cry plentifully, as tickel'd by *Comedy*, or affected by *Tragedy*, if they are displeas'd, they shew more Modesty and good Nature than most other Parts of the House.

THEIR Errors in Behaviour are much of the same Kind with those of their *Dorick* Relations in the Pit, and if they cannot arrive at that Height of Luxury, to swallow Sweetmeats and *Canary*, their Pockets are lin'd with bad Fruit, and by the time their Wives and Daughters have devour'd mellow Apples, and suck'd green Oranges, the Ladies begin to be grip'd, and are oblig'd to move off, for Air and Ease.

I must caution them in the two following Particulars: If they find it necessary to whet their Judgment, or set the Teeth of their Understanding on Edge, by dealing in such Trash, that they

OF AUDIENCES 147

they would not be so liberal of their Fragments of Peel and Core to the Stage and Pit. Or that their lovely Females would not so often mistake the various-colour'd Inhabitants of the Boxes for Beds of Tulips, and water them so plentifully, perhaps in a wrong Season, but restrain from every Thing liquid, that warm Showers may not descend.

I have at last, with much Difficulty, soar'd to the highest Region in the Sphere of Wit and Politeness; and must, according to promise, talk a little to the Gentlemen of the Regiment of the *Rain-bow*, who reign here in their Altitudes, thus, like other Architects, conclude with the Roof of the House.

THEY are introduc'd here as that Part of the Composite Capital, which is borrow'd from the *Corinthian*, and take up the whole Upper-Gallery at the OPERA, and the two Ends at the *Play-House*. The whole Town (or at least the Lovers of POETRY and MUSICK) are indebted to them many severe Reprimands, for their frequent Disorders at both Places, I wish heartily, that my Power could carry my Resentment farther, that they might be thoroughly sensible of my being in Earnest, but being deny'd that Authority, I must be content to have a Lash at them in my Way.

As Liberty and Property are the boasted Priviledges, nay, the very Life and Soul of an *Englishman*, so the most valuable Blessings may be abus'd, and often apply'd to a very wrong Purpose. Nor is this in any Particular more notorious, than as made manifest in the Case now before us.

OUR Servants (because not Slaves) are suffer'd to disturb at Will our politest Amusements:

At an immense Sum we support these *Entertainments*, and they are allow'd *gratis* to put the Negative upon our hearing them: The Bread they eat, the Cloaths they wear are ours, yet, with one in their Belly, and the other on their Back, their Rudeness dare stand betwixt Us and our Pleasures; and the meanest Footman unpunish'd, fly in the Face of the whole Court.

'Tis well I write this, where the Truth from fatal Experience cannot be call'd in Question for no such Liberties or Insolencies would be tolerated in any Part of the Globe, but *Great Britain*.

THEY can bring no Plea for this Priviledge, but Prescription, or being at Hand, if wanted. As to the first, it is never too late to alter a bad Custom, especially when it does not answer the End propos'd. As to the second, proper Methods may be found out to keep them within Call, than their being mounted up three pair of Stairs, could they remain quiet, or improve there, the Imposition might be wink'd at; but as their Delight is to be noisy, let some large Place be fitted up near each THEATRE, where in the Bear-garden Stile, they may amuse one another.

I own, most of those Errors in Judgment charg'd upon that Part of the AUDIENCE, which unfortunately takes up its Station below Stairs, may be occasion'd by the Distractions rais'd by those noisy Fellows: For, who can judge sedately of POETRY or MUSICK in *Bedlam* or a *Brothel*? Or, what is worse, in THEATRES, with Galleries set aside for Livery Servants to Bully and Swear in?

THIS Part of my ESSAY, is not design'd for their Perusal, but their Masters, who might
with

with Ease redress those Grievances, if once heartily and unanimously join'd: Tho' no single Person could well negotiate an Affair of such Consequence, with so large, and so unruly a Body; yet, take them separately, every Man is Master of his own Family, and has Law, Justice, and the Government on his Side.

IF there be any Necessity resulting from some particular Merit, that such Fellows should be indulg'd in Liberties unbecoming their Station; the good-natur'd Condescension would be more properly shewn in Private, where their impertinent Follies can incommode no body, but those who think themselves oblig'd to bear them. If this gentle Usage gains not upon their brutal Tempers, there are Means to tame the wildest Beasts: If their Masters rich Liveries but serve to warm them into ill Manners, and blow them up with Pride, strip them, and put them, on for three Months, a *Bridewell* Jacket, only lac'd with plain Black and Blew, but laid on pretty thick, and in a little time you'll find a strange Alteration.

I do not pretend to prescribe here any Rules for a *Domestick* Regulation, every Man is the properest Judge of what is right or wrong in his own Family. But, were I to propose a Reformation of so publick an Evil as we now complain of, it should be in the Terms of a great Critick, who presented to Cardinal *Richlieu* a Plan for establishing the Grandeur, Use and Decency of the *French* THEATRE —— *and the King shall forbid all Pages or Footmen to enter the* THEATRES *upon pain of Death*

THE canvassing thus the various Mistakes in Behaviour, which infect the several Degrees of an AUDIENCE, makes me reflect, with Indignation, upon the wide Difference betwixt the *Antients* and us on that Head. No Prince there was too great, no Philosopher too wise, nor no Mechanick too ignorant, to be pleas'd and instructed by the Stage; they consider'd what they had in View, in coming there, and behav'd up to that Consideration; the most rigid Stoick would confess an Emotion of Pleasure from what was beautiful, and the lowest of the People demean with the Gravity of an old Senator. Their Silence and Attention were so remarkable, that a *Grecian* or *Roman* AUDIENCE appear'd rather an Assembly of Nobles, met in Consultation about the weightiest Affairs, than a promiscuous Multitude of all Ranks, come there to amuse themselves, no rude Clamour shock'd the listning Ear, all was quiet, except the decent Expression of those Passions the *Drama* was design'd to move, and they were to the Purpose, but never loud. The Contrast betwixt that Age and ours, is so strong, it needs no Illustration to add to the Colouring.

I cannot avoid taking Notice here of the Ignorance, and misapply'd Zeal of some late Divines, who have so strenuously labour'd for a Reformation, or rather Demolition, of the Stage They have all along unhappily chose the wrong Side of the Question, and when they arraign'd our Poets of encouraging Impiety, Immorality, Abuse of the Clergy, Disrespect to our Superiors, *&c.* they should rather have toss'd their Wit and Learning into t'other Scale, and catechiz'd their Flock, who follow'd PLAYS so eagerly, yet so blindly, that every Trifle took them off from attending diligently to that sage Instruction, those moral Precepts, that Love to Virtue, and Hatred to Vice, which every Man

must

must find in most *Entertainments* of the THEATRE.

HAVING lightly touch'd every Particular in the Behaviour of an AUDIENCE, which occurr'd to me, the Affair of CRITICISM in general comes next before me. I run so hastily thro' the different Ranks that fill a crowded House, and the Majority of them are so fully employ'd otherways than in heeding the *Entertainment*, that neither they, nor I were at leisure to criticise, till we got out of Doors. The Chocolate and Coffee-houses, the Drawing-rooms, the Assemblies, the Toilets and the Tea-tables are the Judgment-Seats, where POETRY and MUSICK are try'd, nor is it improper to rank them under the Title of an AUDIENCE, since we are to suppose, they who sit as Judges there, have been present at every Representation, and thoroughly examin'd every Particular upon the Spot, before they make their Opinions publick.

I comprehend then, under two general Heads, all Spectators of *Stage Entertainments*, who pretending to censure or commend any Piece, may be call'd *Judges* or *Criticks*. The first Order takes in the whole World, for every body upon Earth will judge, and if they are not allow'd the Liberty, they will take it. Their Opinions are as various as their Faces, or Humours, as uncertain as the Wind, and as ill founded as common Fame, they speak without thinking, and think without reasoning. The second is, that selected Part of the Whole, who look upon themselves, as the only People capable of that Province, they boast themselves to be the genuine Off-spring of *Aristotle*, or the greatest Men of Antiquity: They talk of nothing but poetick Laws, which must not be infring'd, and

Rules

Rules of Art, to guide blind Nature, and keep within just Bounds the Extravagancies of a great Genius. They erect a formal Tribunal, or Court of Inquisition, before whose Bar all Writers must appear, Nature and Art preside, the Criticks are the Accusers, and the antient Freeholders of *Parnassus* the lawful Jury.

THUS far all goes well. Now let us by their Practice form a just Idea of their Right and Skill in judging and criticising.

THE Method of judging, now most in Vogue, is hearing Sounds by other Ears, relishing Wit by other Understandings, and taking the Beauty of any thing in Perspective from other Eyes than our own; tho' we have no Reason to think they enjoy any Sense to greater Perfection than our selves. Tho' I would have the World in general to appear very discreet in the Matter of Judgment, yet I cannot approve of this slavish Complaisance, to resign the noblest Faculty of the Mind, to a mean Dependance upon a few fashionable Head-pieces, who may chance to be the most ignorant of Men.

IF you offer to censure or applaud any thing in Contradiction to the Sentiments of such and such Persons,—— you are immediately stopp'd short—— *How Sir!*—— *do you consider what you advance?*—— My Lord Driveler, and Sir Timothy Trifle *are entirely of another Opinion* —— That may be, Sir,—— but I judge for myself, as if they were not in being:—— *How shall we then fix upon what is excellent in* POETRY *or* MUSICK, *but from the general Voice of the* Beau-Monde? *and what those Gentlemen determine, no other must contradict.*—— I am sorry for it, Sir, I will not implicitly give into a general Character of any Performance;—— but if any
Man

Man gives a Reason: —— *Reason's a Fool, there's no true Judgment in superior Sense; Superiority of Numbers alone is infallible. Would you have me whipp'd round the Town for a cross-grain'd Puppy, because I think I'm in a right Scent, when the full Cry of the Pack is against me?*

Thus a few eminent Ninnies may lead by the Nose the Judgment of half the Town, and when once they have fix'd the Stamp of Merit upon any dull Work, every fashionable Body must come into it, or bravely dare to stem the Current of popular Opinion. I met once with a small Conversation-Piece at a Tea-Table, the rough Draught of which I'll present my Readers, it being drawn exactly in this neat Manner of judging, and will give a just Taste of the Whole.

Lady Plyant, *and Beau* Modish.

B. Mod. *I suppose, your Ladiship honour'd the new* Opera *with your Presence.*

L. Ply. *Certainly, Mr. Modish, I never miss the first Night.*

B. Mod. *Was your Ladiship mightily pleas'd?*

L. Ply. *I cannot say —— but so so —— tolerable enough —— what I minded of the thing. But I shall not declare my self, till its Character is establish'd by the Town.*

B. Mod. *Was it approv'd of by that Audience?*

L. Ply. *Some strange Creatures seem'd in Raptures, the Claps came from the Gallery, but few Admirers below Stairs, and those, mighty ill dress'd.*

B. Mod. *Then it must be damn'd Stuff! —— there's nothing sure, in Life, so impertinent, as Criticks of either Sex in Long-Lane or Monmouth Street Suits. They pretend to judge of Fashions in* Poetry

POETRY or MUSICK, and cannot put on their own Cloaths, ——— Prepoſterous!

L. Ply. Moſt abſurd and ridiculous!

B. Mod. Dem-me, if I have not heard an aukward Thing in Pattins, and a draggle-tail'd Callicoe, cry, Fogh! at the prettieſt and ſofteſt Air in the World, and a rough-hewn tramontane Fellow call the genteeleſt ſmootheſt Verſe imaginable, inſipid Nonſenſe, who never wore a Pair of clean Gloves in his Life, ſhav'd but once a Month, and ſcarce knew a Barber's Shop from a Chocolate-Houſe, or a Coach from a Wheel-barrow.

L. Ply. Intolerable! for my Part, I would no more applaud what is cenſur'd by the well-bred, well-dreſs'd World, than walk to Court in a Ruff and Fardingale, repeating ſome Lines of Chaucer.

B. Mod. I'm entirely of your Ladiſhip's Mind, a Singularity of Judgment is mighty fooliſh! ——— one looks as ſilly as a Dog on the Stage, the whole Houſe hoots, and the poor Creature knows not which Way to run: I always give my Opinion ſecure, I fortify it in Matters of that Moment with Ravelins of Embroidery, Counterſcarps of Brocade, and Baſtions of Whale-bone, I call to my Alliance a large Stock of perfum'd Powder from my own Sex, and unerring Darts from the Eyes of the Fair; then, undaunted, I dare approve or damn.

L. Ply. You judge perfectly right, Mr Modiſh, you have mighty juſt Notions of Things. I think there's a new PLAY to Night.

B. Mod. So the Bills ſay ——— I ſhall go to view the Company, and I expect to ſee Lady Fanny Faddle there, but I dare ſwear the PLAY is ſomething ſtrangely horrid, for I have not heard it once mention'd by the Wits at Button's, or the Quality at Will's. As for the Author's Character or Family, they are as great Strangers to my Knowledge,

OF AUDIENCES. 155

ledge, as I desire his Poetry *may be to my Ears or Understanding.*

So much I thought necessary to plan out in the fashionable Way of judging, though I could enlarge mightily upon this Head, and tell how * * * * and where * * * * the greatest * * * * and wisest * * * * do and say * * * * * a thousand * * * * better or worse * * * * and thus * * * Fame.

ANOTHER very flagrant Practice us'd in the Art of Judging, is praising or condemning those OPERAS and PLAYS we have been at, but never heard a Note of, nor know one Word of: As if being within the Walls of a THEATRE gave immediately the Faculty of Judgment, as the *Tripos* did the *Pythian* Priestess the Spirit of Prophecy.

SOME honest Gentlemen press by Three o'Clock into the first Row of the Gallery of the *Opera*, or back Seat of the Pit in the *Play-House*, pleased with their Success, and tir'd with expecting the Entertainment, they fall fast asleep before the Overture, or first MUSICK, and fairly take out their Time and Money in Snoring, till rous'd by the CHORUS or DANCE at the End of the PLAY, they start up—— gape—— and cry *Damn'd Musick!* —— a most execrable PLAY!

OTHERS (to be sure People of Fashion, and great Lovers of POETRY and MUSICK) lie the whole time perdue in a Corner with a fine Girl —— Snugg's the Word, and for any thing they know of what's transacted on the Stage, the *Theatre* might have been a *Conventicle*, and the *Entertainment* a plain *Tub-Sermon*, furbelow'd with some sober Sighs and Groans.

YET from the THEATRES these penetrating Judges march to the Coffee, Chocolate, and

Eating-

Eating-Houses, there pass a learned Censure on every Air and Thought, while they preside magisterially at a Table of Fools, where the Words of an absolute Dictator make up for want of common Sense.

A Family of this judicious Tribe, form Schemes of Judging (as an eminent Bard did his heroick Poems) in their Coaches, they drive from House to House, and, like a Shop-Keeper, only give you a small Pattern, by which you are to judge of the whole Piece.

THEY rise from Dinner about Seven, peep in at the *Hay-Market* for one Song, then get a Snip of the Third Act at *Drury-Lane,* and a Morsel of the Fourth at *Lincoln's-Inn-Fields*, then *Presto-Pass,* like a Juggler's Ball, they finish with the *Opera.* You may ask their Sentiments of the *Three Entertainments*, they'll give them very freely and gravely, but you might be as well satisfied of the Truth by their Coach-Horses. Yet to the Drawing-Room or Assemblies they fly, there dissect, mathematically, every Scene, expatiate on the ill Taste of such an Air, had not S——*no* exerted himself, and pity the Fate of two beautiful Songs murder'd by C——*oni*'s having a Cold, and F——*ina*'s being out of Tune, then tell you of the charmingest PLAY, how fine, yet natural the Thoughts!—— how sublime, yet easy the Diction!—— how surprizing and moral the Fable!—— Thus they decry or extol, as it pleases the Weather they should be in, or out of Humour, those Barometers in POETRY and MUSICK, upon whose Tempers being fair or foul, the Rise or Fall of Wit and Sounds depend.

I met one of these judging Gentlemen, after a New PLAY, at the Coffee-House, so ask'd Sir *William*

William how he lik'd the new PLAY?————
Extreamly well, Sir, a mighty full House————Did
Mrs Ol————ld's Part become her?———— I never saw her look with better Red and White in my
Life—— W——ks, they say, appear'd to great Advantage in his—— Certainly, the prettiest fancy'd
Suit of Cloaths he ever wore!———— Was not M——lls
prodigiously clapp'd?———— He spoke some fine things,
and I must own, the Cock of his Hat and Dangle
of his Cane were not amiss But C————is, sure,
the comicalest, impudentest Dog, that ever was born.

BUT had I ask'd Sir *William*, whether it was
Tragedy or *Comedy* he saw, the Baronet would
have been mightily embarrass'd for an Answer,
and thought it very absurd to put such a Question to a fine Gentleman Yet by such Judges
must the best Composer's MUSICK live or die;
though their Ears cannot distinguish betwixt *Castruccio*'s Fiddle and *David*'s Bass.

UPON this Foundation must the greatest Poet's
Success be rais'd, before such Judges must he,
trembling, wait his Doom, and, as the Wind
blows, or according to the Time of the Moon,
meet with a Twenty Day's Run———— or, perhaps,
not a Third Night to recompence a Year's Labour, by paying his Washing and Garret-Rent.

COULD Time be recall'd, such Judges would
let *Otway* starve, and *Lee* run mad again, while
an *Italian* Singer, or *French* Dancer, would be
caress'd, and loaded with Riches. Could the
Dead be rais'd, DRYDEN would once more
be reduc'd by such Judges, to the extreamest Want,
and his immortal Genius vilify'd, while *Settle*
would grow fat, and *Shadwell* be crown'd with
Lawrel. Did Fate put it in our Power to reform
some past Errors, yet would such Judges over
and over repeat their Follies, the second Time

P   Damn

Damn *Phædra* and *Hippolitus*, and give the Author of *Ch——t Ch——t* a Thousand Pound. Such Judges would again drop the *Provok'd Husband* for the miserable low Scenes in the *B——r's O——a*, and swallow greedily the wretched Dregs of MUSICK, which have occasion'd this incredible Run, while *Rhadamistus* and *Siroe* are perform'd to almost *Empty Benches* An Infamy to the *English* Nation, not to be wip'd off by the greatest Length of Time, and a Crime against every thing polite, not to be expiated by the severest Repentance.

IF a Man is not qualify'd to be a Judge, what the D——l has he to do in medling with Affairs above his Capacity, and which concern him not? Let him consider an Entertainment cooly, give his Opinion of it modestly, and in saying it pleases or displeases him, at least give a sort of a Reason for what he advances: A Judgment formed in this Light will be impartial, and proportioned to every Man's Abilities.

BUT it is not sufficient for some Mortals to be born Fools, to have their Friends and Acquaintance satisfied of the Truth, till by attempting Things out of their Sphere, the Fact is made publick, and, by Beat of Drum, and Sound of Trumpet, the Monster is shewn to the World

As no Law of the Land obliges these Gentlemen to commend what displeases them, so no Law of just Criticism obliges them to be pleas'd, whether they will or no, but their Judgments in such Matters should never go beyond the Length of their own Noses, the Eyes of their Understanding seldom seeing farther.

I have at last, with much Difficulty, press'd through a Crowd of Judges, to the Seat of Judicature, where their elder Brothers, the Criticks, preside.

preside. No Art is more frequently and publickly profess'd than *Criticism*, or less understood. It was first design'd to illustrate the Works of the POETS, by bringing forth hidden Beauties to Light, and rescuing some obscure Passages from false Interpretations; they sounded loud the modest Poet's Praise, and shielded his Name from the Venom of the Censorious, such as the proper Criticks of this Age. How chang'd!---how fallen now from what they originally were!

SOME People may wonder, that I should thus censure that Fraternity, of which I seem ambitious to be thought a Member. Did they keep up to the genuine Behaviour of the antient Criticks, it would be my Pride to be esteem'd the least meritorious of the Name; but as it is practis'd and understood at this Time of Day, I disclaim the Title. The true Critick is out of the Question, I only lash the ignorant Pretender.

I look upon our present Race of Criticks to be either formal, deep finish'd Blockheads by Nature, or those, who from tolerable natural Parts, are made so by Art, wrong understood, and Talents misapply'd.

THE first stupid Set only criticise, because they will do so; they have just Sense enough to imagine, that Scandal is easier hit off than Praise, and that Satyr will sooner procure a Man the Name of a Wit, than Panegyrick: Besides, their Tempers lean strongly to Ill-Nature, while Envy and Ignorance push them forward. Being incapable of penetrating into the Merit or Beauties of any Work, they look at all with Jaundic'd Eyes, and think them silly, because they are so. Being determin'd to find Fault, their critical Opinions are quickly deliver'd, and, like Chain-shot, destroy all within their Reach: They examine nothing

thing Piece-meal; they judge by the Lump, and demolish all they judge.

The Criticks of the second Class come into the World with tolerable natural Parts, and a Disposition for Instruction, but in Place of being improv'd by true Learning, they are sour'd with Pedantry, and puff'd up with Pride. Thus their Judgments are thrown into a wrong Bias, while they have not a Stock of good Sense or good Nature to keep them steady, and ballance against opposite Imperfections. They immediately establish critical Rules, by which the World must be guided, the old Laws are refin'd upon, new made, and stated Limits fix'd, over which no enterprizing Genius must leap, tho' of ever so great Advantage to the Republick of Letters, if he does, the Fate attends him by which the *Roman* suffer'd, who conquer'd without Leave of the General. No POET is to be pardon'd, who in the least passes such Bounds, though in the God-like Heat of Fury and Inspiration, there's no Reprieve, once Sentence is given, nor are their Punishments made equal to the Crimes, but, like *Draco*, all Faults they punish with Death: Those *Turk* Criticks, who never give Quarter to a poor captive Bard.

They never take notice of the visible and real Beauties in any POET, that ridiculous Curiosity is banish'd the Province of their Enquiries; as if *Criticism* was invented only to spy Blemishes, and that it is a Crime in a Critick to be pleas'd. These ill-grounded, unjust Notions have so far infected their Judgments, and their Practice has had that Influence on the Generality of the World, that the Art and its Professors are become odious and shocking to all Men of common Sense. In short, the Name is now commonly

monly receiv'd, as a genteeler Conveyance to our Ears, of an ill-natur'd Blockhead.

THERE is another Branch of this flourishing Tree, who being bless'd with large Fortunes, and little Brains, think, like *Simon Magus*, that every thing is to be purchas'd with Money.

THESE Gentlemen, at the Expence of much Labour and Birch, are whipp'd at School into bad Translations, false *Latin* and dull Themes, from thence they run the Gantlope through all the pedantick Forms of an University-Education: There they grow familiar with the Title-Pages of antient and modern Authors, and will talk of *Aristotle, Longinus, Horace, Scaliger, Rapin, Bossu, Dacier*, as freely, as if bosom Acquaintance. Their Mouths are fill'd with the Fable, the Moral, Catastrophe, Unity, Probability, Poetick, Justice, true Sublime, Bombast, Simplicity, Magnificence, and all the critical Jargon, which is learn'd in a quarter of an Hour, and serves to talk of one's whole Life after.

WITH this Stock they set up as Overseers of *Parnassus*, and what then? —— why then! —— they criticise and take Snuff —— and afterwards —— they take Snuff and criticise.

THESE Tinsel Criticks (who only shine with a false Glare of Learning, and whose Stings can but penetrate the Skin of the polite Arts) are very loud at the top Chocolate and Coffee-Houses, and teize Men of Sense to Death, with their Shew of Wit and false Reasoning. Yet I must confess, that of all bad Criticks, they are the best. For if a Poet is but communicative, submits his Works to their better Judgments, or begs a bad Copy of recommendatory Verses, he infallibly makes a Knot of them his best Friends. But if a Man of Merit neglects such nauseous Flattery, or scorns such infamous Slavery, he's proclaimed an insignificant, stupid Dog, to all Intents and Purposes.

ANOTHER large Tribe (the Spawn of the last nam'd) fix the Standard of their Judgments by the Name, Character, or Circumstances of an Author: If he is of Rank in the Eyes of the World, either as to Fame or Fortune, his Works pass their critical Muster without Examination, or if examin'd, they must be good, it is impossible for such a Man to err.

BUT if the young, or poor Poet, is unknown in the Temple of Fame, or wanting in the Blessings of Fortune, so must his Merit and Poverty remain at a Stand, till perhaps, like *MILTON*, he's found out to be worth looking into, some forty Years after his Death.

No Part of *Criticism* is more absurd, unjust or detestable, than where Censure or Praise is implicitly founded upon the Name of any Author dead or living. Every Man of sound Reason must form to himself a strange Idea of that *Critick*, who defers his Opinion of any Piece, till he is satisfied whose it is. Such an Enquiry is foreign to the Business in Hand, before our Judgment is given, that Curiosity is very ill tim'd, and but helps to expose our Weakness, and impose on our Senses; for we are all (both *Poets* and *Criticks*) sensible how Fame is generally acquir'd in this Life, and we never ought to trust to that as a Guide, to shew us the Road to what is beautiful or noble in POETRY, or measure Wit by its Height.

IF any Gentleman is determin'd to criticise, let him judge the Work, and not the Man, let him try every Line and Thought, by the Standard of those natural Graces and artful Proprieties which should make one a *Poet*, and t'other a *Critick*,

Critick. If he proceeds by any other Rules, he will be easily led, by an *Ignis Fatuus*, into the deepest Pit of Error; he will not condemn Nonsense, but Obscurity and Poverty, or extol Merit, but Fame and Fortune.

A natural Inclination to Idleness, or a real Want of Business in their several Vocations, force vast Numbers into the critical Service, who else would never have dreamt of such an Employment

THE Saunterers head this Troop, who lie a Bed one half of the Day, studying how to spend the other, and that is doz'd away, but if rouz'd by any extraordinary Accident, from Sloth into the Spleen, their Venom is spit at all, who, to make Life agreeable, choose never to be idle.

PHYSICIANS without Patients, Lawyers without Clients, and Parsons without Parishes, swell this Body to a large Bulk, and with them may be joined several young Students of the Inns of Court, and both Universities, who are as much out of Humour, that other People can write, as that they are oblig'd to read.

CRITICISM is an open Port, all are free Traders there, and no Business lies more natural, or ready for those who have nothing to do: Any Man commences Master when he will, without serving a Prenticeship, and is sure of a Majority of Customers against a fair Dealer

OF all Criticks, I acknowledge, that ill Writers are the most severe, especially where real Merit is found out and applauded: They greedily prey upon the smallest Faults in a great Genius, they'll turn and torture them a thousand Ways, to please their Malice, and satisfy their Spite They have no other Way of being reveng'd upon

the

the World, and, like the fallen Angels, curse, and strive to blast that Heaven they cannot climb.

I believe, under some one of these general Heads, all Species of Criticks may be rank'd. And as every considerate Author, Reader, or Spectator, must be satisfy'd of the Use, Beauty, and Merit of solid, unprejudic'd Criticism, so must they be distasted, when Ill-nature and Ignorance usurp the Intendancy over the polite Arts, to the utter Destruction of true Learning and just Wit.

If we place this Art and its Professors in a proper Light, we shall quickly perceive, that the Criticism of the Antients was an agreeable Dose of Physick, given by a skilful regular Physician, which carry'd off insensibly all noxious Humours, without any Injury to the Constitution: But modern Criticism is a rank Poison, administer'd by an illiterate Quack, which indeed gets the better of the Distemper, but the Operation destroys Life.

A just Critick, like an industrious Bee in his unbounded Flights, ranges Gardens, Groves and Meads, tries every Flower, or Herb, or Shrub, tastes all their Sweets, and ransacks all their odoriferous Stores, then culls what's excellent, preserves it from the rude Spoiler's Waste, and Teeth of Time, loads his little Thighs with Nature's choicest Gifts, then, in his artful Cell, out of them furnishes a Banquet for a Prince. But the *Snarler*, like a sluggish, waspish Drone, drags along a bloated Carcass, dully, in the same beaten Track, the fairest Fruit, and richest Scents, he shuns, or touches but to blast, and, in the Midst of Nature's flowery Pride, scorns all her Dainties, to fatten on a Dunghill.

BEFORE

BEFORE I conclude this ESSAY, there remain two very material Points unobserv'd.

THE first is, That I am perswaded the profess'd Criticks of this Age have brought upon us, from Time to Time, those Showers of bad PLAYS, which have almost wash'd the Shadow of *Dramatick Poetry* from off the Earth. They adhere so strictly to the severest Letter of Criticism, and press so earnestly the Observation of their Rules alone, that all our young Writers think nothing else but Art requir'd, and that a Heaven-born Genius (which breaks through all their Cob-web Fetters) is useless in *Parnassus*.

UPON this, any Gentleman that has nothing else to do, very gravely gets the critical Receipts by Rote for all Kinds of POETRY, he takes half a Dozen fresh Characters, and keeps what's for his Purpose, a proper Quantity of new Fable, if to be got; if not, he skims the best of the old; of the true sublime, a handful, very fine shred, that it may go the farther, Half a Pound of Terror, to a Quarter of Pity, he mixes them all very well together, and thickens the Plot with a Quarter of a Peck of fine Language, observes nicely, Time, Place, and Action, then melts down a Pound of Rhime, with two Ounces of Similies dissolv'd in it, to sweeten the latter Ends of Acts, and sprinkles it over the Whole. Lastly, to give it a poignant and wholesome Relish, he seasons it with about the Bigness of a Nutmeg of Morality. He may add a Spoonful or two of Satyr, or Panegyrick (as his Taste is) or let them alone.

THUS furnish'd, he sits down with the same Form and Serenity to write a *Tragedy*, that his Cook-Maid does to make a Plumb-pudding.

My second Observation is, That whatever Disparity may be betwixt the antient and modern POETS, I am convinc'd, that in the Way of Comparison of Merits, the Difference is as wide betwixt the Criticks of former Ages and this, nor will it be disputed, should I assert, that the Generality of late Bards, would have met with Applause and Encouragement more adequate to their Performances, had every Man of their Judges been an *ARISTOTLE*, and every Woman a *DACIER*.

BUT, at the same Time, I beg Leave to hint, that by the modern POETS, I cast not an Eye towards the Majority of Verse, or Play-wrights, nor can I allow, that the least Beam of that divine Art shines upon, or appears in the Works of every Coxcomb, that tags a Song with Rnimes, scribbles Lampoons, or prevails on the Actors to give the Town a thing call'd a PLAY, because it is divided into Acts and Scenes, with, *Enter King*, and, *Exit first Minister*.

IF that Class of my Readers who form our Theatrical AUDIENCES, persist in their Errors as to Behaviour, when their Faults have been so gently and plainly laid open, I have no means of Redress to hope for, but in humbly proposing to the P——t (as a Matter of the last Consequence to the Publick) that our *Play-Houses* may be enlarg'd after the Manner of the *Grecian* and *Roman* THEATRES, and separate Lodges contriv'd for those who go there only to chat, intrigue, or eat and drink, that impertinent Mirth, publick Amours, or ill-tim'd Gluttony, may no break in upon the Amusements of those, who go there purely for the Sake of the Entertainment.

As

OF AUDIENCES.

As I have been very copious on the Head of *Criticism*, I make no Doubt but this ESSAY will have the Original of every Copy drawn here, upon its Back, but Truth, Justice and Virtue can stand any Shock: I shall readily give up any Point here advanc'd, if the Objection is founded on solid Sense and calm Reasoning, but where Arguments are supported by Vehemence and Scurrility, I am not oblig'd to reply; that being only *Billingsgate* PLAY, where they who talk loudest and fastest, are certain of Victory, and where Wit and Learning proceed from the Lungs, not the Brain

ESSAY

ESSAY VI.
OF MASQUERADES;

Their great Antiquity; their Use and Abuse; capable of being contriv'd so, as to prove of vast Advantage to the Publick: With an Examen *of the bare-fac'd* MASQUERADES, *call'd* RIDOTTOS, *and* PRIVATE ASSEMBLIES. *To which is added, A Proposal for the Encouragement of the* ORATORY.

Have here ventur'd upon the most difficult Task in the World to succeed in, the Subject is ticklish, and must be manag'd with the greatest Caution: It is the critical Moment, upon which depends the Fate of these ESSAYS, it being impossible so to handle this Affair, as not to incur the Displeasure of some considerable People. For

while

OF MASQUERADES. 169

while I am engag'd in the Cause of *Virtue* and *Truth*, I shall of one Side or t'other innocently make the whole Nation my Enemies.

MASQUERADES have for some Years past made a vast Noise in this Kingdom, to the unspeakable Delight of most fine Gentlemen and Ladies, and with equal Dissatisfaction to many of his Majesty's well-meaning Subjects. They have divided us into two furious Factions, as opposite as *Whig* and *Tory*, neither Side admit of any *Medium*, to moderate their flaming Resentments: One Party in general Terms altogether approving of this Diversion, without limiting it to what is useful, or at least simply innocent, the other as absolutely condemning the Design and Consequences of such an Entertainment, and cursing by Bell, Book and Candle, all who frequent it, though with the most harmless Intentions.

BUT Justice (under whose Banner I fight) commands me to censure the Proceedings of both Parties: The first, for maintaining its Cause, where its Freedoms are unbounded, and its Errors manifest, the other, for blindly striking at the Foundation, without Regard to those Advantages which may be drawn from its Influence on the World.

WHO dreads the Viper's Poison, while indulging in a Mess of their envigorating Broth?—— or the Bee's Sting, with a Finger in the Honey Pot?—— Remove the Evil, and enjoy what's good.

BUT thus the Frailties of human Nature will judge at Random, according to the darkened Notions we entertain of Things, the least Gratification, or Discontent, make us fly out into the Extreams of ungovern'd Passions: Nothing can

Q please

please or displease, but it is Heaven or Hell; Lovers can see no Blemishes, and Foes no Beauties, some will pull up a Tree by the Roots, upon account of one rotten Branch, and others let a dead Stump stand in an improper Place, because it once had green Leaves.

But, in this ESSAY, I propose pursuing a Method widely different from this: What is Praiseworthy, I shall encourage, what is blameable, remove, either by turning its Bent towards somewhat perfectly harmless, or substituting in its Place, what may be render'd of Use to the World.

At first View, and to superficial Understandings, MASQUERADES may look with a very modern Face; and, indeed, so they once appeared to me, their Agility of Motions, and Freshness of Complexions induc'd me to be of this Opinion, till pulling off the MASQUE, by penetrating into the very Bowels of Antiquity, and searching into the remotest Records of Time, I found the Design and Consequences of a MASQUERADE, to be of the oldest Standing of any Mistery now in Being, and as antient as the very first Ceremonies of the *Roman, Grecian, Persian,* or *Egyptian* Religions.

From the very Beginning of *Paganism*, the heathen Priests acted always in MASQUERADE, and kept the Secrets of Religion appropriated to themselves, or at least restrain'd to a very few Members, what they thought the most solemn or material Parts of their Devotion.

The Priests of the superstitious *Egyptians* characteriz'd every thing religious, moral, or civil, by Hieroglyphicks, which Custom first (I believe) introduc'd MASQUERADING into the World: No Deity was allow'd to appear to the People, but in the Disguise of an Ox, Dog, Ape, Onion,

Cucum-

Cucumber: And thus the Notions of a supreme Power were convey'd to them in a familiar Dress, that they might seem less terrible.

THE *Persian Magi* in a manner retir'd from the Commerce of Mankind; they hid themselves and their Worship from the most piercing Eyes; they affected a religious Obscurity, in what they communicated to the Vulgar, either by Writings or Traditions, and the Sun, with them, was only a Cloak to veil their *Oromazes* from mortal View.

THE *Grecians*, above all Nations, envelop'd their most sacred Misteries with Darkness, the *Eleusina Sacra*, or Festival of *Ceres*, was the most celebrated of any in *Greece*, so careful were they to conceal their private Rites, that if a Person initiated dar'd to divulge the least Part of this secret Solemnity, he was treated as one sentenc'd by divine Judgment to suffer Death.

THEY had other Festivals of this Nature sacred to *Vesta, Diana, Cotys*, &c. observ'd all in the Night, and with the greatest Secrecy.

THE *Romans* made a Collection of all the Gods of other Nations, and solemniz'd their Misteries according to the Institutions of the different Countries they borrow'd them from: The religious Vizard was in great Request with their Priests; and, to their Piety, were owing several nocturnal misterious Sacrifices to *Venus* and *Adonis, Priapus, Bacchus*, &c. where MASQUERADING was absolutely essential to the Manner of Adoration.

HERE we may observe, that in the religious Ceremonies of the wisest, politest, and most powerful Empires, Secrecy, Night, and a Disguise were held necessary, both in the Initiation and Performance: Nor was the last of them confin'd to these private Solemnities alone, the most publick Festivals were celebrated both by Priests and People

People muffled up in particular Dresses: So that indeed, the whole of Religion with them, was a well-regulated MASQUERADE. And if Ignorance be the Mother of Devotion, what can so powerfully promote that End, as being led blindfold into it.

THE Adversaries to this well-intended Design will readily object, that there were several Impurities acted, and scandalous Liberties allow'd at these private, though seemingly religious Misteries, that, by my own Confession, they are the very Foundation of our modern MASQUERADES, and that the Enormities complain'd of in one, have been continued in the other, in Encouragement, if not in Action—— To all this heavy Charge, I plead, *Guilty*; nor shall I, by any Evasion, recede from what I have urg'd, in relation to the Rise or Progress of this *Entertainment*. My Intention is not to vindicate the Errors in the present Management of it, but to indulge the greatest, wisest, and best-bred Part of the Nation in the Appearance of a Diversion they are so fond of, yet turn the Current into quite a different Channel, while they enjoy only the Name. Let us resolve to discountenance and lay aside whatever is really irregular in this Amusement, which is not impossible: And I shall plainly demonstrate, that it may be render'd not only innocently agreeable in Speculation, but of the last Consequence in Practice, to all Degrees of People, nay, to a higher Pitch of solid Service, if not Instruction, than any other publick Entertainment can pretend to: Nor shall any Part be play'd in a MASQUE, but what conduces to the general Good, when shewn forth in *Propria Persona*

BUT to proceed regularly with the History of MASQUERADING, and bring it down to the present

present Times, it will be necessary to observe, Though Religion (after these dark idolatrous Ages) was rescued from the misterious Juggles of their Priests, and restor'd to its primitive Lustre, and unadorn'd Beauty; yet where Superstition and Ignorance got any Footing, they kept their Ground stifly; and of consequence, Religious MASQUERADES continued in as great Request as ever. To this Day they maintain the highest Reputation in most of the chief Kingdoms of *Europe*, where Religion is so differently dress'd, that, in the same City, the Garbs it puts on are as various as its Professors. It remain'd in the same Situation with us here in *England*, till towards the latter End of the Reign of K———— H———y VIII. when People began to be asham'd, or tir'd of it, and tho' in Q———— M———y's Reign it rais'd its drooping Head a while, it was but the last Blaze of Life, for it soon after languish'd and dy'd. The Well-Wishers to our Peace and Prosperity, hop'd it for ever buried in Obscurity, but some restless Spirits blew up a few neglected Sparks into general Flames, about the Year Forty One; when, in a frantick Fit, the whole Nation run a MASQUERADING, and all Affairs of Church and State were thrown into one Grand JUMBLE, or MASQUERADE, till People danc'd themselves quite out of Breath, and then they came to their Senses. In K——— C————s the S————d's Reign, Religious and Political MASQUERADES were pretty much laid aside for those of another Complexion, and nearer a-kin to those now in Vogue at the H———y M——t. During his Time they flourish'd, and with him they fell, or by Degrees dwindled to nothing, till reviv'd about the latter End of the late Q———'s Reign, by D———— D———t, the F————h A————r, who, by that Means, cunningly introduc'd the

P————r,

P———r, about half a Dozen C———ls, and as many Scores of J———ts and C———ns, all in their proper Robes; which alone were Dresses sufficient to have form'd a large MASQUERADE in G---t B———n. This threw the settled Nation into a Ferment. My Friend Mr H———r wisely took the Hint, and has firmly establish'd that Amusement by his exquisite *Gou*, in what is polite and diverting. But the sober Part of this Kingdom, who wisely view things with both Eyes, carefully look for something more in an Affair of so publick a Nature, than a Supper or a Dance, which has put me upon the following Regulation, not to destroy, but refine upon H———r's Entertainment; thus fix MASQUERADES upon a more durable Basis, by making it equally advantageous to him and us, that we may at least enjoy the Shell of Instruction, while he picks up the Kernel of Profit, which we throw away.

BUT to finish with the Historical Part of this ESSAY, I shall only make a small Remark here, that religious *Masquerading*, at present with us, is reduc'd to a large Band and short black Cloak, disguis'd in the natural Vizard of Hypocrisy.

HAVING given my Readers a just Idea of the Original of a MASQUERADE (which proves not despicable) I shall next enquire into the more immediate Usefulness, which may be reap'd from this Amusement judiciously regulated, at the same Time set Bounds to any licentious Extravagancies that may have been admitted there, and display to my darkened Countrymen, who oppose them, the mutual Benefits Nature and Art must receive in Conjunction, from its Reception, with proper Restrictions, by which Means it may be considered as a general Good, either in publick or private Life.

NAY,

OF MASQUERADES. 175

NAY, should we join with those People, in decrying *Masquerades* in general Terms, and act with all the ignorant Caution, and simple Zeal, which compose their Arguments, yet in answer to their most material Objections, we might offer numberless Advantages arising from such an Amusement, to the poor, or trading Part of any Nation.

ITS Consequences necessarily occasion so great an Expence, such a Circulation of ready Money (which else would lie dead in Bankers Hands, or Iron-Chests) and such a Spirit of Business to all Callings, relating to every Branch of Trade, or *Mechanism*, that this Plea in its Favour, might very well cast an agreeable Lustre upon the darkest Side of this Diversion, and make it pass current with the most scrupulously prudent.

BUT these Topicks have been lately so learnedly and copiously handled in a wonderful Book, where *private Vices* are undoubtedly prov'd to be *publick Benefits*, and the same Arguments being liable to be urg'd in Vindication of the most notorious Crimes, I shall wave making Use of a stol'n or precarious Defence, in proving the Use and Innocence of a MASQUERADE: I shall produce the most substantial Evidences, back'd by undeniable Matters of Fact, to strengthen what I have asserted in the Title of this ESSAY.

NOT to dwell too long upon the *Preface*, but at once to strike into the Body of my Work, and let its Strength and Perspicuity of Reasoning stare my Opponents full in the Face, I pretend to demonstrate, that a well-regulated MASQUERADE, may be of infinite Service to any Kingdom or State, in several different Political, Oeconomical, and Moral Views, whether we consider the Support of the Government, the

Happi-

Happiness of each particular Family, or the Wit and Politeness of every individual Member, in respect to their several Stations in the Commonwealth.

First then, and principally, a MASQUERADE should be encouraged by every Government, to the End that all Employments, Offices, Posts, E——l, C——l or M——y, in C——t, C——y, C——h, B——h, or A——y, may be supply'd with proper and useful Members, in a juster and clearer Method of Choice, than has been yet preach'd or thought of.

I remember to have perus'd in the Original *Spanish*, a very valuable *Treatise*, call'd *Les examen des Ingenios*; where it is laid down as a fundamental Maxim in the Education of Youth, that by the Laws of Nature, Art, good Sense, and Oeconomy, Parents are oblig'd thoroughly to consider the Genius and Constitution of their Children, and nicely weigh Perfections, and Defects in every Capacity, before they attempt the throwing them into Business for Life.

If they indiscreetly force tender Natures into those Callings, or Employments, Heaven never design'd them for; this blind, rash Choice will be generally attended with two very fatal Consequences; a private and publick: In the first, they render their Off-spring miserable in this Life, by putting them upon acting that Part which is entirely disagreeable to them. In the second, they are guilty of a manifest Injury to the Publick, in allowing their Children to fill those Offices, where they are incapable of discharging the Duty.

The Reasons which may be justly alledg'd on this Head, as circumstantial Proofs, are so numerous and obvious, that to quote one, would be

OF MASQUERADES. 177

be impertinent: And it may be very modestly urg'd, in behalf of any young Gentleman whipp'd into a Post after this ill-concerted Manner, that he may succeed by a very lucky Hit; but that the Odds are apparently against him, without the Shadow of a Fault on his Side.

I shall want but few Words then, to make it appear, that in this Case, the MASQUERADE, reduc'd to Order and Decency under the Eye and Wing of publick Authority, is the most ready, natural and proper Trial of Wits and Dispositions. This *Entertainment* in it self being agreeable to most youthful Inclinations, our bearded Boys and Infants of six Foot high will be easily cajol'd into such a School. Then the Variety of Habits allowing of as great a Latitude in the Characters of Life correspondent to them, every Man of any Taste will choose that Dress his Inclinations insensibly prompt him to; and of Course he'll exert himself to act up to what it represents, ambitious to be thought what he only affects to personate, and thus we shall penetrate into the Excellencies of every one's hidden Talent, and judge from thence what bustling, or quiet Scene of Life, Nature cut him out for.

FOR Example, Let us suppose a MASQUERADE conducted after this sober and polite Manner, establish'd in *P——nd*, where their M——arch is Elective, as well as M——rs of S——te, B——ps, or other inferior Officers. All this might be transacted very much to the Purpose, in a large Plain, finely illuminated with Flambeaus, and in the Space of a Summer's Night, all Vacancies might be fill'd up with the greatest Ease, and to the entire Satisfaction of every individual, as well as the Representatives of the People.

FOUR

Four Foot in the Shoulders, with a proportionable Height; a Voice like Thunder, always Fore-runner of a Storm, well-knit Arms and Legs, that in a common Method of walking, would mow down half the Company like so many Stalks of Wheat, would appear to vast Advantage in a *Turkish* Robe and Turban, and naturally speak the very Monarch; for who so proper to defend a Nation as he, who is most capable of offending them? according to the political Maxims of the *East*.

The nimble *Arlequin* (who has his Nose at every Man's Ear, and a Slap at every Man's Rump; who, like the *Camelion*, can change to any Colour, and with *Proteus* assumes all Shapes) by the dexterous Management of a simple wooden Stick, would readily point out to us a first M——r.

The sober Behaviour, grave Aspect, and venerable Garb of a *Scaramouch*, determine us in a worthy M——n.

The subtil Innocence of an artful *Pierro*, who pries into all Secrets, yet keeps himself conceal'd, would decypher to us at once, a rare S——te, S——y, or C——t J——r.

The meddling *Punchinello's*, who are every Bodies humble Servants, always at Court, always busy, and nothing to do, would furnish us with a perpetual Fund of Gapers for Places, who are pleas'd with dancing over a daily C——t Attendance, and content to be Slaves, without the Name of an Employment.

These few Instances will quickly let People of any tolerable Degree of Penetration, into the Use and Beauty of my Design, and demonstrate with what Ease any P——ce might grace his C——t with C——ns, T——rs, C——rs, S——vs,

OF MASQUERADES. 179

S———ys, E———ys, S———ds, by observing, cautiously, the proper Management of a Key, a white Switch, a Purse, a Goose-quill, a Spur, a Stick of Wax, and so on, to the smallest Officer of the Ex———se.

But, in order to render this Scheme compleat, and not leave the least Cranny for the Shadow of an Objection to creep in at, there must be establish'd by R———l and P———ry Authority, a select Number of Commissioners to to inspect this Entertainment, in the several Branches of it, which particularly concern the Publick, to see that the Whole is carried on with the strictest Decency and exactest Order; that all irregular Persons are banish'd the Place, that every one behaves up to the Propriety and *Decorum* of that Habit which denotes his Characters, both in Action and Speech, from whence they may judge of the Merit of every Performer, as to Understanding, Behaviour, Strength, &c. by the Help of a refin'd Sagacity, quick Eye, and staunch Nose, which Qualifications are essential to those dignify'd with so laborious an Office. Indeed these Commissioners will have vastly the Advantage over those design'd in the second Essay, to choose Actors for the Stage, as to properly distinguishing different Talents, because all People appear at a MASQUERADE in Propriety of Dress and Character. They assume what is natural to them, and acting in Disguise, act without Reserve: They can add the Beauty of an artificial Affectation to their borrow'd Persons, whereas the others have no Oportunity of shewing but what is pure Nature. Tho' if this my Project meets with due Encouragement, where any Blemish (as to Integrity, Honesty, or other trifling Virtues) affects the Reputations

of

of those pick'd up at a MASQUERADE for great Employments, they'll serve to supply the *Play-house*, in personating those Offices, so the Reality and Appearance of all Parts in Life be furnish'd from the same Shop. How justly and acutely would such Gentlemen distinguish the awful, silent Senator, in the solemn *Venetian* Robe! The uncorrupted Judge, in the spotless *Ermin*! the invincible Hero, in Buff and Scarlet! The able Lawyer, in the learn'd Full-bottom! The mortify'd retir'd P——on, in the *Capuchin*'s Thread-bare Cowl! and the rough Sea-Captain, in the Skippers tarry Jacket! Nay, the fawning Courtier, formal Citizen, tricking Attorney, plodding Usurer, thoughtful Merchant, or biting Stock-jobber, will be manifested in some Particularity of Garb or Address: Industrious Nature, like Oil, will rise uppermost, and make apparent each different Quality she form'd.

As I intend that this Project should be universal in its Improvement, and diffusive in all Kinds of Benefits, the lowest Parts of Life need not be excluded from their Shares in a general Good: But to this prudent Method of Choice, I would trust the fixing on all civil Capacities, from the Justice of Peace to the Petty-Constable, and the first Magistrate of a Corporation, to the Bell-man.

Nor would I put a Lad out to any Trade, from my *Lord Mayor*'s, to a Seller of Matches, till his Genius pass'd Examination at a MASQUERADE, where it would certainly shine out, though in a MASQUE, by turning its natural Bent, in an especial Manner, towards that Part of the Entertainment which it affected. A Devourer of Oranges and Apples will grow up to a Fruiterer, as he that swallows Jellies, and pockets Sweet-meats, must have a fine Taste for a Confectioner. The

Frequenter of the Side-Boards has undoubtedly a Turn to a Vintner, as the quick Dispatch of a cold Fowl or Lobster will distinguish the Poulterer from the Fishmonger: Moreover, the Expence of that MASQUERADE, by which their prevailing Inclinations are try'd, will save the Trouble of giving them a Surfeit, at their Entrance into Business, in order to hinder them from eating out their Master's Profit, as Grocers use to stuff their young Apprentices full of Plums.

LET us now turn my Proposal from what may still be done, to those Inconveniencies, which by our Prudence might have been remedy'd. Thus, by curiously viewing it on both Sides, the Contrast will fix in a more affecting Point of View, both the Disease and Cure.

HAD this Manner of Choosing, and fitting young Gentlemen for all Employments, been observ'd, then several strong-lung'd P---ns would have been excluded mounting a P——t, who might have made a bright Figure at the B——r; and instead of deafening, or tiring a Congregation, have prattled Tautology and Nonsense by the Hour to some Purpose. And some dull, heavy L——rs, who stupidly dose over their Clients Affairs, might have lovingly slept with their P——sh the whole Length of a S——on.

SOME graduate Doctors, that have had very bad Success as Physicians, might have supply'd our Markets with admirable Butchers, as several tender-hearted Butchers might, in Return, furnish the Colledge with very clever Anatomists.

MANY M——ates, whose Behaviour and Understanding disgrace the B——h, might shine out in a Farm, and several sensible Yeomen, who fatten Hogs, whiten Veal and grope Turkies,

R

lies, make Generosity and Justice the Ornaments of a C———rt.

SOME pretty, smart Fellows would be whipp'd from the Plough-tail, as sad, idle Dogs, that would sparkle in the Side-box, or at the Head of a C———ny of G———ds, and many of our Lollers in Gilt-chariots whistle over an OPERA Air, to a Team of Oxen or Horses.

WHAT Numbers of spruce, polite Journeymen might be remov'd from behind Counters, in order to fill several considerable Vacancies at St. J———'s, with the weighty Forms of Goodbreeding, and the material Nothingness of proper S———te Ceremonies, and several aukward, simple C———t Of———rs be doom'd to their paternal Business, cast Accounts, weigh Plums, and measure Silks for Life.

THUS, in the dark Reign of old *Chaos*, a vast Concourse of unruly Atoms being jumbled together, at last danc'd themselves all into their proper Places, and form'd this beautiful, regular Plan of the World, so compleat in all its Parts.

THE Arguments and Examples I have here produc'd, sure must prove sufficient to confute the most prejudic'd and obstinate, in Relation to the Merits of a MASQUERADE.

IT is impossible to fix upon any other Scheme so perfect, or adapted to the Design of worthily filling all Places, E———l, P———l, C———l or M———y: For every Genius would have Room and Oportunity to exert it self in the Business of a Piece with its Nature, all would behave with Pleasure to themselves, and with Alacrity discharge their Duty to the Publick. No Man would go unwillingly or ignorantly into his Office, but then we should see the ✶✶✶✶✶✶✶✶ and our ✶✶✶✶✶✶✶✶ and such ✶✶✶✶✶ nor would ✶✶✶✶

******** nor such ********** and then ***** perhaps ******* better supply'd

WE will suppose then MASQUERADES settled upon so lasting a Foundation, that the whole Nation may be assur'd of their being continued, protected and supported by the highest Powers, that they shall be the Touch-stone of Capacity, in all Pretensions to Employments, of whatsoever Dignity or Profit (if not hereditary to the Fools of some particular Families) that the severest Penalties shall be inflicted upon all Offenders, who shall dare to disturb these Entertainments, or disobey Orders in Matters of Judgment, Election or Amusement.

THEN People would be proud of preserving the Reputation that this political Diversion would claim from such Encouragement, nay, in a few Years it would be common, to run to the *Masquerade-house* for every Man's Character, as to Wisdom, Honesty, Courage, *&c* — Nor am I in the least solicitous about every Thing's being transacted with the utmost *Decorums*, being certain, that the most disorderly Mortals upon Earth will be kept in Awe, and restrain'd to a Carriage highly decent, by the Fear of being for ever banish'd the MASQUERADE, should the least Shock to Modesty be prov'd upon them. And I am satisfied, there needs no other Punishment be mention'd, to terrify licentious Riot it self into Sobriety: For, as they would by this Means be depriv'd of the most delightful Entertainment in the World, so on the other Hand, they would lose the Prospect of being Candidates for any honourable, or profitable Employment.

I here in the strongest Terms insist, that all Love Intrigues be utterly discarded and forbid, as Appendixes to this Diversion, excepting, where a Gentleman is desirous to penetrate gently, or pry into a Lady's Perfections, or she to experience his Abilities, with a full View to Matrimony; and that Vigour or Capacity are to be made manifest, in order to their becoming Man and Wife.

WHICH Thought naturally leads me to my second Assertion in Favour of MASQUERADES, viz. That they will be a great Promoter of pure and unspotted Wedlock Joys, and more especially aiding in the two principal Points of that holy State, --- a happy and fruitful Life.

UNSETTLED are the Desires, and as various the Fancies of Men in the Pursuit of a Wife: We expect a hundred Perfections in Woman, and often meet with a fair Female bless'd with one of the Number, but we cannot find the Ninety and Nine: The Passions of the other Sex are as changeable, and their Tempers as difficult to be pleas'd, so that in short, the Whole of Marriage, as to a well-judg'd Choice, consists in a lucky Hit. Or, if we are resolv'd to choose with Caution, and not trust to Fortune, I can only say to my Readers, what a wise *Presbyterian* Parson prudently hinted to a youthful Congregation, on this Head, in a bridal Sermon, when, after learnedly stating the whole Case he proceeded thus: *My beloved, it signifieth not, though your Wives be young, lovely, virtuous and religious, if they be not fit Wives, therefore look ye out with Care for fit Wives, and then ye will become as one Body.* Now where can any Man so properly try to catch a fit Wife, as at a MASQUERADE? —— If he loves Reservedness, there are *Spanish Prudes*: Would he have Life and Air? there are *French Coquets*: Hunts he after Innocence? there are
Milk-

OF MASQUERADES. 185

Milk-Maids, and Shepherdesses: Is ignorant Youth his Game? there are large Babies in Leading-Strings: Covets he Riches and Virtue? there are venerable Matrons, old and ugly: Does he think Knowledge convenient? there are Widows, just come from their Husbands Funerals. Seeks he the obedient Slave? there are *Turkish* Ladies just elop'd from a *Seraglio*. Is Religion alone his Aim? there are Nuns and Quakers: But would he have all Perfections in one Habit? there are *Domines*.

A proper Method of negotiating a matrimonial Conjunction, is allow'd to be a very nice Point, and apt to breed bad Blood betwixt the Parties concern'd, if not handled to the Purpose: Therefore what Project can be more *apropos*, to prevent the Consequences arising from the Animosities, Discontents, Heart-burnings, Jealousies, Elopements, Divorces, and separate Maintenances, which so often clog the married State, and are of infinite Prejudice to its Reputation, and Detriment to the publick Welfare, as but too few can boast of living altogether free from some of the Grievances just nam'd.

LET us then imagine a Gentleman in Pursuit of a Wife at a MASQUERADE, at last he springs his Game, to all Appearance she promises well, the Air, the Motion, the Wit of the Lady charm him, nor are his Person and Conversation disagreeable to her, so far of the Treaty proving satisfactory, it is necessary to push the Matter Home. They retire, Preliminaries are soon settled, the Congress is open'd, both Parties agree to go to the Bottom of the Affair in Hand. If all secret Articles are settled to their mutual Satisfaction, those that are publick, and of less Concern, follow of Course, but if some Allies are deny'd their Pretensions, or refuse to be Guarantees of the Treaty; Matters being at a Stand once, and not put in regular Motion, must drop: Thus either Way, all ends well. If those Things that are of a private Nature, are brought to bear to both their Contents, upon being produc'd, 'tis a Match, if not, the Familiarities that pass'd betwixt them must remain a Secret, the Parties being utter Strangers to one another

This Method of proceeding in an Affair of so great Importance, is too well supported, to be treated as chimerical by any of my Adversaries. This discreet Trial of Tempers and Constitutions before Marriage, would prevent all those small Differences which too often attend it, and put to Silence those very civil Speeches that by way of Interjections lard connubial Love ———— *Very fine!* ———— *indeed!* ———— *is it possible?* ———— *Infinite Assurance!* ———— *had I known that* ———— *Horrid Creature!* ———— *before I'd have done it!* ———— *My G——d!* ———— *I'd be burnt alive first!* ———— *Always foul Weather at Home!* ———— *Is this Matrimony?* ———— *Look ye, Madam!* ———— *Dem-me!* ———— *Fool, Fool!* ———— *Yes, I have it!* ———— *Devil! Catch me a second Time!* ————

We all know, that but one happy Pair have ever yet claim'd the Flitch of Bacon, though the Custom is of several Centuries standing. But were due Encouragement given to what I have here propos'd, in a little Time every married Couple would at least put in for a Rasher.

The seven wise Men of *Greece* would have approv'd of this Scheme, though none of them had the Head-piece to think of it, that being reserved as an eternal Monument of Glory, sacred to the Family of the *Primcocks.*

INDEED the wisest of the old *Grecian* Philosophers (in his Regulation of that Commonwealth, whose Rules were the most strictly severe) squinted a little this way, in establishing a Sort of a political RIDOTTO, in which the young Men and Maidens promiscuously met, in order to provoke them into Matrimony.

BUT so shocking to all Modesty was this prudent Law-giver's State-Cookery, that it must surfeit any Stomach but that of the grossest Feeder, he not only forbidding the Use of MASKS to conceal Names, and hide Blues, but even stripp'd them of their Petticoats and Breeches, and left blind Nature to instruct them.

MY decent Expedient, I hope, will be receiv'd suitable to its Merit, its Conveniency, as well as Reservedness, answering better to all Purposes in the End. By this Means it will be in the Power of a Bride and Bridegroom to come together with some Prospect of living happy, they being the last consulted, if at all, in the matrimonial Bargain, because they are most deeply concern'd, Parents thinking it but just that their Children should be pleas'd with the Person, if they are with the Fortune.

NO Man takes, upon the Judgment of another, a Pair of Shoes, or Gloves, he first tries them on, then says, whether they fit or not: Yet must he, without the least Trial or Experience, be clapp'd into the Marriage-Doublet for Life, and scarcely be allow'd to make a wry Face, when the Yoke pinches, or slip his Neck out of the Collar, when it is too wide for him.

IF a MASQUERADE, rightly dispos'd, can produce such wonderful Effects in filling all vacant Employments with Persons of Genius and Capacity for the Business (as has been fully pro-

proved) I believe it may be supported by Arguments as self-evident, that it is the only Place in the World, where any Youth may be thoroughly qualify'd for all publick Affairs.

I may venture to affirm, that this *Intertainment* will form in those who frequent it, the truest Judgments of all Part in polite Life, sharpen them to the finest Edge of Wit, properly set for the genteelest Conversation, and be the surest Guide in conducting them to Perfection in all the liberal Arts: So that a MASQUERADE may be depended upon as a perpetual Fund of good Sense, the Whet-stone of Repartee, and a real Academy of Sciences.

THE various Characters that are there seemingly represented, the different Inclinations, Desires and Interests that fill every Breast, and that Medley of Nations, Languages and Judgments, must form the most agreeable Mixture of Conversation imaginable, giving every one a true Taste of easy Dialogue, and of consequence inspiring them with a sprightly Turn, and fixing the Standard of each Member's talking pertinently in his Character or Profession

IN order to compleat this laudable Design, every Person must not only humour and strictly adhere, in the minutest Particulars, to what he appears, but where he finds a Body of People harping upon the same String, and to the Tune of his Inclinations, he must strike in there, and herd with them, as the surest and easiest Method of attaining to that Knowledge he thirsts after

IN one Corner may be heard a Consultation of Physicians, determining Life and Death, their Heads full of Receipts, and Mouths of hard Words, all agreeing in the Ends of their Patients, but differing in the Ways thither: In another, a
noisy

noisy Bench of Lawyers, torturing and commenting upon old Charters, Statutes, Deeds, Records-Wills, &c. and spitting at one another, *Judgments, Arrests, Scire Facias's, Noli-prosequis, Demurrers*, &c.

Here they may spy a Tribe of Natural Philosophers weighing Air, making Experiments upon Kittens and Puppy-Dogs; boasting of their Mummies, venemous Animals, and monstrous Births, astonish'd at the wonderful Variety of Nature in Minerals, Fossils, Shells, Feathers, &c. There a Group of *Virtuosi*, poring their Eyes out on Medals, Seals, Intaglias, Cameas, &c. praising every thing antique, damning every thing modern, reducing what is beautiful in this World to still Life, in Pictures, Statues, Bass-Relieves, and other Curiosities of Art.

In one Room they'll find a Circle of Mathematicians surrounded with Globes, Quadrants, Sectors, Dials, Theodolites, Microscopes, Telescopes, &c. demonstrating the Proportions, Lines, Figures of Squares, Angles, Cones, Numbers, Measures, Weights, &c. explaining the Problems of *Euclid*, and making familiar, to the meanest Capacity, the Difficulties of *Algebra*, talking more in a Quarter of an Hour, than can be understood in an Age: In another, they may reconnoitre a Troop of military Men forming Camps, ordering Battles, quartering Soldiers, laying Sieges, raising Blockades, nothing to be heard but Thunder, Blood, Fire, Batteries, Bombardments, and Great Guns.

In this Apartment a Band of musical Gentlemen will be very loud, with Concords and Discords, Flats and Sharps, Crotchets and Quavers, Times and Movements, Air and Composition, chiming together as melodiously as a Set of Pack-Horses, with each a Bell at his Ear, to keep him in Tune. In that a double Line of Poets will be no less noisy in matching Crambos, weighing Cadences, and trying Words, like Earthen Pipkins, by the Sound, to know if they are good for any thing. Here a Man may learn to rhime, fill Pocket-Books with Thoughts, for Ode, Pastoral Elegy, or Epigram, and perhaps some Sentences, proper for the Epick or Dramatick.

THUS in a few MASQUERADE Evenings, a young Gentleman of tolerable natural Parts, by applying himself to a particular Study, may either qualify himself for any Employment or Calling, and afterwards, by exerting those Talents there, pop at once into good Business, or if he is dispos'd for universal Knowledge, carry home with him the Marrow of all Sciences, to fit him for the brightest Conversation, without the tedious Forms of a Scholastick Education.

IF the Behaviour, Customs and Languages of all foreign Nations were punctually observ'd in a MASQUERADE, young Gentlemen need not lose Money and Time in travelling so far from Home, to admire one, and acquire t'other. Our Infants of Q————y, that are willing to improve, need go no farther than the *Hay-Market* to be instructed, where they dance best, or sing sweetest, or bow the genteelest, or dress the richest, or eat the nicest, or walk the stateliest, *Paris, Rome, Venice, Naples, Vienna* and *Madrid* would all be found in that inchanted Spot.

NOR should we forget the Advantages this would bring to the *English* Tongue, as our Speech is a Purloiner from all Languages, antique and modern, daily getting, yet still wanting, where could we hope for so beautiful an Introduction of foreign Words and Phrases, as from that Variety of Characters and Representations of different Nations

Nations at a MASQUERADE? Then we need not steal, but boldly use what we lik'd, as the Properties of those Persons whose Habits we wear, nor should an expressive Monosyllable escape being naturaliz'd, from the old *Greeks* to the present *Hottentots*.

THAT even the most barbarous Sounds add a Greatness, or Grace to our Language, is evident from a late Collection of Travels, where the most uncouth and tramontane Expressions have been greedily receiv'd, and universally us'd. If Captain *Gulliver* had never travell'd, our *Beaus* and *Belles* would never have pronounc'd *Lilliput*, *Brobdingnag*, *Blamerfescu*, or *Hoyhnms*, *Glumdalclish* might have wept her Eyes out for us, our Ignorance would never have dream'd of the Flying Island of *Laputa*, nor profited by the wonderful Discoveries of the Natural Philosophers of *Balnibari*, and we should have mistook a *Hoyhnm* for a Horse, and a *Yahoo* for a rational Creature, to the End of Time.

As nothing is more essential to the Growth of all Arts (from their first springing up to their Maturity) than Freedom, so a MASQUERADE being a perfect Commonwealth (as every Body is there upon the Level) is the very Country of Liberty, in which they must flourish, and consequently, by a well-judg'd Encouragement and strictly-regulated Institution, this Entertainment may prove the Root, from whence all Branches of the Sciences may spread faster and farther, than by any Method now practis'd in the known World.

THE Reasons I have given, and the Proofs made use of in supporting the general Use of a MASQUERADE, being as clear as strong, I need
speak

speak no farther in Praise of Truths so undeniable and self-evident.

WHILE I am busy with the Merits of this illustrious Family, it may be expected, that some honourable Mention should be made of a near Relation, call'd Sign*r* *Ridotto*, which is indeed a tolerable pretty Jumble of MUSICK, DANCING, GAMING, &c. But at best a bare-fac'd MASQUERADE, where People are admitted disguis'd, without a Vizard, and hide their Hearts by their natural Faces.

As all the Members of this Society make their Appearance in the same Character, dress'd in the same Habits, and acting in their proper Persons, they must do every thing with Constraint, and cannot be susceptible of the Advantages entail'd upon a MASQUERADE, this its younger Brother having the natural Tendency to all the Extravagancies and Irregularities of the elder, without the Fortune to support them, or the Sense to improve by them. Therefore I may affirm, that all those Benefits which may accrue to a Nation from a MASQUERADE, cannot be acquir'd at this Amusement, yet Vice and Folly shine there in full Splendor

IN short, a *Ridotto* is as stupidly insipid, as the other is wittily brillant; and as insignificant as the other is necessary: Where one may find Love without Gallantry; a numerous Assembly, without Life or Gaiety, and Conversation without Wit. It is indeed as different from a MASQUERADE, as *Ash-Wednesday* from *Easter-Holidays*, and may serve as a *Lenten Entertainment* in *Italy*, but will not please in *England*, where we keep *Carnival* all the Year round.

How it is carry'd on Abroad, or why introduc'd here, I think is not very material, or worth enqui-

enquiring into: I look upon it as an Interloper, nor will it ever be admitted as a Publick Diversion amongst us, as long as we can meet with what is more agreeable, or instructing.

SINCE I am got into this Road of Amusements, many of my Readers will be desirous, that I should not pass by Drawing-rooms, Assemblies and Visiting-days, without calling in: But as these *Entertainments* are at most of a private Nature, and confin'd to particular Sets of People, to touch upon them would be taking me out of my Way.

THEREFORE I shall only remark, they are upon as dull a Footing as *Ridottos*, if not worse, where the Corner of a Room may do as much Mischief as the Middle of a MASQUERADE, where Honour and Respect are gain'd by a fortunate Card, or a lucky Cast, where good Sense and good Breeding are measur'd by the Sounds of Titles, and Shew of Fortune, where Scandal and a Grin are taken for Wit and genteel Behaviour, where Brocade and Embroidery make the fine Lady and fine Gentleman: And where a common Sharper, with a long Purse of Gold, is admitted as an Equal to the first Peer in the Kingdom.

As I began this ESSAY with the Article of R——n, so I must return to the same Topick, before I take my final Leave of the Amusements of People of the biggest Fashion, and consider how far they ought to be indulg'd, in going to C——h meerly as a Diversion, then close with a modest Proposal.

I own this is look'd upon as an Affair of that Consequence (especially one Day of the Week) that it would be absurd to let it pass unregarded.

ed: Tho' I know it will be immediately objected, This is not my Province, to inspect Matters of so high, solemn, and grave a Nature. I own, the Charge, and dare only touch upon it here, as they have dress'd it up to my Hands: And, as they have turn'd the most serious Part of Life into a trifling Amusement, none of the publick *Entertainments* is frequented with so little Prospect of Improvement, or Design to be instructed. The P———t is more neglected than the Stage, and the P———r than the *Opera-book*. Had they not turn'd the Service of the C————h into a bare Amusement, and made it to consist of a Smile or Frown, a Whisper or Ogle, a Bow, or Curtesy, to see and be seen, I should not have presum'd to mention it here as such. I have no Warrant to inspect C---hes (*quatenus* C—hes,) but am at Liberty to animadvert upon the Behaviour of the greatest and finest Part of the Congregation, who turn them into THEATRES, or Idolatrous Temples, while they do nothing but worship one another: Nor will it be held Presumption in me, to say, that the Whole of their Duty might be better discharg'd by keeping at Home, than coming there to set ill Examples in Devo---n, and by their Forms and Grimaces, divert the Eyes of the ill-bred, ill-dress'd Part of the Assembly, from the Business of the Place.

But as the Genius of the polite Part of this Nation has a prodigious Tendency to every thing mighty new, I hope they'll meet at the Or---ry in N———rt—m—t, with those Novelties that may tempt them thither, amuse them while there, and fix their Attention to what is then spoken or acted, nor sickly change, till the Bloom of Youth

at

at least is gone, and the ripening Fruit is ready to be thrown away.

I hope, tho' this *Entertainment* boasts a little of the Face of R———n, that will be no Objection to the ingenious Inventor and Founder of the *Oratorians*, whom I recommend to the Quality and Gentry of both Sexes, in the most particular Manner.

His Academical P———t has form'd the most happy Alliance betwixt R———n, Morality, and the *Belles-Lettres* And as he inculcates the Quintessence of all Arts and Sciences with his Div———ty, there is this particular Benefit to be reap'd from his Doctrine, that we go to C———h and School at the same Time.

If any Thing that has the Appearance of a Ch———pel can please, this must, where a polite Variety quickens our Dev———n, inspires Zeal, and furnishes our Libraries with a new Liturgy

It would be wonderful, if so bold, so disinterested, so publick-spirited an Undertaking should fail of Success, where R———n is stripp'd f all superfluous Ornaments, and only allow'd a few necessary Furbeloes, to hide what may prove disagreeable to the Squeamish and Ignorant, yet light and easy to the Wearer.

It sounds well of this Gentleman's Side, and shews the Solidity of his Principles, that the Cl———gy are in general averse to his Design, and are to a Man join'd to decry the H———ly-nists.

But we are sensible that they hate Improvement, for fear of Reformation; and under the Pretence of avoiding Innovations, would give us R———n as it was about Eighteen Hundred Years ago,

ago, without allowing for those Amendments, or Additions, which particular Humours or Occasions may require.

I could not forbear touching lightly in this Place, these two last mention'd Heads, which are of greater Moment than most People at first fight imagine. Nor can I think Affairs of this Nature improperly tack'd to the Tail of an Essay upon MASQUERADES.

ESSAY

ESSAY VII.

Of the GYMNASIA, THEATRES, AMPHITHEATRES, NAUMACHIÆ *and* STADIA *of the Antients; but particularly of the antique* CIRCUS, *and modern* BEAR-GARDEN: *A Comparison between the* GLADIATORS *and our* PRIZE-FIGHTERS; *The Italian* STROLERS, *and our Mountebank* STAGES: *With a small Sketch of our* COCK-PITS, PUPPET-SHEWS, FAIRS, *and* PUBLICK AUCTIONS.

I SO far profess my self a bigotted Admirer of the *Antients,* and all their Performances, that every Thing which bears the Authentick Mark, or boasts the least Resemblance of Antiquity, touches me with Veneration, Surprize, or Pleasure: Of Consequence, when we narrow-soul'd, half-witted Mortals,

Mortals, the Moderns, follow, tho' at the greatest Distance, or imitate in the aukwardest Manner, any Custom, Amusement, or Work of theirs, I own my self secretly prepossessed in Favour of that Affair, even to a Degree of Partiality.

HAVING in the Six former ESSAYS, gone thro' most of the Publick *Entertainments*, (at least those resorted to by the *Beau-monde*) this small INTRODUCTION was occasion'd by my recollecting a Diversion truly *English*, the last mention'd, because supported mostly by the Commonalty; but which I look upon with Veneration, and frequent with Delight. Nor can the rude, vulgar Apellation of the *Bear-garden* give any Distaste to my Ears, since it was certainly design'd with a clear View to the *Antique Circus*.

As our *Bear-garden* may be justly esteem'd no bad Copy of the *Antient Circus*, it plainly demonstrates, that the Souls of the lowest of our People are inspir'd with a natural Propensity to the greatest and finest *Entertainments* of Antiquity, and should be accordingly distinguish'd, by a particular Politeness in their *Gou* from all other Nations.

To set this Matter in a true Light, and give my Readers a just Notion of the Reasons for this Comparison betwixt two Places, which may seem at first View widely different, it will be absolutely necessary to run over, in an historical Manner, the various Shews which gave first Birth to so spacious a Building, and trace them Step by Step, thro' the several Ages and Parts of the World, where these Spectacles have been exhibited with greatest Splendor and Applause.

THE Original Institution of a *Circus* was undoubtedly *Grecian*, whether we consider the Place, or the general *Entertainment*, at least upon the
Foun-

Foundation they had laid. The *Romans* erected their Superstructure, and furnish'd it likewise with proper Materials for the Inside, as shall be easily made manifest.

THE Design, Use, and Exercises of the *Grecian* GYMNASIA and STADIA, were in most Particulars the same, as to Building and Games, with the CIRCUS and AMPHITHEATRES of the *Romans*. And as for all the other Sports made use of in the latter, and wanting in the first, they were, without Dispute, borrow'd from the sacred Solemnities of the *Pythian, Nemean, Isthmian*, but particularly from the Trials of Skill, in all Feats of Activity, at the celebrated *Olympick Games*.

BUT in Order to qualify my Readers to be competent Judges of what I have here advanc'd, I'll as briefly as possible recapitulate what Authors of Antiquity and greatest Credit have handed down to us on each Head, without canvassing different Opinions, as to Time, Place, Etymology, or Institution of every Particular, then leave the Parallel to their Discretion.

THE GYMNASIA were common in every City of *Greece*, but first Founded at *Lacedemon*: They consisted of several different Piles of Building united together, each of which serv'd for a several Purpose. They were properly a Kind of *Academy*, and all Sciences for the Improvement of the Mind, as well as all Exercises for strengthening the Body, were cultivated here with the greatest Assiduity. The *Porticos* were fill'd with Seats for the Conveniency of the Scholars, who study'd, discours'd, or attended the Lectures of the Philosophers, Rhetoricians, Grammarians, or other Professors. The other Parts were particularly fitted up for exercising their Youth in all those

those bodily Arts which ennur'd them to Hardships, knit their Limbs, confirm'd their Healths, and train'd them up to appear in the Lists of Fame, at the Games of their greatest Festivals. In one they Wrestled, Run, Leap'd, Box'd, &c. in another, play'd at Ball, in a third, Danc'd: Nor were they without their separate and convenient Apartments for Bathing, Anointing Dusting, Dressing, and for making their Matches, fixing what Sport they would contend in, and the Prize of Conquest. These were so order'd, that the Whole of the Affair was transacted without any Confusion, or Interruption to one another, tho' the chief *Gymnasium* was generally capable of accomodating several Thousands of Spectators at once, besides Numbers of Students and Combatants.

THE *Stadium* was either that Part of the *Gymnasium*, of a large semicircular Form, in which all the fore-mention'd Exercises were perform'd, and where Seats were rais'd above one another, for the Convenience of Multitudes, who flock'd thither to see those Practices in Skill and Strength, or else were built apart from all other publick Edifices, in the Form of a *Circus*, and for the same Uses; of which the most remarkable was at *Athens*, built all of white Marble, being very long, with two parallel Sides clos'd up circularly to the East End, and open towards the other So far the *Stadium* of the *Grecians* answers to the CIRCUS and AMPHITHEATRES of the *Romans*, as being the undoubted Foundation of them, both as to Building and Use. Let us now inspect the solemn Festivals of *Greece*, and see what Materials were borrow'd from them for supplying the *Circus* with Variety of Amusements. The most noted of these publick, sacred Games, were the

Olym-

Olympian, dedicated to *Jupiter Olympius*, for his Conquest over the Sons of *Titan*, which was the most celebrated Meeting in *Greece*, all States in general crowding thither. They were solemniz'd every fifth Year, and lasted five Days, no Woman, upon Pain of Death, was suffer'd to appear at this Solemnity. The *Pythian* Games were consecrated to *Apollo*, in Memory of his destroying the Serpent *Python*, they were held near *Delphi*, and perform'd every Ninth, or afterwards, every fifth Year. The *Nemean* Games were instituted by *Hercules*, in Honour of *Jupiter*, after he had overcome the *Nemean* Lion, and were celebrated every third Year, near the Village of *Nemea*, where *Jupiter* had a Magnificent Temple.

THE *Isthmian Games* were so call'd from the *Isthmus* of *Corinth*, where they were solemniz'd. They were instituted in Honour of *Melicertes*, by *Sisyphus*, King of *Corinth*, or *Neptune*, by *Theseus*. They were observ'd every third or fifth Year, and held inviolable.

Now let us take a short View of the principal Exercises us'd in these sacred *Games*, and the Honours paid to the Conquerors in those Glorious Contentions.

THE principal Exercises made use of in these sacred *Games*, consisted of Leaping, Running, Boxing, Darting, Throwing, Dancing, Wrestling, and Racing. Leaping was perform'd with heavy Weights upon their Heads and Shoulders, and sometimes carry'd in their Hands. They were usually of an Oval Figure, with Holes in them to put their Fingers through, or Thongs to fasten them by. Running was in the highest Esteem with the antient *Grecians*, Swiftness being thought a great Qualification in a Warrior, either as to a sudden Onset, or nimble Retreat

The Course they ran was call'd the *Stadium*, being of the same Number of Paces with that Measure; tho' the Extent of the Race very often varied. Boxing was perform'd by the Combatants having great Balls of Iron, or Lead, in their Hands, to add Weight to their Blows. Their Hands, Wrists, and Arms were bound round with Thongs of Leather, as high as the Shoulder. This small Armour was call'd *Cestus*, and help'd to defend themselves, and annoy their Antagonists. In Darting, they went several Ways to work; they sometimes threw a Javelin, Rod, or other long Instrument out of their naked Hands, or by the Help of a Thong tied round its Middle, at other times, they sent out of a Bow, or cast out of a Sling, an Arrow, small Spear, or Dart.

In Throwing, the *Discus* was made use of, being a *Quoit* of Brass, Iron, or Stone, which they threw, by the Help of a Thong put thro' a Hole in the Middle of it. This was hurl'd in the Manner of a Bowl, not with the Hands lifted up and extended, as in Darting. Some of these *Disci* were of a Spherical Figure, others foursquare. If Agility of Body was in so great Request at these Games, DANCING could not be forgot. This was always perform'd in Armour; nor did the Weight of so cumbersome a Dress hinder them from shewing the lightest, nimblest Motions. The chief Dance of this Kind was the *Pyrrhica Saltatio*. In Wrestling, they first contended only, by Strength of Nature, to throw their Antagonists; but afterwards the Art was introduc'd, by which the Weaker were enabled to foil those Superior in Strength. They never Wrestled till all their Joints and Members were well rubb'd and fomented with Oil; and three

three Falls were requir'd to claim a Prize. *Racing* consisted either in running single Horse against Horse, or by two Horses, one for the Race, the other to leap on at the Goal, or by Chariots, in which were two, three, four or more Horses, coupled together, not Pair after Pair, as we put Sets in a Coach, but all a-row in one Front. The greatest Skill in this Exercise was shewn, in dextrously avoiding the touching the Goal, in which if they fail'd, the Danger was as imminent as the Disgrace. Besides these Exercises already mention'd, often *Poets, Musicians, Orators,* and *Historians,* by repeating their Works, speaking *extempore* on any Subject, or by comparing Notes, contended for the Victory: But generally those Sports which most conduc'd to fitting Mankind for warlike Exploits, were regarded with a favourable Eye, and look'd upon as the greatest Accomplishments. Thus we see that the Games practis'd at these publick Solemnities, were the same with the Sports of the GYMNASIA, the Youth exercising themselves in the latter, to ripen them to Manhood, and qualify them for Victory in the former. The Honours paid to the Conquerors at any of these solemn Festivals, were of the highest Order allow'd to Mortals, and wanted but little of Divine Adoration to the principal Deities. They enter'd the City in a triumphal Chariot, the Walls being broke down, to make them a free Entrance; the greatest Posts in the Army were assign'd them, and the first Places at all publick Shews, magnificent Presents were offer'd them by their Native Cities, and they were ever after maintain'd at the publick Charge. A single, or repeated Conquest, was look'd upon as a prodigious Happiness, and equal to the greatest Triumph,

umph, in Point of Fame: But to come off Victor in all the Exercises, was thought attaining to the highest Pitch of Felicity, and Merit, that human Nature could be capable of: Nay, being exalted to a Degree above the State of Men. Nor was this wonderful Respect confin'd to themselves alone; it extended to every Thing that related to them, it render'd the Place which gave them Birth, noted, their whole Family fortunate, and their Parents thrice happy, in the Eyes of the World. Fame indeed was what they all contended for; the Prizes adjudg'd the Conquerors at any of the Games, being in their intrinsick Value inconsiderable, being generally Crowns, Garlands, or Wreaths of Laurel, Palm, Beech-leaves, Parsly, Pine-leaves, which were thought sufficient to distinguish the Hero, and give him Immortality.

HAVING drawn this little Sketch of the *Grecian* Exercises, Games and Diversions, let us in the same concise Manner inspect those of the *Roman* State, then observe where they agree, or differ, upon the Parallel.

No Nation upon Earth ever so much delighted in all publick Spectacles as the *Romans*, or exhibited Shews with that expensive Magnificence, or diversify'd them with that agreeable Variety: Especially after being establish'd some Centuries, their primitive Rudeness was a little worn off; and by their frequent Recesses from War, and Intercourse with other Nations, they became insensibly softened, and of Consequence, easily moulded into all the politest Customs of the *East*.

THEY had THEATRES and AMPHITHEATRES erected at a vast Expence, and design'd with an Air of Grandeur, but indeed, all their publick Buildings distinguish'd them as Masters of the World. These Edifices are often mention'd by Authors thro' Mistake, as *Synonomous* Terms, yet differ'd very much both in Form and Use. The THEATRES were entirely appropriated to all Kinds of *Dramatick* Poetry; the AMPHITHEATRES were reserv'd as particularly for the Combats of the *Gladiators*, or those of Beast against Beast, or Men and Beasts. The first were of a *Semicircular* Form, or rather half of an Oval; the last was made up of two of these exactly join'd. In the first rude Ages of that Republick, these Structures were like the People, plain and ordinary, generally made of Wood, to serve a present Occasion: But with the Empire their Magnificence rose, as those of *Pompey, Marcellus, Tiberius, Claudius, Cornelius, Balbus, Titus*, &c. —as the Descriptions of their justest Writers, and the Remains of some of them to this Day, testify.

THERE were likewise several *Xysti* in *Rome*, which were large *Porticos* for Wrestlers, and the Performers of the other Exercises to practise in, when the extream Heat of the Sun, or wet Weather hinder'd their performing in open Air.

OF their *Odeum*, I can give but an imperfect Account, as I have already hinted in the second ESSAY. I meet with it often in Authors, call'd a Musick THEATRE, and describ'd much in the common Form of other THEATRES; but as to their satisfying us in the particular *Entertainments* there usually exhibited, they might talk as much to the Purpose, in telling us what a *Musick-house* is at *Amsterdam*.

BUT of all publick Amusements, none were so much the Favourites with the *Roman* People in general, from the Emperor to the Lictor, as

T   those

those call'd the *Circensian* Shews; under which Title I comprehend all Representations in the *Circus*, the *Naumachiæ*, the *Stadia*, or the AMPHITHEATRES, they differing more in the Name, than the Design, or Application.

THE Shews exhibited in the *Circus*, or the AMPHITHEATRES, were much the same; the latter only being erected for the more convenient Celebration of some particular Sports or Exercises, which were before presented in the former. All the Pastimes, or Feats of Strength and Activity in Vogue there, were an exact Copy of those us'd at the *Grecian* Games, and just now describ'd, and were generally comprehended under the Title of the *Pentathlum*, or *Quinquertium*, which included Running, Leaping, Wrestling, Throwing, Boxing, Darting, &c. The Manner of contending, the Laws for regulating the Victory, and the Prizes of Conquest were in Effect the same with those of *Greece*.

THE *Chariot-Races* were in as high Esteem with the *Romans* as any of the *Circensian Sports*. The *Charioteers* were divided into four Companies, and all *Rome* into as many Factions, in Favour each of his darling Colour, which distinguish'd them. They made use in their Chariots of two, four, six or seven Horses. And *Suetonius* says, That *Nero* drove a Chariot drawn with ten Horses coupled together, at the publick Games: Nay, the same Emperor at least oblig'd Pairs of Camels to perform in the same Service: And *Heliogabalus* refin'd upon him, and introduc'd Elephants.

THE Extent of the Races, and the Number of Matches perform'd at once, was uncertain, being vary'd upon extraordinary Occasions, or at the Pleasure of the Emperor. The Conquerors

rors in this Sport were rewarded with Crowns, Coronets, and Garlands, as was customary in *Greece*, or sometimes with very considerable Sums of Money.

THE *Troja Lulus* was said to be invented by *Asinius*, and was celebrated by Companies of noble Youths, neatly fitted out with proper Armour and Weapons, and headed either by the next Heir of the Empire, or the Son of some eminent Senator, who was stil'd, *Princeps juventutis*. This Game was perform'd on Horse-back, in which all Motions of a warlike Onset or Retreat were made use of, in order to instruct them in Martial Exercises, and answers to the *Pyrrhica Saltatio* of the *Greeks*, only the latter was exhibited on Foot.

THE Shews of wild Beasts were in general design'd to the Honour of *Diana*, Patroness of Hunting, and to answer that Institution, all Species of them were, at an immense Expence, brought from the most remote and most different Parts of the World.

SOME of these Creatures were presented meerly to gratify the Curiosity of the People, who doated on such strange Sights, as Crocodiles, Unicorns, and Flying-dragons: Others were produc'd for the Combat, as Lions, Tygers, Leopards, Lynxes, Rhinoceros, others purely for the Delight and Use of the Spectators, who were allow'd to catch what Deer, Hares, or Rabbits they pleas'd

A Shew of Beasts then may be reduc'd to three Heads, the first, when the People were thus allow'd to carry off what Boars, Oxen, or Sheep they could catch for their own private Use, the second, when Beasts fought against Beasts, as a Lion match'd with a Tyger, a wild Bull with an Elephant, a Rhinoceros with a Bear, or Deer hunted by a Pack of Dogs: The third, when the Combat was betwixt Man and Beast. The Men engag'd in this Enterprize had the general Name of *bestiarii*, and were either condemn'd Persons, or those who hired themselves out, like the *Gladiators*, for a set Pay, and at last the Nobility, Gentry, and even their Women, had the Bravery to engage voluntarily in these glorious Encounters.

But of all the *Circensian* Shews, that of *Gladiators* was the Favourite *Entertainment* of the *Roman* People in general. Their Rise was owing to the very antient Custom of sacrificing Captives or Slaves at the Funerals or Tombs of eminent Men, the old Heathens fansying the Ghosts of the Deceas'd to be pleas'd with the spilling human Blood. Then finding the People highly delighted with such cruel Diversions, it grew into a Custom, not only for the Heirs of the principal Magistrates, but even of the wealthy Citizens, to present them with these bloody *Entertainments* Nay, even the Priests themselves were often Exhibitors of such sanguinary Amusements.

At last the *Consuls, Dictators* and *Emperors*, in order to ingratiate themselves with the Commonalty, made a Birth-day, a Triumph, or a Consecration of any publick Edifice, a Pretence for exhibiting a Shew of *Gladiators* And, as their Return grew more frequent, so did the Number of Combatants, and Days of the Solemnity encrease; the first rising from three Pair to three Hundred and twenty, and the latter, from one Day to One Hundred and twenty three.

The several Kinds of *Gladiators* are not necessary to be mention'd here; as to their Condi-
tion,

tion, they were at first, either Captives of War, condemn'd to that Life, or Slaves bought, instructed by able Masters, and let out to hire for that Purpose.

BUT in a little time the Freemen themselves claim'd the Priviledge of being kill'd, to divert their Fellow Citizens, and took Pay for so doing at the AMPHITHEATRES, nay, the Knights, Senators, and Ladies of Quality, blush'd not to enter the Lists, and own the Profession, till restrain'd by a publick Edict of *Augustus*.

THE *Naumachia*, as to their Form, are no where particularly describ'd, but are suppos'd to differ very little in that from the *Circos*, or AMPHITHEATRES, only the lower Part, or Ground-plat, was fill'd with Water for the Representation of Naval Fights, or a Contention of Rowing for Victory. They were at first design'd to initiate their Men in a Knowledge of Sea-Affairs, in their Wars against the *Carthaginians*, and were afterwards improv'd into one of their solemn Shews, as well to gratify the People, as to encrease Naval Experience and Discipline: And some of the Emperors affecting Popularity, were at vast Trouble and Expence to court the People by *Entertainments* of this Nature.

THE Emperor *Claudius* made Use of the *Fucine* Lake, on which he presented a most magnificent Sea-Engagement, to an infinite Multitude of Spectators. *Domitian* form'd by Art a Sea of Waters, then produc'd a Number of Vessels on either Side, sufficient to have furnish'd out two compleat Navies for a real Fight: But *Heliogabalus*, in his Representation of a *Naumachia*, fill'd the Channel with Wine in place of Water, and thus *out-did* all his other *Out-doings*. The *Stadia* were Places in Form of a *Circus*, appropripropriated entirely to the Running of Men and Horses; the most noble of which was built by *Domitian*.

THE *Campus Martius*, consecrated to the God *Mars*, was mightily resorted to by the *Romans*, on Account of the Sports and Exercises perform'd there. Here the young Nobility practis'd all Feats of Activity, and learn'd the Use of Arms, and Rudiments of War. Here, often, the Races for Chariots, or single Horses, were undertaken; which pleasing Variety of Sights, made it one of the most agreeable Places in or about the City.

I have been as concise as possible on this Head; but in an Affair of this Consequence, Obscurity is more to be avoided than Prolixity: Therefore I shall at once proceed to consider the Diversions of our *Bear-garden*, upon a Parallel with those of the *Antique Circus*, as succinctly as a necessary Perspicuity will admit of.

I must here caution my Readers to remember, that under the general Title of the Shews of the *Circus*, or *Bear-garden*, I comprehend all those *Entertainments* I have spoke to in this ESSAY, as far as they related to the *Antients*, or that I shall speak to, as copied from them by the Moderns: And when I talk of either of these Places in the singular Number, that represents the rest of the Brotherhood in *Athens, Rome* or *London*. It will be altogether foreign to the Business in Hand, to recapitulate, or enlarge upon the Part the *Grecians* play'd at all *Entertainments* of this Nature. What I have already advanc'd on this Subject, is sufficient to shew, that the publick Exercises to which they train'd up their Youth, in order to appear as Candidates for

Fame

Fame at all their Games, were undoubtedly the Noble Original of the *Roman Circus* and *British Bear-garden.*

THE Great *Circus* in *Rome*, was a very large Oblong Square, with Noble Galleries, of the finest Architecture and Materials for the Spectators of the Games, according to their several Degrees; and under them, the Caves and Dungeons for the Beasts and Malefactors, who furnish'd out the *Entertainments*. In the Middle were several Ornamental Pillars, Altars, &c. with the *Meta*, round which the Chariots in their Races turn'd, where they set out, and where the Race concluded. In the *Arena* (which was strew'd with Sand, to suck up the Combatant's Blood, and hinder their Feet from slipping) were all the usual Exercises perform'd.

To this, in Use, if not in Grandeur and Beauty, answers our *Bear-garden*, the same the Design, End and Form, tho' I cannot say much as to the Buildings, Ornaments, or Encouragement which the other boasted. Tho' I will venture to affirm, that our Copy is upon an equal Foot of Merit with their Original. We have indeed some sorry Balconies and wooden Galleries for the Use of the Spectators, and a Pit for the exhibiting our Shews, but all conformable to the Appearance of those who are the chief Support of these Amusements, the lowest of the Vulgar, which as it is a Shame, it is a pity, and as it is a Pity, it is a Shame.

IN the *Circus*, the chief Spectacles were Men against Men; —— Men against Beasts —— and Beasts against Beasts: Chariot, or Horse-races, Leaping, Wrestling, and other Exercises of the like Nature.

ESSAY VII.

In the *Bear-garden*, our *Prize-fighters* Tally with their *Gladiators*, shewing as much Sport, and spilling less Blood; our Courage being made manifest thus to the World, without their Cruelty.

Men indeed seldom enter our Lists against Beasts, unless Butchers against Bull-dogs, in brotherly Alliance with their own Curs, whose Preservation and Honour are justly as dear to them as those of their Wife and Children.

But as for Beasts against Beasts —— I think we may modestly say, we equal, if not exceed any Thing they ever produc'd on that Head, our charming Bears, our noble Bulls, and nobler Mastiffs, must give those Spectators (who have Sense enough to frequent all publick Amusements, to be instructed as well as delighted) the truest Notions of an invincible Bravery, join'd to the most sagacious Conduct. On the other Hand, the Tygers, Leopards, Rhinoceros, Lions and Elephants of the *Antients*, never afforded that Variety of Diversion, the whole of that Affair being the same brutal Fierceness repeated, void of all just Courage and fine Contrivance.

Then our teizing of a tame Ass into Madness, with Dogs at his Heels, and lighted Squibs and Crackers all round him —— the baiting a wild Bear with Wheel-barrows, and teaching Horses to Dance, play at Cards, and tell Fortunes —— are *Entertainments* of that Novelty, Beauty and Grandeur, as never were known to the most Expensive and Luxurious of the Old *Roman* Emperors.

If we cannot boast of their Chariot-races, we can, to the Immortal Honour of our Country shew, that the Noble Sports of Wrestling, Cudgel-playing, Fisty-cuffs, Leaping, &c. flourish

rish in *Britain*, more, perhaps, than ever they did in *Greece*. Diversions that have more Humanity and Discipline in them, than the well-tim'd Crack of a Whip, or the nice Turning of a Post.

THESE should have been the principal Foundation of their *Circus*, as they were of the *Grecian* Games, and are of our *Bear-garden*. And tho' they have been the Admiration of Antiquity, not a Shadow of them now remains, but as happily preserv'd in their Original Purity by the *British* Nation.

As these publick Games were the Delight of *Greece* for many Ages; on which principally depended the Education of their Youth, and the Amusements of the Old, being maintain'd by the joint Consent of all the separate States, tho' ever so much disunited on other Accounts, and this at a Time, when at their Height for Power, Learning and Magnificence.

So with the *Romans*, the Representations of the *Circus* were the Darlings of their People, when their Wit was clear, their Studies solid, their Pleasures polite, and their Sway universal. And in either Empire with these they flourish'd, and with them fell, bravely surmounting all Difficulties, and withstanding all Shocks, till swallow'd up in that of a general Ruin.

PEOPLE of Genius and Spirit may shew a reasonable Surprize, that the Amusements of the *Bear-gardens* are so strangely neglected by People of Sense and Distinction, especially, as they are prov'd just Copies of such Glorious Originals. But what will they say, when I shall plainly demonstrate, that they may be render'd of the utmost Importance to this Nation, by keeping up the true Old *English* Spirit, and training up

every

every individual *Briton* to be a General! ——— a Hero!

If the vast Disparity betwixt the *Circus* and *Bear-garden*, in the Articles of Grandeur and Expence, is objected to us, let us but consider the prodigious Encouragement given to their SHEWS by *Senators, Consuls, Dictators, Emperors*, and their whole State: Nay, the World in Conjunction with them, strove who should add greatest Lustre to their Games.

And as we can boast the same Foundation, I think our People of Quality, Fortune, and publick Spirit, should with the greatest Zeal promote these Diversions, if not with a View of pleasing or instructing themselves, yet with a due Regard to the Delight and Improvement of the *Populace*, and the Honour of their Country.

Thus will the In-bred Valour and Martial Genius of this Nation be rous'd up and fix'd: Thus will the lowest of the People be inur'd to behold with Raptures, gash'd Faces, spouting Veins, goary Sculls, hack'd Limbs, *&c*. Thus will they be harden'd to the most fearless Contempt of Danger and Death: Thus will our Bulldogs, those Noble Creatures, our other selves (Beasts by Nature appropriated to this Nation) be kept in perfect Order, and that valuable Race preserv'd: Thus will such Spectacles add to the Native Fierceness of both, and breath a new Soul into the whole Kingdom.

And indeed, if we enter'd a little more particularly into the real Merits of the *Circus* and *Bear-garden*, we shall find, that in Variety, the Original Design, and desir'd End, they differ not widely, however we fall short in Point of Luxury and Magnificence.

FIRST,

FIRST, then, let us examine the antient State of the *Gladiators*, upon the Parallel with our Modern *Prize-fighters*, they being the main Pillars of the *Circus* and *Bear-garden*.

I have already shewn, that the Rise of the *Gladiators* was owing to that barbarous Custom practis'd in all Ages of Antiquity, of sacrificing Captives, or Slaves, at the Funerals and Tombs of great Men. The *Romans*, who exceeded in Humanity most other Nations, scorning such mean Butchery, commanded them to kill one another like Men. Their first *Gladiators*, tho' they were of the same Rank with those who grac'd the foreign Funeral Altars, being either Slaves by Birth, Captives of War, or Malefactors condemn'd by Justice to Death. The first fought for Liberty, the others for Life. As they came more into Reputation, People voluntarily enter'd themselves into the Service for Pay, were regularly enlisted as Soldiers, and an *Academy* establish'd for instructing them in the Art of cutting Throats cleverly and decently. At last, to oblige some of the Emperors, Persons of Figure and Distinction enter'd the *Circus* as *Gladiators*, greedy of Immortal Fame: And *Nero* once compell'd a Thousand *Knights* and *Senators* in one Day, to grace his SHEWS, and cut, slash and slay one another in the most beautiful Manner, for the Good of their Country.

THE Combats were attended with Freedom to the Conquerors, if Slaves, or Donatives from the Emperor and People, if hir'd Persons: But Death to the Vanquish'd, if Life was not granted upon imploring Mercy from the Spectators; and this happen'd just as their Fingers and Thumbs chanc'd to be in Humour.

ESSAY VII.

THO' during the whole Course of the *Roman* Empire, all the *Circenſian Shews* were the Delight of the People, yet this of the *Gladiators* was look'd on with the moſt favourable Eye, always receiv'd with uncommon Raptures; and, at all Triumphs, Feſtivals, Funerals, or any publick Demonſtration of Joy, or Grief, the Solemnity was counted imperfect without it.

THUS with ſome ſmall Intermiſſions (and viſible Tokens of Decay, as the Empire it ſelf grew feeble and aged) the *Gladiators* ſtood their Ground till the Year Five Hundred, that a King of the *Oſtrogoths* totally baniſh'd them from *Italy*: And, certainly, nothing but a *Goth* could have been ſo barbarous as to have thus rudely deſtroy'd a Diverſion, which for ſo many Ages charm'd the wiſeſt, politeſt, and moſt powerful State upon Earth! But in my poor Judgment, the Manner of their Deſtruction is an undeniable Proof of the Merit and Politeneſs of the *Entertainments*.

THUS in *Italy* the *Gladiators* roſe, flouriſh'd, fell, and for ſeveral Centuries lay bury'd, till luckily reviv'd in *England*: The only Nation upon Earth that can boaſt the raiſing from the Dead an Amuſement in it ſelf equally uſeful and genteel; an Amuſement, which from its intrinſick Worth ſo long claim'd a due Reſpect from the Maſters of the World.

THIS my laſt Aſſertion may meet with ſome Oppoſers, who will readily object to me the *Juſts* and *Tournaments* ſo much in Vogue for ſeveral Centuries, and which have been altogether dropp'd for theſe two Hundred Years paſt; as likewiſe the Bull-Feaſts that are held in ſo great Requeſt, at preſent, all over *Spain* and *Portugal*.

As

As to the first of these, I cannot in the least Feature find out a Resemblance betwixt them and the old *Gladiators*, either in the Design, the Conduct, or the Consequence of the Combat; but am more apt to think them rather an Imition of the *Pyrrhica-Saltatio*, or *Troja-Ludus* before describ'd; only in these, there never was any Blood shed, which but too often happen'd in their *Justs* and *Tilts*.

As to the latter, the *Spanish* Cavaliers indeed set forth in dreadful Array to encounter their wild Bulls, come very near one material Article of the SHEWS of the *Circus*, that of Men against Beasts: But I am inclinable to think, that with the *Romans* the *Bestiarii* were not allow'd to be mounted so compleatly arm'd, or well attended to defeat, in an apparent Danger, the furious Onset of a Villainous-minded Bull, as the bold-spirited Dons are.

It remains for me now to speak to our Modern *Prize-Fighters* in a way of Comparison with the Antient *Gladiators*, and at the same time come to the material Design of this ESSAY, and shew that we can carry this *Entertainment* to a greater Height, both as to Pleasure and Profit, than has been known to former Ages, where there should no Cruelty appear but in the Way of Justice, no Blood shed but for Instruction; and Life or Death only consider'd, as every Man is devoted to the Good of his Country.

OUR Modern *Prize Fighters*, those happy Copies of the Old *Gladiators*, shew a Spirit superior to the boasted Bravery of the *Romans* For as they are not Slaves, of Consequence not oblig'd to Fight; they only Fight for Fighting's sake.

BUT as I would embellish the *Bear-garden Scene* with the greatest Variety of *Actors*; and have always in Reserve a Number sufficient, not only to amuse the People, but to answer the unexpected Exigencies of the State, in Case of a Rebellion, Invasion, &c. So we must not too far trust barely to Hirelings for that Service. All Ages and Nations have experienc'd that Supply to be precarious, and especially in a Country of Liberty and Property, will altogether depend upon Whim and Humour. Therefore I propose, as a Matter of the last Importance to this Nation, and as the greatest Promoter of beautiful Justice——First——That all our Malefactors condemned to Death, be forc'd to stab, hack and hew themselves to Pieces for the Good of their Fellow Subjects, then their Deaths will infallibly prove of a more general Use to their Country, than their Lives could have been pernicious. By this Means the most profligate Wretches may die the truest Patriots; and every *Blueskin*, or *Sheppard*, go off the Stage, a *Curtius*, or *Martius-Scævola*. Thus argued *Tully* himself, when the Charge of Barbarity was laid to the SHEWS of GLADIATORS.—— *These* SHEWS, says he, *may seem to some People very inhuman, but where only guilty Persons compose the Number of the Combatants, 'tis impossible that any Thing should fortify us with more Success, against the Assaults of Grief or Death.* And he might have added —— *or more effectually instill a warlike Disposition into the Minds of the People.*

SECONDLY,—— I would oblige all State Criminals adjug'd to Transportation, or other corporal Punishments, to Lift themselves in the Service of the BEAR-GARDEN, in order, by small Play, to be instructed themselves in the Rudiments

diments of War. Thus a little Gash, Cut, or Thrust, will inure them to the bearing of greater Wounds, be a Punishment in some Respect adequate to their past Crimes, and at the same time delight the *Populace*; train them up to Martial Exercises, and arm them against all cowardly Ideas.

THIRDLY,—— to encourage Spectators to come there with a sincere Design to improve, the Go———nt should allow any Man that is willing to be enroll'd as an Out-pensioner, to be call'd upon in Cases of Necessity, to be free of the BEAR-GARDEN, both as to Diversion and Instruction, and that he should be absolutely at Liberty to have a crack'd Skull, a Thump on the Ribs, or broken Shins, whenever he demanded them, *gratis*.

I have already shewn what particular Influences this Proposal, well executed, may have on the Minds of the Commonalty of *England* in general. I now beg Leave to hint at the principal Advantage to which the whole Scheme must naturally tend.

As the Scituation of this Kingdom, the fundamental Constitution of our State, and the Temper of our People require not a great Number of Standing Forces, kept in constant Pay, so if, upon any Emergency, our Affairs should stand in Need of a larger Supply than is usually kept on Foot, where shall we find Recruits to answer the pressing Necessities of the State, and form, in a Hurry, a large Army? All Ages and Nations have experienc'd, and smarted for the Folly of trusting too far, to raw and undisciplin'd Troops:—— Where then can we hope for a seasonable Relief in such a Scene of Distress, but from a well-regulated BEAR-GARDEN, whose

Auxiliaries may prove new-rais'd Troops, but veteran Heroes? 'Tis evident, that it may be brought to that Pass, as to form an *Academy* for the Army, a Nursery for Infant-Warriors, as *Chelsea-College* is for the Old. Let but our Encouragement rise to an equal Height with that of the *Romans*, in the SHEWS of their GLADIATORS, and we should never be reduc'd to so low an Ebb as to beat up for Voluntiers: Several Regiments, at a short Warning, might be borrow'd from the BEAR-GARDEN UNIVERSITY, every Man at least a Batchelor of Arts in the Sciences offensive and defensive, and a sufficient Number always kept in *petto*, as a *Corps de Reserve*.

SOME People may sneer at my Project, as absurd or chimerical, but let those merry Gentlemen consider, how often the *Romans* were oblig'd to Lift their GLADIATORS, when their Legions out-stretch'd *Arithmetick*, and they were Masters of the World.

LET any Man but read over attentively the Bills of Defiance from any of our BEAR-GARDENS, or AMPHITHEATRES, and the brave Replies of their Antagonists; if there be the smallest Spark of Courage *latent* in his Soul, such intrepid Terms of Honour must blow it up to a Flame of Glory. The World may talk of *Alexander*, *Scipio*, *Hannibal*, and *Julius Cæsar*, whilst I set fearless in their View, *Kned Sutton*, *Jack Fig*, *Tim Buck*, and *Bob Stokes*.

As I have before provided the Army with Of———rs from the *Mas*———*de*; so I have now furnish'd it with private Men from the BEAR-GARDEN, which will be a certain Fund upon all Emergencies, without any real Expence to the Nation.

WERE

Of the BEAR-GARDEN, &c.

WERE it thought necessary to cultivate the Genius of those design'd for Sea Affairs, in the same Method of Education, 'tis but turning our Eyes towards the *Naumachia* of the *Antients*, and observing nicely all the Rules establish'd in the BEAR-GARDEN only with Respect to the Difference between Sea and Land-service. I fancy we may then produce something on the *Thames*, which could not have been so well executed on the *Tiber*.

I must own, all the other *Entertainments* of the BEAR-GARDEN, are prudently imagin'd, and becoming the Bent of a brave People; and all conduce to the great Design, of mixing Instruction with our Amusements: And, that Men may be instructed by Brutes, *Æsop, Lemuel Gulliver,* and *Hockly in the Hole* shew us. Who can view Dogs tearing Bulls, Bulls goaring Dogs, or Mastiffs throtling Bears, without being animated with their daring Spirits! And what is brutal Fiercness in them, may produce true human Courage in us. Were the BEAR-GARDEN once rightly establish'd, the Managers of it might venture to introduce Lions, Tygers, Unicorns and Rhinocero's in formal Combat: This, with an Elephant or two to shew Postures, and a Flying-dragon for the high Ropes, would give the justest Notions of, and put us upon a Level with Antiquity, in the Articles of Grandeur and Variety.

BUT not to dwell altogether on the Merits of the BEAR-GARDEN, or our AMPHITHEATRES for PRIZE-FIGHTERS, as founded on the *Entertainments* of the antique CIRCUS, before I entirely quit the Regions of fighting Men, and fighting Beasts, I must not pass by, unregarded, our fighting Fowls.

ESSAY VII.

THE Diversions of our COCK-PITS are really *English*, as to the Invention, Excellency, and Application: And as no Nation can pretend to match us in a Sprightly, Noble, Martial Race of *Cocks*; so I think, the Amusement they give us, may vie with any thing Antique or Modern, as to Humanity and Politeness. Our Taste on that Head is so refin'd, so adapted to People of the first Quality, and most elegant Education, that the Assurance of some Countries is to me amazing, where they would be distinguish'd by a *picquant Gou*, and an universal Knowledge in every Thing polite, as to our killing Time in the most agreeable Manner; ―――― yet have not the least Notion of COCK-FIGHTING.

THE Pride, the Life, the Courage of these little Creatures, would inflame a Coward, and spur him on to the most daring Attempts. Who could, unmov'd, behold these seemingly insignificant Birds, cut, slash, and tear one another to Pieces! It must animate a *Thersites* with the Soul of *Hector*, to view them all over one gaping Wound, yet disdaining to yield their Hold or Ground, tho' in the Pangs of Death! No Spectacle can be more becoming a Man, except the Refinement upon this Diversion, as practis'd on Shrove-Tuesday, *the bravely knocking them on the Head with Clubs*; an Amusement parallel to which no Time, or Nation of Antiquity can boast of.

I am so elevated with this Subject, that when once I am fairly enter'd, I could talk of it without ceasing; and, perhaps, in my Fury be transported to say something not over much to the Purpose: But such a World of Matter crowds this ESSAY, that I am oblig'd to proceed in examining the Merits of another *Entertainment*,
which

Of the BEAR-GARDEN, &c.

which indeed disgraces the BEAR-GARDEN, in being mention'd in such bad Company, as our *Italian* Strolers.

IN the third ESSAY upon DANCING, I took some small Notice of the Original and Conduct of the true *Italian Stage,* which always appear'd to me a tolerable Copy of the Old *Mimes*, as these travelling Stagers seem to be only proper Appendixes to the Retinue of a *Mountebank.*

WE have been often promis'd the Top Company of *Europe* in their Way, and as often deceiv'd, being still forc'd to take up with the Refuse which foreign Stages had cast away: Nay, those merry Gentlemen who lately engross'd the *Opera-House,* in so magnificent a Manner, were but the Gleanings of those Rabble Sets, who had the Honour of entertaining the *French* Nobility in the Neighbourhood of *Soho,* at the *Ginger-bread* THEATRE, on the other side the *Hay-market.*

TO form a true Idea of these itinerant Players, and undeceive that Part of the World which may expect mighty Matters from them, I am inclinable to think, that most of them were got under Hedges, born in Barns, and brought up in Houses of Correction: Nor should they ever dare to shew their Faces in any Place but a wooden Booth.

FOR, undoubtedly, the buskind *Ragamuffins* that *Thespis* first carted about the World, must have been *Demi-gods* and *Heroes,* to these Pedlars in Poetry, and Gipsies of the Stage.

IT is impossible to enter into a regular Criticism, either on their Action, or *Drama*; to get thro' such Heaps of Rubbish, would require more than *Herculean* Help: The Confusion of such Nonsensical Scenes cannot be view'd forwards,

wards, they will not bear the least Light, nor have they the Merit even of a Witch's Prayer, to be read backwards.

THEREFORE to set them off to the best Advantage, let us only consider them as deck'd out in the most glaring Ornaments, and painted in the gayest Colours, in their own publick Bills; --- of which the following is but a Specimen ———— *This Evening* Argentina *will represent a particular Fatigue, call'd the* Hobgoblin; *with a Prologue by all the Devils in Hell: A Comedy of that Variety of Incidents, that she personates all Nations upon Earth, with Singing and Dancing in all their different Manners.* ——— Another Evening, Pantalon *undertakes his particular Fatigue by performing a* Comedy *in a* Comedy; *where he's engag'd by Honour,* Argentia *suppos'd a Countess by Mistake of a Picture;* Diana, *a cheated Lady;* Arlequin, *a mistaken Eunuch; in which Signior* Franchelino *danc'd with a Machine on his Head, the Favourite of the King of* Morocco. ——— Arlequin *in the* Proteo Novello, *personated a French Officer, a Chimny-sweeper, a walking Statue, a Blackmoor Stand, an Astrologer, an Infant, a* Diana; *to which was added, the comical Scene of a stuttering Musick-master, by* Brighella. Argentina *went thro' another very particular Fatigue, in the Affectation of a new Title, wherein the Doctor, by the Name of* Tabarin, *perform'd a new Character, both very comical and jocose, never yet seen on any Stage.* Then Brighella, *in the surprizing Disguises of* Cartouche, *counterfeited the Personages of a* Turk, *a petit-maitre, a Merchant, a* Swiss, *an* Armenian, *a* Florentine, *a Venetian Gondolier, an* English *Water-man, a* French *Dwarf, and a fine Lady; in which Signior* Grimaldo *of* Malta *danc'd a wonderful Dance within a dark Lanthorn, never yet*

yet seen, with the diverting *Humour of the Mistress Devil, and the Maid Devil.*

LET any Pretender to common Sense judge of the Merit of their Performances, from this Theatrical *Gallimafry* of Poetry, Musick and Dancing, as ingeniously express'd in *Phrases* peculiar to themselves.

DID they strictly adhere, in any Point, to the Old Institution and Art of the *Pantomimes*, they might be introduc'd in most *Stage-Entertainments*, by Way of an Interlude, with great Success; particularly, they might with Propriety fill up the Vacancies betwixt the Acts in the *Italian Operas*, which would prove an agreeable Variety to most of the *Audience*.

BUT in the Manner their *Dramatical* Jumbles are conducted, they are a Scandal to any Stage, an Encroachment upon our THEATRES, and a Banter on all Kinds of *Poetry*. As the Affair of Theatrical *Dancing* is carry'd far beyond their weak Attempts in our own *Play-houses*; so there is nothing else left for them, in which they dare pretend to please.

WE having once fairly got rid of them, it may be thought unnecessary, even to have condescended to mention them; but having formerly found several Patrons, it is necessarily proper to prepare People to receive them suitable to their Merits, in case of a second Visit.

WHILE I am engag'd in this stroling Family, I cannot in Conscience neglect the most valuable Branch of it, a *Mountebank*'s Travelling-Stage; which we shall readily perceive to be in all Respects superior to their Relations from Abroad.

FOR, if we nicely and impartially examine the Conduct of these Gentlemen (from Doctor *Smith*,
who

who keeps his Coach and Six, to the Old Pimple-fac'd *Quack*, who paces from Market to Market on his py-ball'd Pad) we must be convinc'd, that they are the most publick-spirited Men upon Earth; that they only profess *Physick* for the Good of their Country, and throw *gratis* their Labour, Tumblers, Rope-dancers, and Jack-puddings into the Bargain.

This is honourable; this is acting without Reserve, for the Benefit of Mankind: Nay, they are often so generous of the Fruits of their Labour, that in order to provoke People to rectify what is amiss in their Constitutions, they part with their *Physick* for less than what it cost them.

Nothing can be more judiciously imagin'd than their additional Stage-Amusements, nor more apropos to the Affair in Hand. They prudently consider, that *Physick* never operates so well, as when the Patient is in good Humour. Thus with every Medicine they give you an equal Dose of Mirth, to prepare you by proper Motions for its working. A *Merry-Andrew* will whip out your Tooth, as he catches you laughing at his dry Jest; or whilst a Country-fellow is gaping at the Rope-dancer, he may have a Paper of Pills, or a black Potion thrown down his Throat.

Then the Doctor's Solemnity of Address, Gravity of Countenance, and Rich Cloths, give the Vulgar so just an Idea of his profound Capacity, that they must at least prove the better half of the Cure in any Disease: For, undoubtedly an implicit Faith in our Physician, is the most valuable Part of his Pacquet, or Prescription.

Were we to enter into a formal Comparison of these Rival Twins, we should find that the *Mountebank-Stage*, in every Particular exceeds the

Itinerant

Itinerant Italian. The Design, the Conduct, the End propos'd in all publick Amusements, are judg'd with greater Propriety, and executed more to the Purpose, in the first than the last; they aim at something, and seldom miss the Mark.

One acts always in Cover, the other in open Air; a strong Argument in Favour of them whose Deeds and Words can bear the nicest Scrutiny in Day-light, and stand the publick Test of the World.

SOME People may assert, that there is no essential Difference betwixt them, the Action and Expression of both being extravagantly low and ridiculous, consisting altogether of Grimace and Nonsense. But even here the *Mountebank* triumphs, he executes what he designs, his Pretences to Wit and Action, are calculated to be upon the Level with the Understandings of the Mob, and all their Tricks and Jokes are so many Baits artfully dispos'd for the catching greedy Gudgeons.

THEREFORE as I have been often a Spectator of both Performances, and consider'd them in a just, critical Light, I will maintain, that the *Mountebank* Drollery is in all Points more natural, genteeler, and better hit off than that of their scurvy Imitators, the *Italian Farce-Actors*.

THERE remains nothing now for me to add to what has been advanc'd on this Subject, but wishing those Gentlemen Strolers so much Business at Home, that they may never have Leisure or Inclination, to favour us with another Visit.

I am of Opinion, That from some small Hints scatter'd up and down this ESSAY, and some of the former, most of my Readers will be convinc'd, that no Man can be in a worse Scituation,

tion, as to a polite Taste in publick Amusements, than an Admirer of *Operas* at L——n's-I——n-F——ds, *Grotesque* Dancing at D——y--L——ne, and *Italian* Plays in the H——y--M——t.

IN the whole Course of my Travels, nothing ever excited my Curiosity in a higher Degree, or gave me more sensible Delight, than taking particular Notice of the several Diversions of every Country, in order from thence to form a Judgment of the various Dispositions of different Nations.

THE Mechanical Genius of the *English* is obvious to every body in many Cases, but in none more properly, than in the Contrivance and Conduct of our PUPPET-SHEWS: The Improvement of which is certainly owing to us, if not the Invention; and, indeed, it has often prov'd our Province to refine upon the first Thoughts of others, in Works of Art and Ingenuity.

I confess, I cannot view a well-executed PUPPET-SHEW, without extravagant Emotions of Pleasure: To see our Artists, like so many *Prometheus's*, animate a Bit of Wood, and give Life, Speech and Motion, perhaps, to what was the Leg of a Joint-stool, strikes me with a pleasing Surprize, and prepossesses me wonderfully in Favour of these little wooden Actors, and their *Primum-mobile*.

THESE portable Stages are of infinite Advantage to most Country Towns, where *Play-houses* cannot be maintain'd, and, in my Mind, superior to any Company of Strolers: The Amusement is innocent and instructive, the Expence is moderate, and the whole Equipage easily carry'd about, as I have seen some Couples of Kings and Queens, with a suitable Retinue of Courtiers and Guards, very well accommodated in a

single

Of the BEAR-GARDEN, &c.

single Band-box, with Room for *Punch* and his Family, in the same Machine. The Plans of their little Pieces do not barely aim at Morality, but enforce even Religion: And, it is impossible to view their Representations of *Bateman*'s Ghost, *Doctor Faustus*'s Death, or Mother *Shipton*'s Tragical End, but that the bravest Body alive must be terribly afraid of going to the D———l.

It is necessary to observe here, That the Plans upon which these little *Tragi-Comedies* are form'd, are generally borrow'd from those Subjects I recommended in the first ESSAY to the *Opera-house*. Those Domestick Matters of Fact always prove the Favourites of the People, which induc'd me to believe, that they might appear with equal Success on the Stage of the great PUPPET-SHEW in the H———y-m———t.

I have already hinted at the beautiful Imitation of an *Antique-Chorus*, so justly executed by the Prompter of the PUPPET-SHEW, in the Person of *Punch*; who, exactly in the Manner of the *Coryphæus* of the *Antients*, has something to say in every Scene, and makes every bodies Business his own.

As I have particularly taken Notice of *Ropedancers, Strolers, Mountebanks, Puppet-shews*, &c. and mention'd them with all the Respect due to their Merits; it would be look'd upon as the highest Ingratitude, carelesly to pass unregarded those Places where they oftenest shine, and in greatest Splendor, I mean our publick *Fairs*.

HAVING only profess'd to reform the Errors, or point out the Beauties in our publick Diversions, no Man will expect, that I should in the least touch upon the Article of Trade, it being quite foreign to my Design, and the *Fairs* I speak of, commonly of a Nature opposite to it, tho' even in that Point, they may be render'd very advantagious, by bringing of well-dispos'd People together, for their mutual Profit and Amusement: For where such Meetings are prudently, and conveniently contriv'd, there will be Trades of some Sort or other continually going forward. Nor do I intend to inspect the yearly *Rendezvous* at *Sturbridge*, *Bury*, or other large Towns; they not falling naturally within the Precincts of my Enquiries: Nor, indeed, dare I venture so far out of my Depth, as to go beyond the Limits of the Bills of Mortality.

I have in my Days seen *May-Fair*, that Favourite of *Nobility* and *Mobility*, quite demolish'd, to the general Regret of all, but those Powers to whom, with Patience, we must submit. Nay, my Old Friend *Bartholomew*'s Wings are close clipp'd; his Liberties retrench'd, and Priviledges invaded. How alter'd! —— how sunk from his former Golden State! —— Those merry, drunken, whoring Days! —— when immortal *Ben* thought it no mean Subject for his comick *Muse*. We live in Hopes, the Losses there sustain'd will be made up to us t'other side the *Thames*, and that *Southwark* may be what *May* and *Bartholomew Fairs* have been. It happens at that dead Time of Year, when Business and Diversions in *London* sink under the Weight of a long Vacation, when Trade lies dead, and Pleasure languishes; whilst there they raise their drooping autumnal Heads, and revive to charm us with new budding Delights, as in the Spring.

There Scepter'd Kings, and Long-tail'd Queens fill the capacious Stage, to awe with their tinsel Grandeur, the admiring Populace. There Love-sick Heroes, and sighing Princesses too, in friendly Murmurs, to break the Hearts of

amorous

amorous Prentices, and draw Floods of Tears from good-natur'd Chamber-maids. There the humorous Clowns and cunning Sharpers display their Talents of Joke and Trick, till tickell'd *Cockneys* stretch their Sides with immoderate Laughter. There the Beaus and Belles (who have only breath'd the dusty Air of *Hide-Park*, all Summer) may find themselves lost in the Middle of the *Fair*, and not discover where they are, or what they have been about, till the Mist is clear'd from before their Eyes, and the agreeable Vision vanish'd.

To enter into a curious Detail of every particular Amusement to be met with in these *Fairs*, would swell this pigmy Volume to an enormous Bulk. Therefore I shall close this Scene with observing, that from my nicest Remarks upon these publick Meetings, and the Variety of Spectators and Amusements that attend them, I cannot avoid saying, that they nearly resemble the *Secular Games* of the *Romans*, and the *Jubilees* of their modern Successors, only what they enjoy'd in the Revolution of every Hundred, Fifty, or Twenty five Years, we can command at different Places and Seasons, often in the Compass of twelve Months, whilst we can justly laugh at the pompous Proclamation of their SHEWS, which no Man could hope to live to see a second Time.

JUST as I had resolv'd to shut up this my last ESSAY upon our publick Diversions, I recollected, that I was about disobliging five Parts in Six of the numerous Inhabitants of this *Metropolis*, by neglecting to make honourable Mention of our *Publick Auctions*, which of late Years are become one of the principal Amusements of all Ranks, from the Duke and Dutchess to the Pick-pocket and Street-walker.

I am sensible that many People (whose Judgments are actuated by Prejudice, or their private Interest) will immediately object to the Progress these *Auctions* have made, and call loudly for a Stop to be put to so growing an Evil. They'll assert, That in Time, their irregular Motions will cause a Stagnation in Trade, hinder Money to circulate justly, and ruin even those of large Fortunes, by buying so many good Bargains.

They'll pretend to argue, That the Notion of Oeconomy, wrong understood, has so far infected all Degrees of People with the Hopes of buying every thing immoderately cheap, that they crowd to *Auctions* to purchase what they do not want, rather than miss of a charming Pennyworth. That fine Ladies go there only to get the better of some idle Hours, and that fine Gentlemen will follow them: Both are oblig'd in Honour to bid for something, tho' ever so unnecessary, and when they are so happy as to meet with a delicious Bargain, they do not know what to do with their Purchase, and would give Fifty *per Cent.* to have this Piece of good Fortune taken off their Hands.

THESE Foes to our publick *Auctions* insinuate, that the *Virtuosi* go there to part with their old Curiosities at a dear Rate, and pick up others more valuable for a Trifle; breaking Tradesmen to get ready Money for stale Goods: The Setters to bid for every Thing and buy nothing; and the *Auctioneer*——— to be the only gaining Person: Nay, they add, that the Infatuation is now so general, there is no Way left of opening the Eyes of the World in this Lethargick

thargick State, till the Smart of their Follies awakens them.

THUS will some Mortals rail at, or ridicule every thing that is carry'd on successfully for the publick Good: Critick-like they live by finding Fault, ill Nature works in them, as Poison does in a Toad; they must spit their Venom, or they swell,——they burst,——they die.

FOR my Part, how they can be thought prejudicial to Trade, is to me miraculous, when the Furniture of our Houses (which generally consists of our own Manufactures) is bought up in such Profusion, that the Frequenters of *Auctions*, not only over-stock all their Apartments, but lay up whole Magazines, and turn every Garret into a Lumber-room. If the Buyers at *Actions* merit not the Title of *Oeconomists*, as to the Article of laying out their Money, yet they certainly may claim it, as to the Management of their Time, which is abundantly more precious. These *Entertainments* are so calculated for the Use of the *Idle* and *Indolent*, that Morning, Noon and Night, they may know where to be most agreeably busy.

WHETHER the Sticklers for, or against publick *Auctions* prevail, I care not, but think my self oblig'd in Honour to do Justice to a near Relation of our Family, before I drop this Subject, the worthy Mr. *Cock* of *Broad-street*, near *Golden square*. He is allow'd by all the World, to be a very clever Gentleman in his Business, and manages his little Hammer as much to the Purpose as any Instrument can possibly attain to His Flourishes are genteel, yet significant, his Manner of Address easy and well-bred, but intrepid his Phrases manly without Rudeness, and expressive without Obscurity, or Circumlocution. Not *Tully* himself could fill a *Rostrum* with more

Grace

Grace, or Eloquence. And we may venture to affirm, for the Glory of this Age, and our own Nation, that if assisted by the Endeavours of the Reverend Mr. H——ly, Restorer of the antient Elocution and Action; that the Industry and Capacity of these two Gentlemen will raise *Pulpit-Oratory* to a higher Pitch of Fame than Mankind yet has known.

I fear most of my Readers will seem shock'd, when after this copious List of Town Diversions I must confess, that I have not touch'd upon the most material Part of all, which gives the greatest Delight to the Majority of Audiences, or Assemblies of every Kind: And without which, the most perfect *Entertainment* is look'd upon as ridiculous and insipid: But I hope their Surprize will readily abate, when I set full in their View the Beauty of a Crowd: —— A Crowd! —— which never fails to give Harmony to flat OPERAS Spirit, to dull Plays, and Life, to heavy Dances. Nothing could be added more *apropos* to the Nature and Design of these ESSAYS: For even with those who would be esteem'd the principal Judges of all publick Amusements, a Crowd is generally the Touch-stone of Merit.

WHAT would our fine Ladies say to an *Assembly*, or *Opera*, where they are not crowded to Death? *Lard!* —— *'tis so agreeable to be jostled, and squeez'd, and push'd, and pull'd to Pieces*. In what a silly Light would *Cato* appear to our genteel Criticks, with vacant Benches!——How dull the brightest Preacher, with a thin Congregation?——and how ugly a reigning Toast in an empty Drawing-room?

A Crowd is the Soul of *Musick* and *Poetry*, the Quintessence of good Sense, and the Wit of a *Masquerade*. In short, it is the *Je ne sçay quoy*
in

in every thing that pretends to the Name of a polite Amusement, and the *tout ensemble* of Perfections in all publick *Entertainments*.

I think it altogether needless, to canvass any farther those Diversions of the Town, which I have already touch'd upon, or hunt out for others, which are not of Consequence enough to be look'd into. I hope that every Part (of those which are most frequented) have their Beauties, Defects and Amendments made sufficiently manifest, and every Point so supported by undeniable Circumstances and Examples, that no Proof can be more self-evident.

I make no Doubt, but several of my Readers will look upon my Method of handling this Topick as too circumstantial and prolix, while others will think me too concise, and perhaps very defective, in omitting what they call a publick Amusement. I have, in these ESSAYS, furnish'd out a Magnificent Banquet, to which the whole Town is invited: Every Man will either barely commend the Dish he likes, and find fault with all the rest, or if his singular Palate is not touch'd with some particular Kickshaw, damn the whole Treat.

THE wise Cabals of our *News-mongers* (who feed upon our publick Papers, and gravely hold forth in the principal Corners of our Top Coffee and Chocolate-Houses) will be struck with Amazement, that in the present Posture of Affairs, the State of *Europe* is not look'd into, War and Peace never mention'd, and the Ballance of Power forgot; when these Points, artfully vary'd, serve to amuse four Parts in five of the deepest Heads in *Great-Britain*.

OUR natural Philosophers will sneer at my total Neglect of *Mary* of *Godliman*, and the whole

whole Rabbit-scene. *What! not a Page of his Book set aside, to inspect the Affairs of the wonderful Rabbit-woman?——No Notice taken of* D——r M——in's *Physical, or Monsieur St.* A——e's *Anatomical Discoveries?——Stupid Creature!——He writes* ESSAYS *upon publick Diversions, and never names* Cunny Moll; *who, like the* B——r's O——ra, *engross'd all Conversation for six Months; after whom all Degrees of People ran so fast and so long, that both the* Entertainment *and they were quite out of Breath.*

THE *Literati* and *Politicians* will expect a full Detection of the artificial, natural, and political Mysteries in *Gulliver's* Travels. They undoubtedly will be astonish'd at my so negligently touching an Affair of that Moment to Mankind in general, and to this Nation in particular, or that I should in so careless a Manner, only throw in a few loose Hints, in Relation to that wonderful Book, which has in some Measure surpriz'd, diverted, or instructed every *Briton* great and small, rich and poor, young and old, whether they understood it or no.

Nay, *Fawks's Dexterity of Hand*, the *moving Pictures, Musical-Clocks,* Solomon's Temple, the *Wax-work, all alive*, the *High-german Artist, born without Hands or Feet*, the *Cow with five Legs*, the *Hare that beats a Drum*, the *Savoyard's Rareshow*, and all other Curiosities of Art and Nature, will find their Admirers, who would demand a formal ESSAY in their Favour, to illustrate their Beauties, and make manifest their Use and Instruction.

BUT were I to canvass the Merits of such Trifles, what I propos'd as a necessary Pocket-companion, would soon fill a Folio Shelf in a Library. My Design was, to animadvert upon

the

the Standard *Entertainments* of the present Age, in Comparison with those of Antiquity, not to take Notice of every Mushroom Amusement in my Way, which dies, perhaps, the Day it springs up, or if set fairly a going, yet can't outlive its first Run.

HAVING, to the utmost of my weak Endeavours, strove to execute so laudable a Design, I shall conclude here, preferring an expressive Brevity to an unmeaning Circumlocution. The World, by this rude Sketch, may readily guess at the absolute Necessity of a Work of this Nature, and, perhaps, the Out-lines I have here so unskilfully drawn, may tempt a masterly Hand to touch up these Figures with some finishing Strokes. It is Honour sufficient for me to have led the Way in so great an Undertaking, in Hopes that those who have Power and Capacity, may one Day fix our publick *Entertainments* upon a Basis as lasting, as beneficial to Mankind.

F I N I S.

For Product Safety Concerns and Information please contact our EU representative GPSR@taylorandfrancis.com
Taylor & Francis Verlag GmbH, Kaufingerstraße 24, 80331 München, Germany

www.ingramcontent.com/pod-product-compliance
Lightning Source LLC
Chambersburg PA
CBHW081803300426
44116CB00014B/2224